BEYOND "JUSTIFICATION"

BEYOND "JUSTIFICATION"

DIMENSIONS OF EPISTEMIC EVALUATION

WILLIAM P. ALSTON

CORNELL UNIVERSITY PRESS
ITHACA AND LONDON

Copyright © 2005 by Cornell University

All rights reserved. Except for brief quotations in a review, this book, or parts thereof, must not be reproduced in any form without permission in writing from the publisher. For information, address Cornell University Press, Sage House, 512 East State Street, Ithaca, New York 14850.

First published 2005 by Cornell University Press
First printing, Cornell paperbacks, 2006

Printed in the United States of America

Library of Congress Cataloging-in-Publication Data

Alston, William P.
  Beyond "justification" : dimensions of epistemic evaluation / William P. Alston.
    p. cm.
  Includes bibliographic references and index.
   ISBN-13: 978-0-8014-4291-9 (cloth : alk. paper)
   ISBN-10: 0-8014-4291-5 (cloth : alk. paper)
   ISBN-13: 978-0-8014-7332-6 (pbk. : alk. paper)
   ISBN-10: 0-8014-7332-2 (pbk. : alk. paper)
  1. Justification (Theory of knowledge) 2. Knowledge, Theory of. 3. Epistemics. 4. Belief and doubt. I. Title.
  BD212.A45   2005
  121—dc22   2004015591

Cornell University Press strives to use environmentally responsible suppliers and materials to the fullest extent possible in the publishing of its books. Such materials include vegetable-based, low-VOC inks and acid-free papers that are recycled, totally chlorine-free, or partly composed of nonwood fibers. For further information, visit our website at www.cornellpress.cornell.edu.

Cloth printing   10 9 8 7 6 5 4 3 2 1
Paperback printing   10 9 8 7 6 5 4 3 2 1

To Alvin Plantinga
Lodestar, Inspiration, and Faithful Friend

CONTENTS

Preface   XI
List of Abbreviations   XV

INTRODUCTION   1
  i. What Counts as Epistemology?   1
  ii. Concentration on the Epistemology of Belief   5
  iii. Basic Organization of the Book   6

Part I. The Naturalistic Approach

CHAPTER 1. DISPENSING WITH "JUSTIFICATION"   11
  i. Conceptions of Epistemic Justification   11
  ii. Comments on These Conceptions   15
  iii. Conditions for the Justification of a Belief   19
  iv. Attempts to Identify Epistemic Justification   21

CHAPTER 2. THE EPISTEMIC POINT OF VIEW   29
  i. True Belief as the Basic Goal of Cognition   29
  ii. Truth and Other Goals of Cognition   34
  iii. Objects of Epistemic Evaluation   37

CHAPTER 3. THE EPISTEMIC DESIDERATA APPROACH — 39
   i. A List of Epistemic Desiderata — 39
   ii. An Outline of the Epistemic Desiderata Approach — 47
   iii. Interrelations of Desiderata — 49
   iv. Internalism and Externalism — 51
   v. Internalism and Externalism on Justificationism and on the Epistemic Desiderata Approach — 53

CHAPTER 4. DEONTOLOGICAL DESIDERATA — 58
   i. Preliminaries — 58
   ii. Basic Voluntary Control of Believing — 62
   iii. Other Modes of Voluntary Control of Believing — 67
   iv. Indirect Voluntary Influence on Believing — 73

CHAPTER 5. ADEQUACY OF GROUNDS OF BELIEF — 81
   i. Grounds and the Basing Relation — 81
   ii. Having Evidence and Basing a Belief on It — 89
   iii. Adequacy of Grounds and Truth — 92
   iv. Adequacy of Grounds—Preliminaries — 94
   v. Adequacy of Grounds and Epistemic Probability — 98
   vi. The Logical Construal of Epistemic Probability — 104
   vii. A Frequency Construal of Epistemic Probability — 109

CHAPTER 6. RELIABILITY AND OTHER TRUTH-CONDUCIVE DESIDERATA — 114
   i. The Problem of Generality — 114
   ii. Belief-Forming Processes — 120
   iii. Belief-Forming Mechanisms as Psychologically Realized Functions — 125
   iv. The Problem of Generality Solved — 129
   v. Identity of Adequacy of Ground and Reliability of Process — 132
   vi. Objections and Complications — 138
   vii. Some More Serious Complications — 143
   viii. Proper Functioning of Cognitive Faculties — 148
   ix. Intellectual Virtues: Sosa and Goldman — 152
   x. Intellectual Virtues: Zagzebski — 157
   xi. Conclusion on Intellectual Virtue — 161

CHAPTER 7. ADDITIONAL EPISTEMIC DESIDERATA — 162
   i. Group III Desiderata — 162
   ii. Group V Desiderata — 165

CONTENTS

CHAPTER 8. WHERE PARTICULAR DESIDERATA ARE OF
SPECIAL IMPORTANCE   170
  i. Introduction   170
  ii. Reliability   171
  iii. Group III Desiderata   172
  iv. Deontological Desiderata   174
  v. General Philosophical Assessment of Beliefs   175
  vi. Assessment of Perceptual Beliefs: Preliminaries   178
  vii. The Nature of Perception   180
  viii. The Truth Conducivity of Grounds of Perceptual Beliefs   184

Part II. Ultimate Questions: The Epistemology of Epistemology

CHAPTER 9. CRITICAL QUESTIONS ABOUT EPISTEMOLOGICAL
METHODOLOGY   191
  i. The Demand for a Final Settlement   191
  ii. The Inevitability of a Regress   194
  iii. Attempts to Avoid the Regress: Doxastic Practices   196
  iv. Epistemic Circularity   201
  v. Avoiding Epistemic Circularity   204
  vi. The Pervasiveness of Epistemic Circularity   207

CHAPTER 10. SKEPTICISM   211
  i. Types of Skepticism   211
  ii. Disarming the Pyrrhonian Skeptic   217
  iii. Humean Skepticism   221
  iv. Skepticism Concerning Various Epistemic Desiderata   224

CHAPTER 11. THE EPISTEMIC DESIDERATA APPROACH AND
THE OVERALL EPISTEMIC ORGANIZATION OF BELIEF   230
  i. Types of Foundationalism   230
  ii. Coherentism and Contextualism   235
  iii. Does the Epistemic Desiderata Approach Make a Difference?   239
  iv. Are We Committed to Contextualism?   240

Envoi   243
Bibliography   247
Index   251

PREFACE

This book is a culmination of more than thirty years of active publishing and teaching in epistemology and, in a larger sense, of more than fifty years of off-and-on concern with epistemological issues. Through the first twenty of those fifty years I was primarily concerned with other things, philosophy of language, philosophy of mind, and philosophy of religion mostly. And in the last thirty I have been actively involved in philosophy of religion and philosophy of language as well as in issues concerning truth and realism. But epistemology has been a primary area for me in the last thirty years, one to which I have repeatedly returned. It will be clear from the first chapter that this book represents a decisive break with the orientation in epistemology that informs most of the work prior to "Epistemic Desiderata" (Alston 1993b) and much of the work since. It was in that essay that I announced an abandonment of the idea that the central positive epistemic status for belief was something called 'being *justified*,' so that the primary task for the epistemology of belief is to get straight as to what it is for a belief to be justified and as to the conditions for one or another type of belief to enjoy that status. Unfortunately, I continued to speak in terms of epistemic justification in most of the epistemological articles I published in the next ten years because I did not want to clutter up the primary concerns of those articles with philippics against "epistemic justification". But in this book I have finally cut the umbilical cord, making at least a start of laying out an epistemology of belief in terms of the alternative pluralistic epistemic desiderata approach without making use of the supposition that 'justified' succeeds in picking out a centrally important epistemic status of belief. As I point out in the book, this does not mean that my previous work, and the work of the many other epistemologists who have been laboring under the justificationist banner, is without value. On the contrary, as I point out at the end of the book, many of the treatments in this book make use of, and build on, results obtained by people trying to understand what it is for a belief to be justified. Many of these results can be fairly simply translated into my "epistemic desiderata" terms, and others readily suggest applications in the new look.

If I were to try to acknowledge all the help I have received from innumerable people, both from personal contact and from writings, in the decades preceding the turn represented in this book, I would extend this preface beyond acceptable bounds. But I will just mention some twentieth-century philosophers who have exercised a powerful influence on my thinking about epistemology, both in agreement and in disagreement: Robert Audi, Laurence BonJour, Roderick Chisholm, Fred Dretske, Richard Feldman, Roderick Firth, Richard Foley, Carl Ginet, Alvin Goldman, Peter Klein, C. I. Lewis, Paul Moser, Alvin Plantinga, and Ernest Sosa. Many other names could be added to the list, but these are the ones that stand out in my mind at the moment as having been prominent in my thoughts, writings, and teaching. As for this book specifically and the orientation in epistemology that is represented there, I want to acknowledge my indebtedness to graduate students in my epistemology classes and seminars in the 1990s, who reacted to my new ideas, not always, fortunately, with starry-eyed praise but not infrequently with tough questions. Though my initial manifesto in Alston 1993b was intended as a bombshell in epistemological circles, it mostly evoked only deadening silence, though a few dissents have found their way into print.[1] On the other side I must proffer fervent thanks to my friend and long-time colleague Jonathan Bennett for his enthusiastic approval of dispensing with epistemic justification. A little agreement, especially from as vigorous a critic as Jonathan, is most gratifying. And speaking more generally of Jonathan Bennett, though our frequent and fruitful interactions have been mostly on matters other than meta-epistemology, he has been a faithful reader and valuable reactor to my efforts in this area, as well as in many others, for all of which I remain profoundly grateful.

My thanks go to an anonymous reader of the manuscript for Cornell University Press, who made many penetrating comments on the same, one

---

[1] See especially Alvin Goldman, "Disagreement in Philosophy", a contribution to *Perspectives on the Philosophy of William Alston*, ed. Heather Battaly and Michael Lynch (Lanham, Md.: Rowman & Littlefield, forthcoming).

of which is responsible for the presence of Chapter 6, section vii, in the book. And special thanks go to the director of the Press, John G. Ackerman, for his unfailing support and encouragement. And as usual I am more grateful than I can say to my wife, Valerie, for putting up with my all too frequent over-obsession with trying to get everything completely straight in what I am writing, with all the absences from what are, no doubt, more important involvements.

Finally, I want to take the opportunity to record my appreciation for the long association with my former student and continuing friend and fellow laborer in the vineyard, Alvin Plantinga. Through the years I have found Al to be a steady beacon light to which I have constantly returned for reorientation in the course of the many false starts and reversals in my wanderings. More specifically, he has provided invaluable encouragement to my endeavors, along with equally valuable critical reactions. A prime example of the latter with special reference to the present work is the way he saved me from embarrassing misstatements in the sections on probability in Chapter 5. But I shouldn't give the impression that Al has been hypnotically focused on my career. His achievements in metaphysics, philosophical logic, epistemology, and philosophical theology are familiar to everyone on the current philosophical scene and beyond. Al is largely responsible for the return to prominence of the philosophy of religion in the academy and for the burgeoning field of Christian philosophy. To paraphrase W. S. Gilbert, he is the very model of a modern Christian philosopher. It is with great pleasure that I dedicate this book to him.

WILLIAM P. ALSTON

Syracuse, New York

ABBREVIATIONS

DP   doxastic practice
ED   epistemic desiderata
O   object
PB   perceptual belief
PE   perceptual experience
PES positive epistemic status
S   cognitive subject
TC   truth-conducive

BEYOND "JUSTIFICATION"

INTRODUCTION

Explaining the title comprises two main tasks: (1) bringing out what makes an evaluation *epistemic* and (2) identifying what items are subject to evaluation in that way. Chapter 2 will be devoted to the first task, and some groundwork for the second will be laid here. But my main concern here is to explore the ways in which my concern with epistemic evaluation fits into the larger context of epistemology in general. In addition I will provide a brief preview of the overall organization of the book.

i. What Counts as Epistemology?

Epistemology is typical of fields of philosophy (and, to a greater or lesser extent, of fields of intellectual inquiry generally) in lacking precise boundaries. There is a clear historical reason for this. Thinkers were engaged in what *we* tend to call "epistemology" long before anyone applied that label to what they were doing or, indeed, distinguished these efforts from other intellectual inquiries by any designation whatever. The earliest example of the term given in the OED is from Ferrier's *Institutes of Metaphysics*, where it is explained as answering "the general question 'What is Knowing and the Known?,' or more shortly 'What is Knowledge?' " (1856). I am not prepared to go to the stake for the claim that the term was not used for a branch of philosophy prior to the nineteenth century, but it is clear that the major philosophers prior to that century never label any of their work as such. And if anything is clear with respect to those portions of the work of Plato, Aristotle, Aquinas, Descartes, Leibniz, Locke, and Reid—to mention a few—that have been treated in the twentieth century as contributions to epistemology, it is not only that they are intimately connected with cognitive psychology but that they are best classified as cognitive psychology, with the result that extensive surgery is required to extract those portions that we are inclined to regard as "pure" epistemology. It will suffice to mention that the primary source for Aristotle's epistemology is a treatise entitled *On the Soul*, that Aquinas's epistemology is found primarily in a general treatment of the human mind, that the main source for Locke's epistemology is his *Essay Concerning Human Understanding*, a large part of which concerns the nature, classification, and origin of ideas while what we would call the more specifically epistemological part, Book IV, is as much concerned with distinguishing cognitive faculties as with "strictly epistemological" questions. Again, Hume gets into his most famous epistemological discussion—on induction—by raising questions about the *psychological* roots of our acceptance of inductive generalizations, and Reid's major contributions to what we call 'epistemology' are contained in *An Inquiry into the Human Mind* and the *Essay on the Intellectual Powers of Man*. Since we are in the position of forming our conceptions of epistemology by picking and choosing what to count as such from what must appear to a contemporary philosopher as a heterogeneous grab bag of disparate materials, it is the reverse of surprising that there should be considerable differences and considerable uncertainty as to what does and does not fall within that province.

Before leaving these historical considerations I should acknowledge that there are works by some major pre-nineteenth-century thinkers that do not present what seems to us a mélange of epistemology and cognitive psychology like the works mentioned above. These are treatments of methods of intellectual inquiry or of the logic of science, for example Aristotle's *Posterior Analytics*, Descartes's *Discourse on Method* and *Rules for the Direction of Mind*, and Spinoza's *The Emendation of the Understanding*. But for the dominant twentieth-century intuitions as to what clearly counts as epistemology, at least in English-speaking circles, these works are outside the pale. At least they are not regarded as "pure" epistemology.

Against this background, what can be said on the subject of what does and does not count as epistemology? I think the best we can do is the following. What we call 'epistemology' consists of some selection from the problems, issues, and subject matters dealt with by philosophers that have to do with what we might call the cognitive side of human life: the operation and condition of our cognitive faculties—perception, reasoning, belief formation; the products thereof—beliefs, arguments, theories, explanations, knowledge; and the evaluation of all that. And so a very broad conception of epistemology would be *philosophical reflection on the cognitive aspects of human life*, thus putting the burden of discrimination on what counts as philosophical, something that I will not get into here. But I said that what we call 'epistemology' consists of "some selection" from this. And that is where we get into disagreements and uncertainty.

It is clear that for twentieth-century English-speaking philosophical sensibilities, the center of the selected portions will have to do with what in the twentieth century has been called (unfortunately, as I shall make explicit in Chapter 1) the *justification* (warrant, rationality . . .) of *belief*, and, as the term 'epistemology' suggests, *knowledge*. These are the twin concerns that have preoccupied most Anglo-American epistemologists in the twentieth century. This focus stems largely from the fact that from at least the seventeenth century epistemological reflection has been stimulated by concern with skeptical doubts about knowledge and the rationality of beliefs. But the exclusive attention to these matters has been challenged recently from a variety of directions, and we can see these challenges as reflecting one or another neglected segment of the larger territory adumbrated above, one or another stretch of that territory that was overlooked in the rush to respond to skeptical worries.

One such segment comprises the "intellectual virtues", such as openmindedness, a disposition to consider reasons against one's own position, carefulness, and so on—virtues the exercise of which are conducive to success in attaining our cognitive goals. Flushed by the discovery of a subject matter that has not been overworked by recent epistemology, and encouraged by the recent revival of "virtue ethics", a number of thinkers have been vigorously cultivating the soil of "virtue epistemology"[1]. The more modest of these enthusiasts simply take the intellectual virtues to be one topic among others to be explored by epistemologists, an activity that is in no way incompatible with or in competition with other epistemological topics. But bolder partisans of the new look, well represented by Zagzebski 1996, present the intellectual virtues as the center of a new sort of complete epistemology. Zagzebski and others seek to provide an analysis of, for example, knowledge and justified belief in terms of the virtues and their exercise. I find these more imperialist pretensions to be unconvincing, but there is no doubt that the intellectual virtues are among the important objects of philosophical reflection on the cognitive aspect of our lives. And their neglect by epistemology in the last few centuries needs

---

[1] See, e.g., Sosa 1991, Monmarquet 1993, and Kvanvig 1992.

to be remedied. Note that as far as epistemic evaluation is concerned, putting intellectual virtues into the picture will involve adding epistemic *subjects*, cognitive *agents*, *persons* to the list of targets of epistemic evaluation.

Another part of the larger territory that, though neglected by contemporary epistemologists, had been extensively explored by earlier thinkers is *inquiry*, the process of seeking answers to questions, solutions to problems, or, more ambitiously, the construction of systematic theories. Earlier I alluded to the efforts of Aristotle, Descartes, and Spinoza along this line. The nineteenth and twentieth centuries have not been lacking in such treatments, but they have generally been assigned to the philosophy of science or logic. In the nineteenth century one thinks of Mill's *System of Logic* and Whewell's *Philosophy of the Inductive Sciences*. In the twentieth century, just to pick two items out of a crowd, there are Karl Popper's *The Logic of Scientific Discovery* and N. R. Hanson's *Patterns of Discovery*. It has become a popular sport in certain circles to berate the epistemological establishment for neglecting "serious" problems as to how inquiry is most successfully conducted and concentrating instead on answering skepticism and becoming hypnotically obsessed with trying to understand simple, commonsense perceptual knowledge. Since I think that the world is full of things to explore and reflect on philosophically and that there is no reason for the study of one to exclude studies of the others, I will not enter into these polemics but instead note that the study of inquiry provides a rich harvest of objects of epistemic evaluation. Indeed, insofar as it distinguishes itself from the psychology or sociology or history of inquiry, it is pretty much taken up with evaluative questions as to how researches are best or most successfully pursued.

Another recent trend in epistemology that complicates the terrain of epistemic evaluation, one with less in the way of traditional roots, is *social epistemology*, the study of knowledge and epistemically valuable belief as a social phenomenon. From the ancient Greeks on, epistemology has focused on the individual cognitive agent, her cognitive activities and cognitive products. Social epistemology aims to go beyond this in taking seriously the idea of, for example, scientific knowledge or religious belief as a social reality that cannot be properly understood without taking into account the ways in which social interaction is involved.[2] If we take this seriously, we will be involved in issues such as those treated in a landmark work of this movement, Goldman 1999A. There we find chapters treating a variety of ways in which forms of social interaction and organization affect the search for knowledge and well-grounded belief—Testimony,

---

[2] See, e.g., Fuller 1988 and Schmitt, ed., 1994.

Argumentation, The Technology and Economics of Communication, Speech Regulation and the Marketplace of Ideas. These are followed by chapters applying all this to the development of science, the law, the political process, and education. Here too we have a rich field of possible objects of epistemic evaluation—the various social institutions, processes, and interactions that are involved in the search for knowledge and attempts at systematizing and communicating it. It is worthy of note that much of the material in Goldman's book would be rejected by many contemporary epistemologists as "not real epistemology", and relegated to sociology, social psychology, or other social sciences, or perhaps to the philosophical foundations thereof. This is a prominent example of my earlier point that the boundaries of "epistemology" are fuzzy and controversial, and drawn by different thinkers and from different perspectives in different ways. I will not get embroiled in the question of just where to draw those boundaries. I prefer to note that anything called 'epistemology' by anyone belongs to some portion of the vast sprawling territory that we can identify as philosophical reflection on the cognitive aspect of human life.

ii. Concentration on the Epistemology of Belief

Having noted some attempts to move beyond the narrow focus of most twentieth-century English-speaking epistemology, I will now proceed to disappoint some of my readers and reassure others by announcing that this book will share the more familiar focus. Or rather it will have an even narrower focus. Leaving knowledge for another occasion, I will be dealing with those issues in epistemology that concern *the epistemic evaluation of belief*. Given the prominence in twentieth-century Anglo-American philosophy of the view that knowledge is true belief that satisfies further conditions, including being justified, it might seem strange to produce a book-length treatment of the epistemic evaluation of belief without considering its contribution to knowledge. But the view of knowledge just mentioned is controversial, and should be more controverted than it has been.[3] And though I would like eventually to make a major contribution to that controversy, the epistemic evaluation of belief will more than occupy me for this book. At most there will be only hints as to its bearing on knowledge.

Let me assure my readers with other interests and sympathies that in restricting the book in the way just noted I by no means denigrate concern

---

[3] For an outstanding recent attack on this tradition, see Williamson 2000.

with intellectual virtues, methods of inquiry, social aspects of knowledge, and so on. I make no claim that what I will be discussing is the whole of what can properly be called 'epistemology'. But I do think that the various epistemic desiderata of belief are of central importance in philosophical reflection on human cognition. The other matters that are of interest to epistemologists have that interest, in large part, because of their relations to epistemically positively valued beliefs. Intellectual virtues count as such because their exercise tends to eventuate in the epistemically right sorts of beliefs. Social aspects of cognition are of special interest because of the ways in which they influence the acquisition of epistemically desirable beliefs. And so on. Thus in focusing my attention on the epistemology of belief, I am dealing with matters that are of central importance to other epistemological concerns.

But there is another more "strategic" or, to put a less favorable spin on it, "opportunistic" reason for the focus. My primary aim in the book is to explore and explicate the modes of epistemic evaluation of belief and to develop a better framework for understanding and using them than is prevalent in the present state of the subject. The present endeavor grows out of dissatisfaction with the way in which the epistemology of belief has been construed and handled in the mainstream of Anglo-American twentieth-century epistemology. Therefore, in order to make the desired contact with what I am trying to modify and improve, I need to concentrate on the same targets of evaluation as the procedures I seek to reform. Just as one who seeks to propose a better way of construing and pursuing social psychology needs to concentrate on the problems and current state of that field rather than, say, the psychology of perception, however important the latter might be, so with my current endeavor.

I will make one further point about my chosen topic. In restricting myself to beliefs, I do not mean to restrict myself to individual beliefs one by one, in isolation from each other. My interests include more or less systematic bodies of belief as well. There are important epistemic desiderata that apply only to larger units than individual beliefs—*coherence* in any of the many understandings of that term, *explanatory fecundity*, *simplicity*, and so on. Even though most of the attention will be on individual beliefs, I will not exclude the more holistic modes of evaluation.

iii. Basic Organization of the Book

Now for a brief preview of the organization of the book. The distinction of the two parts reflects a distinction between two perspectives from which we may approach the epistemic evaluation of beliefs. On the one hand, we can set about to determine whether one or another belief is, for example, well grounded, based on adequate evidence or reasons, by using whatever we take ourselves to know or believe on adequate grounds. The epistemic evaluation will proceed on the assumption that we already know quite a bit that is of relevance to it. (If we don't, we might as well abstain from attempting it.) If we try to determine whether a certain political prediction is well grounded, we presuppose that we know a great deal about what makes such predictions more or less likely to be true, about the sampling procedures for determining the likely attitudes of voters to certain candidates or certain issues, what issues are likely to be most salient in the minds of possible or likely voters, and so on. This is the way we standardly proceed in trying to answer a question. If we didn't or couldn't presuppose a background of relevant knowledge, we would be in no position to investigate the issue. This point applies equally to attempts to determine the epistemic status of beliefs.

Part I takes up the bulk of the book. This reflects the fact that I consider the above perspective to be the only reasonable one to adopt. Hence the detailed treatment of various epistemic desiderata and their interrelations will appear in this part.

The other perspective is one that reflects the attempt to respond to radical skeptical doubts by showing, without presupposing that we already know various things, that we have genuine knowledge or well-grounded belief. This is the effort classically illustrated by Descartes' attempt in his *Meditations* to show, in the face of even the most extreme doubts, that we do have some genuine knowledge. To be sure, a moment's reflection should be sufficient to reveal the futility of trying to show that we have knowledge, or show anything else whatever, without presupposing some knowledge (well-founded belief). Otherwise we would have no premises on which to rely for the showing. And so if it is not to be a mug's game, we have to rethink the enterprise. We have to think of it as an attempt to decide what to say about skeptical demands to show that we know something, without giving all the cards to the skeptic by agreeing to play the game on his terms, which allow us nothing to work with. In Part II of the book I will consider various options for dealing with the skeptic and will develop one of these, which, briefly, consists in the point that since we can't take a single step in intellectual inquiry without presupposing some knowledge or well-grounded belief, the problem is one of finding a basis for deciding which presuppositions to make. I will then explore the bearing of this on how we should think about various modes of epistemic evaluation of belief.

Finally, a couple of preliminary comments about these two perspectives.

1. The first perspective is one aspect of what has been called 'naturalized epistemology,' not the extreme version put on the map, unfortunately, by Quine in his too well known essay "Epistemology Naturalized" in Quine 1969, but a more moderate version that is distinguished precisely by avoiding the temptation to play the skeptic's game. One declines to pursue epistemology as "first philosophy", an attempt to get conclusions as to what we know or how we know before we address ourselves to getting any knowledge about anything else. Instead, one approaches epistemology in the same "natural" spirit as any other problem area—by working with any of our knowledge, beliefs, or assumptions that seem to be of relevance to the problems at hand; remembering, of course, that any of them can be called into question at a further stage of inquiry.

2. The second perspective need not be adopted by way of attempting to respond to radical skepticism, though that does give it a dramatic appeal that never fails to attract beginning students. Instead, one can accomplish the same thing by asking what epistemic status epistemic principles or judgments have. Do we have knowledge (or well-grounded belief) of them, and if so, on what basis, and if not, what can be said in their defense? Thus, for example, instead of trying to respond to skeptical doubts about what we take to be perceptual knowledge, we could ask what grounds we do or could have for the principles we ordinarily presuppose as to the conditions under which one has perceptual knowledge.

PART I

THE NATURALISTIC APPROACH

CHAPTER 1

DISPENSING WITH "JUSTIFICATION"

i. Conceptions of Epistemic Justification

In the last half of the twentieth century the epistemic evaluation of belief has been so dominated by the terms 'justification' and 'justified' that my exploration of dimensions of epistemic evaluation must either highlight these terms or explain why I abstain from doing so. My choice is for the latter. In fact, not only will I defend a preference for ignoring 'justification' in epistemology. I will go on the offensive and argue that the widespread supposition that 'justified' picks out an objective feature of belief that is of central epistemic importance is a thoroughly misguided one. I shall argue that the perennial quest for what it is for a belief to be justified, and what are the necessary and/or sufficient conditions for such a status, is quixotic, of the same order as the search for the Fountain of Youth. The best assessment of the situation is that no such objective property of belief has been identified, and that controversies over what it takes for a belief to be justified are no more than a vain beating of the air. Having dispelled this illusion we will be in a position to reconstruct the epistemic evaluation of belief on a sounder basis. And, by way of preview, though my project sounds radically iconoclastic, and in a way is meant to be so, it does not imply that contemporary epistemologists, including myself, have been completely wasting their time. On the contrary, the investigation of "epistemic justification" has produced many important results, however ill-founded the framework of the inquiry may have been.

I will begin by pointing to the great diversity of attempts to say what it is for a belief to be justified. To avoid possible misunderstandings, let me say that this diversity is not the sole or even the main basis for my conclusion. It is only the first step along the way, one that will lay out the first of the data of which we need to take account. Here is a sample of attempts to say what it is for a belief to be justified. (Some of these formulations are in terms of 'rational' rather than 'justified', but I believe that a close reading of the context in each case will reveal that the authors who use 'rational' mean to be marking out a property of beliefs that has the same, or a very similar, epistemic force as what the other authors are trying to get at with 'justified'.)

1. "One is *justified* in being confident that p if and only if it is not the case that one ought not to be confident that p; one could not be justly reproached for being confident that p" (Ginet 1975, 28).

2. "The rational belief is the belief which does not violate our noetic obligations. The rational belief is the belief which, by reference to our noetic obligations, is permitted. . . . For Locke the rational belief is the belief in accord with the reality-possession and firmness obligations that pertain to one's believings. Rationality consists in not violating *those* duties concerning one's believings. To be rational in one's believings amounts to doing as well in the firmness and reality-possession dimensions of one's believing as can rightly be demanded of one" (Wolterstorff 1983, 144).

3. "A noetic structure is rational if it could be the noetic structure of a person who was completely rational. To be completely rational . . . is to do the right thing with respect to one's believings. It is to violate no epistemic duties . . . a rational person is one whose believings meet the appropriate standards; to criticize a person as irrational is to criticize her for failing to fulfill these duties or responsibilities. . . . To draw the ethical analogy, the irrational is the impermissible; the rational is the permissible" (Plantinga 1983, 52).

4. "The distinguishing characteristic of epistemic justification is thus its essential or internal relation to the cognitive goal of truth. It follows that one's cognitive endeavors are epistemically justified only and to the extent that they are aimed at this goal, which means very roughly that one accepts all and only those beliefs which one has good reason to think are true. To accept a belief in the absence of such a reason . . . is to neglect the pursuit of truth; such acceptance is, one might say, epistemically irresponsible. My

contention here is that the idea of avoiding such irresponsibility, of being epistemically responsible in one's believings, is the core of the notion of epistemic justification" (BonJour 1985, 8).

5. "... epistemic justification is essentially related to the so-called cognitive goal of truth, insofar as an individual belief is epistemically justified only if it is appropriately directed toward the goal of truth. More specifically, on the present conception, one is epistemically justified in believing a proposition only if one has good reason to believe it is true. To accept a proposition in the absence of good reason is to neglect the cognitive goal of truth. Such acceptance ... is epistemically irresponsible. On this conception, one has an epistemic responsibility to believe only those proposition which are likely to be true on one's evidence; and thus one has an epistemic responsibility to believe only those propositions one has good reason to believe are true" (Moser 1985, 4–5).

6. "The epistemic notion of justification derives from ethics and must retain its normative force if the term is to remain univocal. We may distinguish stronger and weaker normative senses in epistemology. In the weaker sense, if a person is unjustified in holding a belief, then he ought to give it up. The stronger sense demands more than the 'right' to have a certain belief: if a subject is justified in holding or has justification for a belief, she must be capable of meeting challenges to it in a rational way. Thus justification in this sense carries an obligation as well as a right (although the obligation is not to form the belief, which may be beyond voluntary control)" (Alan Goldman 1988, 40).

7. "We may assume that every person is subject to a purely intellectual requirement—that of trying his best to bring it about that, for every proposition h that he considers, he accepts h if and only if h is true. . . . One way, then, of re-expressing the locution 'p is more reasonable than q for S at t' is to say this: 'S is so situated at t that his intellectual requirement, his responsibility as an intellectual being, is better fulfilled by p than by q'" ['p' and 'q' range over doxastic attitudes] (Chisholm 1977, 14). Chisholm then proceeds to define various modes of epistemic status, such as 'has some presumption in its favor' and 'evident' in terms of 'more reasonable than'.

8. "S's believing p at t is justified if and only if: (a) S's believing p at t is permitted by a right system of J-rules. (b) This permission is not undermined by S's cognitive state at t" (Alvin Goldman 1986, 63).

9. "What are we asking when we ask whether a belief is justified? What we want to know is whether it is all right to believe it. Justification is a matter of epistemic permissibility. . . . Thus I will think of epistemic justification as being concerned with questions of the form, 'When is it permissible (from an epistemological point of view) to believe P?' . . . Epistemic norms are norms describing when it is epistemically permissible to hold various beliefs. A belief is justified if and only if it is licensed by correct epistemic norms" (Pollock 1986, 124–125).

10. (This is partly in my own words). It is epistemically rational for a person to believe that p at t *iff* S would believe, on sufficiently careful reflection, that believing p at t is an effective way of realizing the goal of now believing those propositions that are true and now not believing those propositions that are false. And that analysans will be satisfied *iff* S "has an uncontroversial argument for p, an argument that he would regard as likely to be truth preserving were he to be appropriately reflective, and an argument whose premises he would uncover no good reasons to be suspicious of were he to be appropriately reflective" (Foley 1987, 66).

11. "An improved alternative to the normative concepts of justification is the notion of justification as *an adequate indication, relative to one's total evidence, that a proposition is true*. Such an adequate indication is provided for one by something that makes a proposition, P, evidentially more probable for one, on one's total evidence, than not only -P but also P's probabilistic competitors . . . on this notion, an epistemic justifier of a proposition is simply a certain sort of truth indicator, or evidential probability-maker for that proposition" (Moser 1989, 42–43).

12. "S's belief that h is epistemically justified at t iff: There is some set of reasons, R, such that:

   (1) S's belief that h is based upon R at t;
   (2) S's believing that h on the basis of R is epistemically justified at t;
   (3) If, at t, S has any other reasons, R', that are relevant to whether S is justified in believing that h, then S would be epistemically justified in believing that h on the basis of R&R' at t. . . .

S's believing that h on the basis of R is epistemically justified at t iff: S's believing that h on the basis of R is a reliable indication that h at t" (Swain 1981, 98–99).

13. "S is Jeg in believing that p iff S's believing that p, as S did, was a good thing from the epistemic point of view, in that S's belief that p was based on adequate grounds and S lacked sufficient overriding reasons to the contrary" (Alston 1985, reprinted in Alston 1989, 105–106).

14. "A belief B has positive epistemic status for S if and only if that belief is produced in S by his epistemic faculties working properly; and B has more positive epistemic status than B* for S iff B has positive epistemic status for S and either B* does not or else S is more strongly inclined to believe B than B*" (Plantinga 1988, 34).

15. "Doxastic attitude D toward proposition p is epistemically justified for S at t if and only if having D toward p fits the evidence S has at t" (Feldman and Conee 1985, 15).

16. "A *justified belief* is what a person who is motivated by intellectual virtue, and who has the understanding of his cognitive situation a virtuous person would have, might believe in like circumstances" (Zagzebski 1996, 241).

ii. Comments on These Conceptions

It is important to emphasize that what we have here are attempts to say *what epistemic justification of belief is* rather than make claims about the necessary and/or sufficient conditions of being justified that go beyond a specification of the nature of that status. Thus, for example, BonJour holds that a belief is justified *iff* it fits in a sufficiently coherent way into a sufficiently coherent system. But that isn't what he says being epistemically justified *is*. That is in terms of being *responsible* in believing. Again, Alvin Goldman's view, roughly speaking, is that a belief is justified *iff* it is formed in a sufficiently reliable way. But his explanation of what it *is* to be justified is in terms of being *permitted by a right system of rules*. To be sure, it is not always obvious, or even clear, whether a formulation is intended to tell us what being justified is, or to lay down conditions for this that go beyond a specification of its nature. Nevertheless, it is often enough determinate on which side of the distinction a particular formulation lies.

The formulations in the above list fall into two main groups. First, there are those I call *deontological*, for they have to do with obligations, responsibility, blame or the absence thereof, and the like. 1–9 constitute this group. Second, there are those that think of being justified in terms of the belief's being adequately grounded, well supported, being based on sufficient evidence or reasons, there being sufficient evidence or reasons for it, and other features that entail that the belief is at least likely to be true. Let's call this the *truth-conducivity* group. These include 10–15. We should not suppose that the two groups are hermetically sealed against each other. In 4 and 5, for example, we have a definition in terms of responsibility combined with the view that one can believe responsibly only if one believes on the basis of sufficient reasons. But by reading carefully we can distinguish what is definitional from what is true of the belief status so defined.

Both sorts of accounts have strong roots in ordinary language. This is most obvious for the deontological group. It is plausible to suppose that 'justified' came into epistemology from its more unproblematic use with respect to voluntary action. I am justified in doing something, for example, charging my department for a taxi ride to and from the airport, provided my doing so is in accordance with the relevant rules, regulations, or standards, provided it is *permitted* by those rules and hence that I could not rightfully be *blamed* or *held to account* for it, and was acting *responsibly* in doing so. The rules or norms could be institutional, as in the above example, or legal or moral. Thus I might be morally justified in objecting to your blocking my driveway provided my doing so doesn't violate any moral rule. Because of this provenance it is natural to think of believing, when taken to be subject to being justified or unjustified, as subject to requirement, prohibition, and permission. We say things like "You shouldn't have supposed so readily that he would not return", "You have no right to assume that", "You shouldn't jump to conclusions", and "I ought to have trusted him more than I did". Locutions like these seem to be interchangeable with speaking of a belief as being, or not being, justified.

The truth-conducivity construals cannot claim any such etymological support, and as a result there is something of a linguistic strain in speaking of justification in these terms. Nevertheless, the evidentialist can call on support from current linguistic tendencies. It is not implausible to hear "He isn't justified in believing that" as "He lacks sufficient evidence (grounds, reasons . . .) for believing that". And there is an equal plausibility for equating "I am justified in believing that P" to "P is the case so far as I can tell", or "P seems to be the case, given what I have to go on, given the evidence available to me".

My reference to two *groups* was deliberate. There are differences between particular formulations in each group. Some of the differences may be merely terminological, but others are of considerable importance. Thus there may not be a large difference between equating 'justified' with 'permitted' and 'not subject to blame', or between 'evidence' and 'reasons', depending on how these latter terms are themselves construed. But among the significant differences are the following. First the deontological group.

(1) On some accounts the deontological terms—'permitted', 'required', and 'forbidden'—apply to believing itself. And this certainly seems to presuppose that belief is subject to direct voluntary control. How else could my believing that we will win the war against terrorism be required or permitted? (See Chapter 4 for a detailed discussion of this). But on other accounts in this family these terms are taken to apply rather to voluntary actions that have a bearing on whether the subject acquires a certain belief. On this latter version a belief's being justified depends on whether actions in its causal ancestry were permitted rather than whether *it* is permitted. And there are more fine-grained differences that will be explored in Chapter 4.

The evidentialist group also exhibits significant differences.

(2) Most obviously, there are different accounts of just what it is that entails the likelihood of truth. In 10, 11, 13, and 15 it is a matter of adequate evidence, reasons, or grounds for the belief. In 12 it is the reliability of the way in which the belief was formed. In 14 it is the belief's being acquired by the proper functioning of one's cognitive faculties. In 16 it is the belief's being formed by the exercise of an intellectual virtue. It is not obvious in all cases just from the passages cited that what is being put forward does entail a probability of truth for belief. That will become clear when we treat these conceptions in Chapters 3 and 5.

(3) With respect to the formulations that stress evidence, reasons, and grounds there is the difference between requiring for justification that the belief be *based on* sufficient evidence (reasons), as in 12 and 13, and requiring only that the subject *have* sufficient evidence for it, whether or not this played any role in the acquisition of the belief, as in 10, 11, and 15.

(4) Here is a distinction that cross-cuts the difference between our two main groups and applies equally to both. All the above conceptions of justification can be thought of as being objective. They lay down conditions that must be satisfied; S's believing them to be satisfied is not enough. But each of them is susceptible to "subjectivizations" of various sorts. The simplest subjective transformation of a given set of conditions would consist of S's believing that the conditions are satisfied. A more complex subjectivization is represented by 10.

There are other ways in which philosophers have explained the justification of belief, but I will set them aside for present purposes because they are not addressed to my present topic, which is what it is for a *belief* to *be justified*, what it is for a *belief* to *have the property of being justified*. These other ways include the following.

A. There is the notion of *propositional* as opposed to *doxastic* justification. (a) A proposition, P, may be said to be justified for S provided S is so situated that if he were to make use of that situation to form a belief that P, that belief would be justified. (S can be justified vis-à-vis P in this sense even if one does have a justified belief that P. It is just that in attributing justification in this sense to S one is leaving it open whether S has a belief that P). (b) In the doxastic sense one is justified in believing that P provided one has a belief that P which is justified. It is this latter sense that is my concern here.

B. There is the distinction between being justified as a property or status of a belief (my topic) and the *activity* of *justifying* a belief. The latter involves presenting an argument for the belief or exhibiting the reasons or evidence for it—what renders it justified. The two are obviously connected. By *justifying* a belief one shows that it *is justified*. But it is a confusion to identify the two. S can be justified in believing that p even if neither S nor anyone else has engaged in the activity of justifying that belief. The confusion between the two frequently surfaces in epistemological discussion. Thus in presenting the regress argument for epistemic foundations, one may start out to ask whether all justified belief can owe that status to support from other justified beliefs. It is then pointed out that this leads to an infinite regress (or else to a circle). But in arguing against the possibility of such an infinite regress, it is not uncommon to do so by arguing that it is impossible to continue the *process* of *justifying* beliefs by other beliefs infinitely. The subject will have been surreptitiously shifted from *being justified* to the *activity of justification*. In this discussion the focus will be solely on the former.

It is a little noted but very important point that although the usual focus of attention is on disagreements over what epistemic justification is—and, as we shall see in the next section, what the conditions are for its realization—if we consider the various features of belief listed above that are asserted by some and denied by others to be what it is to be justified, there is virtually no controversy over the epistemic desirability of these features. There is persistent disagreement as to whether having sufficient evidence, being reliably formed, or believing in a way that is permitted is necessary and/or sufficient for a belief's being *justified*. But (almost) everyone recognizes these and the other features of belief in the above accounts to be good things to have in a belief. No one disputes that it is a good thing for the attainment of the aims of cognition that one have sufficient evidence for beliefs, that one conduct one's cognitive activities in such a way as not to violate intellectual obligations, and so on. This point will be the keystone of the new approach to the epistemology of belief developed and defended in this book. My proposal will be that we give up the attempt to determine just what is required for a belief to be "justified", indeed that we give up the supposition that there is any such property of beliefs that we need to get at the nature and conditions of, and instead focus on a variety of *epistemic desiderata* for beliefs, features of belief that are desirable from the epistemic point of view, the point of view defined by the basic aims of cognition. In the next chapter I will explore those aims and the way in which they make features of beliefs like those that figure in accounts of "justification" epistemically desirable. But first I must (a) look at various accounts of conditions for a belief's being justified, conditions that go beyond the nature of epistemic justification, and (b) give some support to the denial that there is any objective and epistemically crucial feature of beliefs picked out by 'justified'.

iii. Conditions for the Justification of a Belief

As for conditions of justification that go beyond the specification of its nature, here too the literature is rife with a variety of incompatible views. I will concentrate on alleged necessary conditions since they are more varied, noting whether they are also typically held to be sufficient. Here is a partial list of such conditions.

1. *Cognitive accessibility*. The subject has some high-grade cognitive access to the reasons, evidence, or grounds for the belief B or for the fact that B has some positive epistemic status. Since the satisfaction of other conditions is presupposed by this one, it cannot be taken to be sufficient but only as necessary. Advocates of this condition differ as to what sort or degree of access is required, as well as just what it is to which one must have that access. For example, where the more basic condition is evidentialist, is access required only to the evidence or also to the fact that the evidence is sufficient?

2. S has *higher-level* knowledge, or well-grounded belief, that (some or all of) the lower-level conditions access to which is required in 1 are satisfied. Here again, for the same reason, this requirement could only be necessary, not also sufficient.

3. S is able to carry out a successful *defense* of the epistemic status of B. But if so, more basic conditions of justification must be satisfied in order that the defense be successful. Hence, again, necessity is the most that could be claimed.

4. *Reliability*. The way in which the belief was formed is one that reliably produces true beliefs.[1] This is often taken as a sufficient as well as a necessary condition of justification. Again, there is room for differences in the exact form of the position. How is the reliability of a way of forming beliefs to be understood? How reliable must that way be if it is to confer justification on its product? Is this sufficient for justification no matter what else, or is it sufficient only for prima facie justification, which holds in the absence of sufficient "overriders"? And so on.

5. *Coherence*. The belief must fit in a sufficiently coherent way into a sufficiently coherent system. This is often taken as sufficient as well as necessary.[2] And, again, there is room for many different versions. How is coherence to be understood? How coherent does the system, and the way the particular belief fits into the system, have to be? And so on.

6. *Virtues*. The belief must be formed as an exercise of an intellectual (epistemic) virtue. Again, this is sometimes taken as sufficient as well as necessary.[3] And, again, there are different, sometimes radically different, versions. How are intellectual virtues to be construed? Just what virtues have this relationship to justification? And so on.

7. On adequate reflection S would believe that B is held on the basis of sufficient evidence, or that other first-level conditions are satisfied.[4]

With respect to 4, 5, 6, and 7, where they are taken to be sufficient, there is a question as to whether the claim is to absolute sufficiency, no matter what else is the case, or only to *prima facie* sufficiency, which will be absolute sufficiency provided there are no sufficient "overriders" in the picture.

The overlaps between this list and the one in the previous section make clear that there is no neat dividing line between what it *is* for a belief to be

---

[1] See Goldman 1979, 1986, 1992a, and 1992b; Swain 1981.
[2] See BonJour 1985; Lehrer 1990.
[3] Note that Zagzebski in the passage cited earlier treats this as what it is for a belief to be justified. But other theorists take it rather as a condition for being justified, explicating the nature of justification in some other way.
[4] Foley 1987.

justified and the conditions for a belief's having that status, conditions that are taken to go beyond a specification of its nature. What one theorist will offer as an account of what justification of belief is, another will offer as a condition for that status that goes beyond its nature. Though I cannot exhibit this possibility for everything on both lists, there are enough actualizations to prevent a rigid separation. In the list of section i Swain explains what justification *is* in terms of reliability, but Goldman in his 1986 takes it to consist in being permitted by rules of a certain sort while taking reliable formation as a necessary and sufficient condition of that permissibility. Again, BonJour in the same list takes a belief's being justified to *be* its being formed responsibly and takes coherence as a necessary and sufficient condition for this. Whereas Lehrer (1990) and Putnam (1981) regard coherence as what a belief's being justified *is*.

iv. Attempts to Identify Epistemic Justification

To return to the main thread of the argument, we are confronted with a wildly chaotic picture of an enormous plurality of incompatible views as to what it is for a belief to be justified, and as to what further conditions are required for a belief's having that status. One could be pardoned for taking this alone as a sufficient reason for abandoning the search for the true account of epistemic justification. If so many brilliant philosophers disagree so radically as to what it is and what it takes to have it, why should we suppose that there is any objective property of beliefs picked out by 'justified'? Wouldn't it be more reasonable to conclude that they are chasing a phantom? But I will resist the tendency to move this quickly. I don't think that we should take radical disagreement, even long-continued radical disagreement, as showing the unreality of its putative object. There are many cases of long-continued disagreement in which it is obvious that there is a unique correct answer to the question. Think of the issue of whether there is intelligent life in the universe outside our planet, or questions about a genetic basis for one or another individual difference. Or, closer to home, consider disputes as to the nature of causality or natural laws or propositional attitudes. Surely there are causal relations and natural laws and propositional attitudes. It is more reasonable to believe in such things than to deny their existence, however persistently thinkers disagree about their nature. So let us not be so hasty to move from persistent disagreement to the nonexistence of its object.

Nevertheless, the persistent disagreement is an important datum for the inquiry. It is a fact that requires an explanation. Why is it that philosophers who think long and deeply about epistemology take such widely different positions on the nature and conditions of epistemic justification? So far as I can see, there are two main candidates for an explanation of the phenomenon.

(1) As is typical for philosophy, it's just a very tough problem. It is extremely difficult to find an adequate basis for a conclusive resolution, one that will command wide, if not universal, assent. But that doesn't show there isn't an objective reality picked out by 'justified' in epistemic contexts. It doesn't show that there are no objective facts about what it is for a belief to be justified and what the conditions are for that, any more than persistent disagreement shows that there are no objective facts as to what is involved when one thing causes another.

(2) The other explanation is this. There isn't any unique, epistemically crucial property of beliefs picked out by 'justified'. Epistemologists who suppose the contrary have been chasing a will-of-the-wisp. What has really been happening is this. Different epistemologists have been emphasizing, concentrating on, "pushing" different *epistemic desiderata*, different features of belief that are positively valuable from the standpoint of the aims of cognition. These include the features we have been listing above in surveying views as to the nature and conditions of justified belief. They include such features as a belief's being permitted by relevant rules or norms, a belief's being based on adequate grounds, a belief's being formed in a reliable way, a belief's fitting coherently in a coherent system, and so on. Somehow the practice has spread of taking one's attachment to a certain epistemic desideratum as deriving from its being part of what it is for a belief to be "justified" or what is required for that. But the supposed connection with "justification" has nothing to do with what makes a desideratum epistemically desirable. There is no substance to that connection; it is an honorific title that carries no remuneration, perks, or further implications along with it. It is not as if one needs to show that, for example, reliability of formation or evidential support or coherence is what matters for *justification* in order to validate its epistemic credentials. There is no such reality as epistemic justification to perform that function. All we have is the plurality of features of belief that are of positive value for the cognitive enterprise. They need no validation from a connection with a supposed master epistemic desideratum picked out by 'justified'. There isn't any such. A belief's being justified has no more objective reality than ether or ghosts.

The question of the right way to pursue the epistemology of belief hangs on the choice between these explanations. Should we keep trying to get straight about the real nature and conditions of epistemic justification, or should we give this up as a misguided enterprise and explore the variety of epistemic desiderata in their own terms, and raise a variety of important questions about their nature, viability, importance, and interrelations? How can we make a reasonable choice here?

My suggestion is that the issue turns on whether we have or can have some theoretically neutral way of getting at this alleged property about which our contestants are disagreeing. It has to be theoretically neutral because if we were to use one of the competing accounts to pick it out, opponents of that account would complain, quite reasonably, that this didn't pick out justification at all but only something that has been erroneously identified as justification. So we can't reasonably claim to have identified what the various theories of justification are trying to characterize by saying that it is reliable belief formation, or having sufficient evidence, or forming a belief in a permissible way, or. . . . So where are we to find an acceptable way of identifying what the arguments are about? Let's consider some possibilities.

Here is a starting point. If I am justified in believing that p, my doxastic state is *one that is desirable from an epistemic point of view*. And what is that point of view? In the next chapter I will defend the thesis that it is defined by the aim at maximizing true belief and minimizing false belief, with some additional qualifications. But this does not even come close to picking out epistemic justification. There are many epistemically desirable features of belief that cannot be identified with being justified, most notably truth. Nothing can be more desirable from the standpoint of the aim just mentioned than truth. And yet, by common consent, justification is distinct from truth. True beliefs can be unjustified, and false beliefs can be justified. That's one of the few things all justification theorists agree on. Indeed, as I have just been pointing out, everything (almost everything?) that goes into the controverted accounts of the nature and conditions of justification is epistemically desirable. But, as we have seen, all of them are disqualified as ways of picking out what the arguments over justification are arguments about.

It has been suggested to me that we might think of epistemic justification as the maximally "thin" epistemic desideratum of belief. This would fit in nicely with my program of concentrating on the various "thick" epistemic properties in their own right rather than seeking to determine which of these, or which combination of these, gives us a thick evaluative property of justification. This would make justification related to, for example, having sufficient evidence, being reliably produced, being permitted, and so on, in something like the way goodness is related to the various forms thereof—usefulness, virtuousness, beauty, pleasure, and so on. My only objection to this proposal is that it is irrelevant to understanding the way 'justified belief' figures in the thought of those epistemologists who give it a central place. I can't imagine any such epistemologist being content with relegating 'justified' to such a thin status. One who thinks that being responsible in one's believing is what it *is* for a belief to be *justified* would not be cheered by the suggestion that for a belief to be justified is for it to have some positively epistemically valuable property or other, of which there are many, all with more or less the same standing. The central importance each of our contestants gives to his account of what it is to be justified would be lost. This concession would be taken as a stone rather than bread.

Some epistemologists try to locate justification, as a preliminary to investigating its nature and conditions, by saying that it is what makes true belief into knowledge. It is whatever solves for X in "True belief + X = knowledge". But there is more than one reason why this will not do. The most obvious one rests on Gettier's celebrated demonstration that true justified belief is not sufficient for knowledge. But this could be taken care of by changing the formula to "True belief + X + what succeeds in dealing with Gettier problems = knowledge". And, provided the concept of a Gettier problem is sufficiently clear, this would handle that difficulty, with the further proviso that knowledge is true belief + certain further conditions, something that is not beyond controversy. But it still doesn't give us a satisfactory way of identifying epistemic justification. That is because justification theorists typically recognize other constraints on what counts as epistemic justification, and if it should turn out that what turns true ungettierized belief into knowledge does not satisfy those constraints, they would not recognize it as epistemic justification. Suppose that a completely convincing case could be made for the thesis that being formed in a reliable way or being formed by the proper functioning of one's faculties is sufficient for turning true ungettierized belief into knowledge. Suppose that the case is so overwhelming that it would convince anti-externalist justification theorists like Chisholm, BonJour, Foley, and Feldman. Would they then be prepared to identify epistemic justification with reliable formation or formation by the proper functioning of one's faculties? Unless one or another of them underwent a fundamental intellectual conversion, I suggest that the answer would be negative. Barring any such drastic event, I am convinced that what they would say instead is that they had been mistaken in thinking that epistemic justification can be uniquely picked out by the above formula. My reading of the situation is that they are more firmly committed to their views as to what epistemic justification is than they are to the idea that justification is what turns true ungettierized belief into knowledge. If I am correct about this, they, and leading justification theorists generally, are not really prepared to recognize what satisfies X in the above formula, *whatever else is the case*, to be epistemic justification. Thus this approach fails for basically the same reason as taking 'justified' to be the thinnest term for a positively epistemically evaluable property; it fails to connect with the way 'justified' is used by philosophers who give it a central place in the epistemology of belief.

I should make it explicit that I have no objection to someone's using 'justified', or some other term like 'warrant', for what turns true ungettierized belief into knowledge. At least, where 'justified' is concerned, no objection other than it's being misleading, since it does not jibe with the way the term is used by justificationist epistemologists. But a philosopher is within her rights to stipulate that sense for that term and then proceed to do with it what she can. My contention here has to do with what the concept 'justified' is typically used to express by epistemologists who give "justification" a central place in epistemology.

Up to this point I have been arguing that none of the most promising attempts to *say*, in theoretically neutral terms, what epistemic justification is are successful. But even if I am right about that, it doesn't follow that we cannot refer to a common target with 'justified'. There are ways of zeroing in on an object of thought other than using a uniquely satisfied definite description. The most obvious of these is to work with one or more paradigm cases and take the whole class of cases to be those that are sufficiently similar to the paradigms. There are many familiar concepts that are used successfully on the basis of paradigms. Natural-kind terms often have this status. Most of us are unable to spell out necessary and sufficient conditions for the application of terms like 'dog' and 'tree'. Instead, we learn and use the terms on the basis of paradigm cases, applying one of them to an object *iff* that object is sufficiently similar to the paradigms. Why shouldn't it be this way with 'epistemic justification'? If we can point out clear cases of justified and unjustified beliefs, that will put us in a position to use 'justified' to pick out a property of beliefs without having spelled out explicitly what it is for a belief to be justified. To be sure, paradigm-based concepts are less than fully determinate because of the vagueness of the notion of one case being "sufficiently similar" to another. But that does not prevent such concepts from being determinate enough to be useful.

The prospects for a paradigm-based status for 'justified' in epistemic contexts suffer from much worse troubles than the degree of indeterminacy it shares with natural-kind terms. For the differences between different accounts of epistemic justification cut deeply into the practice of picking out paradigms and extrapolating from them. Thus BonJour, in attacking reliability theories of justification, presents imaginary cases of beliefs formed by a highly reliable faculty of clairvoyance, cases that he takes to be unjustified. But at least some of these will be taken by a hard-nosed reliabilist to be clear cases of justified belief. Again, internalist critics of reliabilism hold that if we were in a world controlled by a Cartesian demon who arranged things so that our beliefs were generally false, even though we had all the evidence we have for them in the actual world, the beliefs that are justified in the actual world would be equally justified in the demon world even though they are formed in a highly unreliable way; whereas reliabilists will typically deny this. Finally, philosophers on opposite sides of the issue over whether simply *having* enough sufficient evidence is sufficient for justification, whether or not the belief in question is based on that evidence, will differ sharply on the justificatory status of a belief for which one has sufficient evidence but which is based on thoroughly disreputable grounds. I admit that there is a substantial body of cases on the justificatory status of which (almost) all parties will agree. But examples like the above show that there are radically different ways of extrapolating from those cases to others, differences that result from opposition over the correct account of epistemic justification. And these different patterns of extrapolation would determine different statuses of belief called 'justified', not a common referent.

In the light of all this, the most reasonable judgment is that the parties to at least the most radical of the disputes about epistemic justification are using 'justified' to pick out different properties of beliefs, different epistemic desiderata or collections thereof. Instead of having persistent disagreements about a common target, they are arguing past each other. They differ more strongly than disagreeing about a common object; they are talking about different things under the label 'justified'. They have not succeeded in using 'justified' to pick out a common objective feature of beliefs about the nature of, or conditions for which, they are disagreeing. Note that I have restricted this conclusion to "the most radical" of the disputes about epistemic justification. Thinkers who share a deontological or a reliability or an evidential support conception of justification, without differing too strongly in their particular versions thereof, can be credited with genuine disagreements about less fundamental issues. Thus two theorists who have basically similar evidentialist conceptions of justification can have a genuine disagreement over whether simply *having* the evidence is sufficient or whether the belief must also be based on that evidence.

I want to make sure that the above conclusion is understood in as radical a way as I intend it to be. Perhaps the best way to ensure this is to contrast it with weaker positions with which the above might be identified. It has become fairly common recently to deny that there is any single concept of 'justified belief' at work in the literature. Thus in Alvin Goldman 1988, reprinted in Goldman 1992a, there is a distinction between "weak" and "strong" justification, the former roughly amounting to "deontological" justification, as specified above, and the latter to reliabilist justification. In my earlier "Concepts of Epistemic Justification" (1985), reprinted in Alston 1989, I distinguished between a deontological concept of justification and a concept of justification as a belief's being based on an adequate ground. Perhaps the closest approximation to my more radical antijustificationist position is found in Swinburne 2001, in which a mind-boggling variety of kinds of justification are distinguished.

My antijustificationism is distinguished from all these views in two important respects. First, they are all in terms of different *concepts* of justification, whereas my position is a denial of any objective *status* or *property* of beliefs picked out by 'justified'. This may look like a merely verbal difference. For if there are different concepts expressed by 'justified' in epistemic contexts, then it follows that when people who use different concepts from that stock argue as to which has the correct view as to what it is for a belief to be justified or what the conditions are for that, they are not really disagreeing but simply arguing past each other. And isn't that the conclusion I want to draw from my position as well?

Yes, it is. But that conclusion is drawn in different ways from these views and from mine, and these differences have important implications. Before we get to these, some clearing of the air is called for. As I pointed out earlier, there can be no objection to people *stipulating* different senses in which they use 'justified', different concepts they are using the term to express. We can all agree on that. But the thinkers in the last paragraph from whose views I am distinguishing my own are not saying anything that trivial. They take it that there is an established practice of using 'justified' in epistemic contexts to express different concepts and thereby to pick out different properties of beliefs that are "out there" in property space. And I have no objection to that claim either.

It is also true that my argument is directed against theorists who think that arguments over what it is for a belief to justified or over what the conditions are for this are genuine disagreements as to what the right account is of a unique property or status of beliefs that is picked out by 'justified'. And *if* Goldman et al. think that by distinguishing different concepts of justification they are showing that all such disagreements are only apparent, resulting from the contestants not noticing that they are really talking about different things, then, with the exception of the second distinction between our views still to be mentioned, there is no basic difference between their position and mine. But it is clear that they do not satisfy that condition. In "Internalism Exposed" (1999b), published eleven years after "Strong and Weak Justification", Goldman presents a number of arguments against a certain kind of internalist conception of epistemic justification, rather than simply passing off the difference as a matter of the internalist and himself expressing a different conception with 'justified'. And all of Swinburne's dizzying array of concepts of justification are variants of justification as well-grounded belief, thereby leaving to one side deontological conceptions, which Swinburne, presumably, would suppose to be mistaken about what it is for a belief to be justified. So long as there is enough of a unique objective core to the epistemic justifiedness of a belief, even if it is disjunctive, enough to make it possible for there to be genuine disagreements as to how to characterize that core, then the position is thereby distinct from mine, according to which there is no such objective reality picked out by 'justified' in an epistemic context.

The second distinction between my position and those of Goldman, Swinburne et al. has to do with the range of epistemically important desiderata for belief. I mention this only in passing here. It cannot be properly appreciated until I come below to lay out what I take to be the variety of epistemic desiderata, most of which get involved in one treatment or another of "epistemic justification". But just for a taste, none of the thinkers mentioned above suggest *coherence of a belief with a sufficiently coherent system of belief* or *a belief's being formed by the exercise of an intellectual virtue* or *a belief's being formed by the proper functioning of a cognitive faculty* as one of the concepts expressed by 'justified'. But these and other features will appear on the list of epistemic desiderata that I will present as needed to be dealt with in my substitute for justificationism. Thus even if, as I have just asserted not to be the case, Goldman and Swinburne were committed to taking there to be no genuine disagreements over what justification is or what its conditions are, because there is no such subject matter to be argued about, they would still differ from my epistemic desiderata approach in the variety of features of belief they recognize as desiderata from the epistemic point of view.

Most of the remainder of Part I will be devoted to a detailed discussion of these desiderata—their nature, viability, importance, and interrelations. But first I must do something to defend taking all the desiderata with which I am concerned to be *epistemic* desiderata. I have been sensitized to the necessity of this by some of the rejoinders I received from presentations of a prepublication version of "Epistemic Desiderata" (Alston 1993b). It was not uncommon for discussants to say with respect to some item they did not consider required for justification on their account of justification: "Well, that may be desirable in some way, but why suppose it is *epistemically* desirable?". Reliabilists about justification would react in this way to, for example, high-grade cognitive access to what makes for positive epistemic status, while internalists about justification would react in parallel fashion to treating reliability of belief production as an *epistemic* desideratum. The defense of my wide application of 'epistemic desiderata' will be the subject of the next chapter.

CHAPTER 2

THE EPISTEMIC POINT OF VIEW

i. True Belief as the Basic Goal of Cognition

My next task is to elucidate the term 'epistemic evaluation', which figures centrally in the title of the book. I won't be spending much time on 'evaluation'. I will take it for granted that we have enough of an idea of what evaluation is for working purposes. Suffice it to say that we evaluate something when we dub it good, bad, or indifferent for some purpose or from some point of view.

'Epistemic' will require more explanation. We evaluate something epistemically (I will be mostly concerned with evaluation of beliefs) when we judge it to be more or less good or bad from the epistemic point of view, that is, for the attainment of epistemic purposes. And what purposes are those?

We can best approach this question by reminding ourselves that epistemology consists of a critical reflection on human cognition. And the evaluative aspect of epistemology involves an attempt to identify ways in which the conduct and the products of our cognitive activities can be better or worse vis-à-vis the goals of cognition. And what are those goals? Along with many other epistemologists I suggest that the primary function of cognition in human life is to acquire true rather than false beliefs about matters that are of interest or importance to us. Here are some formulations of this basic idea.

> Epistemic evaluation is undertaken from what we might call "the epistemic point of view". That point of view is defined by the aim at maximizing truth and minimizing falsity in a large body of beliefs. (Alston 1989, 83–84)

> Epistemic justification is essentially related to the so-called cognitive goal of truth, insofar as an individual belief is epistemically justified only if it is appropriately directed toward the goal of truth. (Moser 1985, 4)

> Why should we, as cognitive beings, care whether our beliefs are epistemically justified? . . . What makes us cognitive beings at all is our capacity for belief, and the goal of our distinctively cognitive endeavors is *truth:* we want our beliefs to correctly and accurately depict the world. If truth were somehow immediately and unproblematically accessible . . . then the concept of justification would be of little significance. . . . But we have no such immediate and unproblematic access to truth, and it is for this reason that justification comes into the picture. *If our standards of epistemic justification are appropriately chosen,* bringing it about that our beliefs are epistemically justified will also tend to bring it about that they are true. If epistemic justification were not conducive to truth in this way . . . then epistemic justification would be irrelevant to our main cognitive goal and of dubious worth. (BonJour 1985, 7–8)

I don't know how to prove that *the acquisition, retention, and use of true beliefs about matters that are of interest and/or importance* is the most basic and most central goal of cognition. I don't know anything that is more obvious from which it could be derived. But I suggest that anyone can see its obviousness by reflecting on what would happen to human life if we were either without beliefs at all or if our beliefs were all or mostly false. Without beliefs we would be thrown back on instinct as our only guide to behavior. And as far as thought, understanding, linguistic communication, theorizing, science, art, religion—all the aspects of life that require higher-level cognitive processes—are concerned, we would be bereft of them altogether. And if we had beliefs but ones that were mostly false, we would constantly be led astray in our practical endeavors and would be unlikely to survive for long. As Quine puts it, "Creatures inveterately wrong in their inductions have a pathetic but praiseworthy tendency to die before reproducing their kind" (1969, 126). As for the higher life of the mind, it would become a chaos if we had to rely on mostly false beliefs. Our attempts to understand the natural world, to create beauty, and to engage in fruitful and rewarding interactions with our fellows would be frustrated at every turn.

Indeed, the idea that it is important for human flourishing to be guided by correct rather than incorrect suppositions about how things are, where this is of interest or importance to us, is so obvious that it would seem to be unnecessary to belabor the point. And so it would, were it not for the fact that this apparent truism has been denied by reputable philosophers.[1] In

---

[1] See, e.g., Stich 1990.

response I will say only, putting the point of the above paragraph from the other side of the contrast, that where we seek to produce or influence one outcome rather than another, we are much more likely to succeed if we are guided by true rather than false beliefs about the likely consequences of one or another course of action. That is the basic practical importance of truth. And again, with many other philosophers, I take it that there are more purely theoretical reasons for positively evaluating truth. To be sure, theoretical investigation is often undertaken for the sake of its bearing on practical enterprises; and even where it isn't, theoretical results often turn out to have unforeseen practical utility. But the attainment of knowledge and understanding are also of intrinsic value. "All men by nature desire to know", said Aristotle, and this dictum has been reaffirmed by many of his successors. Members of our species seem to have a built-in drive to get the truth about things that pique their curiosity and to understand how and why things are as they are and happen as they do. So it is as close to truistic as we can get in philosophy to take truth as a good-making characteristic, and falsity as a bad-making characteristic, of beliefs and other outputs of cognition.

I should emphasize that in all this I am presupposing what I call in Alston 1996a a "realist conception" of truth. That is the eminently commonsensical conception of a true proposition, belief, or statement as one that "tells it like it is". A proposition is true *iff* what the proposition is about is as the proposition represents it as being. All that it takes for the proposition that lemons are yellow to be true is that lemons *be* yellow. This is an inchoate, or minimalist, "correspondence conception" of truth. It is congenial to a full-blown correspondence theory that aspires to spell out what correspondence consists in, but it stops short of committing itself to any particular way of doing this. Its main rivals on the contemporary scene are various versions of an epistemic conception of truth according to which a true belief is one that enjoys some high-grade positive epistemic status. In Alston 1996a, Chapter 7, I formulate what I regard as fatal objections to this way of thinking of truth. It must be admitted that the epistemic conception makes it easier to show that the epistemic point of view is one that takes the basic goal of cognition to be truth, since that would just amount to saying that the basic aim of belief formation is the formation of beliefs with a high positive epistemic status. But like many things that are too easy, to quote Russell on another topic, "It has all the advantages of theft over honest toil". The realist conception of truth also makes it more difficult to show that beliefs with certain kinds of positive epistemic status are likely to be true. But at least in showing that, we will be establishing a conclusion about real truth and not some impostor.

We must not understand the thesis that truth is the basic goal of cognition in too simplistic a fashion. It is often pointed out that if the multiplication of truths were our sole cognitive goal, we could not better spend our time than by memorizing telephone directories. It was to avoid such implications that the focal aim at acquiring true rather than false beliefs was presented with the qualification "about matters that are of interest or importance to us". And there are other complications that have to be built into a completely adequate formulation of the master goal of cognition. For one thing, there is a certain tension between the aim at maximizing true beliefs and the aim at minimizing false beliefs. It is frequently noted that the latter goal could be maximally achieved by believing nothing. And if that is impossible for us, as it obviously is, still an exclusive attention to the minimization of false beliefs would favor our believing as little as possible.[2] And if maximizing true beliefs were the sole cognitive desideratum, it would be best served by believing as much as possible. Obviously, we need to strike some kind of balance between these aims. We need to be neither too fearful of error nor too hungry for truth. But what is the right balance? Perhaps we could think of it this way. Our basic cognitive goal, with respect to any proposition that is of interest or importance to us, is to believe it if and only if it is true. That would seem to balance the positive goal of getting the truth and the negative one of avoiding false beliefs in just the right way. By relativizing the goal to beliefs that are of significance to us, it can be thought of as each of these beliefs (or as many as possible) being true rather than false.

Here is some further fine-tuning of the thesis about the basic aim of cognition I am defending.

1. In specifying the basic aim as "maximizing true beliefs and minimizing false beliefs about matters of interest and importance", I am thinking of cognition generally. Of course, we don't think in terms of such an overall aim each time we address ourselves to a problem or ask a question. A better way of putting the thesis in micro rather than macro terms would be this. When we engage in inquiry, what we are basically trying to do is to find the correct answer to a particular question or the correct solution to a particular intellectual problem. We are primarily and most centrally interested in getting at the truth about whatever matter we are concerned with at that time.

---

[2] This is not as obvious as it is sometimes supposed to be. For it is conceivable that minimizing the number of our beliefs would, or could, result in a larger proportion of false beliefs than a more extensive body of beliefs.

2. But the formulation in terms of inquiry and indeed in terms of "aims" is not fitted to cover the whole territory. A lot of our cognitive activity is not an attempt to answer a question or solve a problem. We acquire, process, and store a great deal of information without setting out to do so. A great deal of what we learn from perception comes to us without any explicit goal-directed seeking on our part. We can't walk around with our eyes open without obtaining a lot of information about our surroundings that we are not particularly interested in or motivated to make any particular use of, except perhaps momentarily to keep us from bumping into things. And yet there is something analogous to a truth-related aim that is guiding this activity. And that is *function*. The function of sense perception is to provide us with true beliefs about the immediate physical environment, in the same sense in which the function of the heart is to pump blood around the body. It has this built-in aim that it "pursues" without the need for the person to be consciously motivated to attain it. It is basically the same teleological structure that works through consciously motivated voluntary activity in posing and answering questions and attempting to solve problems. And so with that understanding we can say that all cognition, even the sort that works "automatically" without depending on conscious motivation, has as its basic aim the generation of true belief.

To be sure, we could sidestep the problem of accommodating cognitive activity that is not consciously motivated by an aim at certain results by switching from talk of *aims* to talk of *values*. After all, the central topic of the book is the epistemic *evaluation* of beliefs, and so it would seem to be *valuable* features of belief rather than what belief formation *aims* at that is our primary concern. But the consideration of the aims of cognition is not so easily jettisoned. For in order to mark out the distinctively *epistemic* values of beliefs I have been led to do this by reference to the epistemic point of view, which I got at in turn from a consideration of the basic aims of cognition. And I do not see any equally effective way of distinguishing epistemic values of beliefs from others. Hence I will proceed to think in terms of the valuable properties of belief, desiderata, that are epistemically valuable just in that they are in some way related to the most basic and central values that are aimed at in our cognitive activities.

3. It is also true that we are not aiming at forming true beliefs at every moment of our cognitive activity. Much of the time we are searching for possible answers or hypotheses, trying them out, drawing implications from them, considering objections, and so on. But we shouldn't understand the thesis in such a way that it contradicts these truths. We should

understand it as a thesis about the most basic ultimate aim of cognition. The activities enumerated above, and many others like them, are best viewed as preliminary stages in an attempt to get a correct answer to some question, not as ends in themselves. It will remain true that all cognitive activity is aimed, directly or indirectly, at the formation of true beliefs about some topic of concern.

ii. Truth and Other Goals of Cognition

Various difficulties have been raised about the thesis that the basic aim of cognition is true belief (with the further qualifications mentioned above). Perhaps the most serious of these is that it is propositional *knowledge*, not merely true belief, that is the most basic aim of cognition. Knowledge, by common consent, goes beyond true belief. Even if, as is generally assumed, knowledge is a special kind of true belief, it is a kind that involves further conditions. And when we try to get the correct answer to a question, aren't we trying to *know* that it is the correct answer, not just believe truly that it is? Isn't the quest for a correct answer a quest for knowledge? And if so, isn't the view that the basic aim of cognition is true belief an incomplete account of that aim?[3]

Well, yes and no. Inquiry does typically aim at knowledge, at least in its more explicit and sophisticated forms. But I think that knowledge is a prominent aim only in more sophisticated forms of cognitive activity rather than the basic aim of cognition generally. To do a thorough job of showing this I would have to develop an adequate account of propositional knowledge, something that is beyond the scope of this book. But I can at least make explicit one constraint on what makes true belief into knowledge, and in that way bring out something about the place that knowledge holds in the aims of cognition.

The constraint is that true belief counts as knowledge only when it is no accident that the belief is true. This kind of accidentality has to do with the relation between the truth value and the ground of the belief.[4] For a true belief to count as knowledge it has to be true nonaccidentally in the sense that what makes it true either is, or is reflected in the ground on which the belief is based.[5] The various Gettier and Gettier-like examples of true justified belief that do not count as knowledge all trade on a lack of

---

[3] See, e.g., Zagzebski 1996, esp. part II, 4.1.

[4] I assume that all true beliefs that could count as knowledge are based on grounds.

[5] If I were giving an account of knowledge, as I am not in this book, I would have to spell out this truth maker–ground relationship much more fully.

connection between ground and truth. If I am right about this constraint, we can see that an explicit quest for knowledge is a quest for a certain epistemic status of a true belief. And to explicitly set out to achieve a belief that satisfies that constraint, one must be seeking knowledge that the belief satisfies it. I am not saying that one cannot know that p without knowing *that* the true belief that p satisfies that constraint. That would be to fall into a level confusion; it would be to confuse knowing that p with knowing that one knows that p. But the fact remains that one cannot have as one's focal aim to come to know that p without also aiming at knowing that all the necessary conditions for knowing that p are satisfied. Otherwise one could not tell whether the goal has been reached. And so to take knowledge as one's focal aim involves one in an aim at higher-level epistemic knowledge about a lower-level belief. And that aim is restricted to the more developed forms of cognitive activity. It is not present in the most rudimentary forms, such as the acquisition of perceptual beliefs that happens automatically without being guided by any conscious aim at all. And even in the less exalted forms of inquiry in which we are trying to get the correct answer to everyday questions like where one left one's glasses, nothing as elevated as trying to determine whether a belief satisfied all the necessary conditions of knowledge is involved. Hence we must deny that it is generally true that cognition has knowledge as its aim. We can continue to hold to the thesis that true belief is the basic aim of cognition generally, seeing the quest for knowledge as an enriched form of that aim, one that is found in the higher reaches of cognition. We may well suspect that the prominence of knowledge as the central aim of cognition in the thinking of philosophers stems from the fact that the inquiry involved in philosophy and other high-level theoretical enterprises often does explicitly aim at knowledge. But it is an unwarranted parochialism to suppose that this extends to cognition generally.

Another difficulty for thinking of true belief as the basic goal of cognition, raised, for example, in Maitzen 1995, is that it seems to imply that truth is the only thing positively valuable for cognition. Maitzen and others discuss this matter in terms of how to think of the goal in terms of which we evaluate beliefs as *justified*. Maitzen's specific point is that if *justification* is something that is positively valuable from the standpoint of the truth goal, it would have to be identified with truth. For what could be more valuable from the standpoint of an aim at truth than truth? In Chapter 1 I made it explicit that I don't wish to put "justification" front and center as the master epistemic desideratum. Hence I will discuss the matter in more neutral terms as a matter of whether thinking of the basic cognitive goal in this way freezes out candidates for epistemic desiderata other than truth.

A complete validation of my candidates for epistemic desiderata in the light of the idea that true belief, with the qualifications noted, is the primary goal of cognition will have to await the account of the organization and interrelation of the various epistemic desiderata in the next chapter. But enough can be said here to show that truth is not the sole desirable feature of belief from the epistemic point of view, defined in terms of the primary aim of cognition at true belief. The crucial point is that the most *basic* aim of cognition is not the only thing aimed at by cognition, not even the only thing aimed at from the standpoint of that most basic aim. That is because other features of belief are also desirable from the standpoint of that basic aim because they are related in various ways to it. Here I will restrict myself to the most obvious way in which a relation to true belief can make features of belief other than truth desirable from the epistemic point of view, and leave other desiderata for treatment in the next chapter. This most obvious way is that the feature *renders* the belief true, or at least and more usually, *likely* to be true, and in this way entails at least the likelihood of truth. For short of the basic epistemic desideratum of truth itself, no status of a belief can be more favorable vis-à-vis the goal of truth than a status that renders the belief at least likely to be true. Call such properties of beliefs *directly truth-conducive*. (The qualification 'directly' will often be omitted and tacitly understood).

What features of a belief render it at least likely to be true? One that much of my discussion will be highlighting is the belief's *being based on adequate evidence* (reasons, grounds . . .). Provided the notion of adequacy here is such as to entail that B is thereby at least likely to be true, this counts as a truth-conducive (TC) desideratum, one the epistemic desirability of which stems directly from the epistemic point of view's being defined by the goal of true belief. As we will see in Chapter 5, section iii, not all philosophers who stress the importance of a belief's having a strongly favorable positive epistemic status think of it as entailing the probable truth of the belief. And we shall also see that by so thinking of it they put in doubt the epistemic value of that status. Pending that discussion I will think of adequate grounding as a TC desideratum.

Another directly TC feature of a belief is reliability, that is, being formed in a reliable way, a way that can be relied on to produce mostly true beliefs. However that is further spelled out (and much of Chapter 6 will be devoted to that), this feature clearly passes the test for being TC. It is analytically true that if a belief is formed in a way that can be depended on to produce mostly true beliefs, its being so formed renders it probably true and thereby entails its probable truth.

I take it that these examples are sufficient to show that truth itself is not the only property of beliefs that is desirable and valuable from the epistemic point of view, defined in terms of a favorable balance of true over false beliefs being the basic aim of cognition. Further examples will be introduced in the next chapter.

iii. Objects of Epistemic Evaluation

Now I turn to the question of the objects of evaluation on which we will concentrate. In the Introduction I announced my intention to concentrate on beliefs. But other aspects of the cognitive search for truth are subject to evaluation from the epistemic point of view.

First, we can evaluate the process as well as the product. This side of the matter has become prominent in epistemology with the recent development of reliability theories. But the epistemic value of the process is derivative from the epistemic value of its belief outputs. However we precise the notion of a reliable belief-forming process, it has to have something to do with the proportion of true beliefs in the output of that process.[6] Hence the epistemic interest of the reliability of belief-forming processes is derivative from the epistemic interest of the truth value of its outputs rather than being independent of that. Goldman (1986) discusses two other ways of evaluating belief-forming processes—*power* and *speed*. Power has to do with the number and variety of outputs. Speed I take to be self-explanatory. Goldman says that they are "comparable in importance" with reliability (122) (he presumably means epistemic importance), but again it would seem that their epistemic value is derivative from the value of true beliefs. Goldman himself explains powerful cognitive mechanisms as "mechanisms capable of getting a relatively large number of *truths*" (222; emphasis added). And if speed is of distinctively epistemic value, it will presumably be because it rapidly turns out a large proportion of *true* beliefs, not just any old beliefs at random. And so these aspects of belief-forming processes have whatever epistemic value they have in a way that is derivative from the value of true beliefs.

Again, there are evaluations of the cognitive subject that are derivative from the aim of truth. The most salient epistemic evaluations of cognitive

---

[6] When I go into this properly in Chapter 6, I will make explicit that what is epistemically crucial is the proportion of true beliefs that *would* eventuate, not the proportion of true beliefs that in fact are forthcoming.

subjects have to do with their dispositions vis-à-vis the cognitive enterprise. Intellectual virtues are in the foreground here. And it would seem that the dispositions that amount to intellectual virtues *and* that possess epistemic value are those the activation of which involve a motivation to acquire true rather than false beliefs and some considerable success in this quest. Here too the epistemic point of view defined by the search for truth is crucial for the epistemic value of these objects of evaluation. There will be more about intellectual virtues and their place in epistemology in Chapter 6, sections ix and x.

CHAPTER 3

THE EPISTEMIC DESIDERATA APPROACH

i. A List of Epistemic Desiderata

Having concluded that 'justified' as used in epistemic contexts in application to beliefs does not succeed in picking out a unique and centrally important positive epistemic status of beliefs, I am ready to develop a program for an alternative way of pursuing the epistemology of belief. This will involve replacing the focus on "epistemic justification" with a number of different features of beliefs, and systems of beliefs, all of which are valuable from the epistemic point of view and none of which has an exclusive position as the central and preeminent epistemic desideratum. In contrast to the familiar focus on "justification", this will be a radically pluralistic approach in which each item in the plurality deserves some attention as a possible contributor to a positive epistemic status of beliefs. That is not to say that they are all equally valuable nor is it to deny that some are more fundamental than others. We will find that some are more important than others, depending on the context in question, and that there are asymmetrical relations of dependence between them. Most of the desiderata I will consider are taken from attempts by justificationists to say what it is for a belief to be justified, and specifications of the conditions for that status, attempts noted in Chapter 1. But I will not restrict myself to that source, feeling free to range over any features of belief that commend themselves as desirable from the epistemic point of view.

The first step is the compilation of a preliminary list of candidates for the status of epistemic desiderata (ED). I use the qualification 'candidates for' advisedly. I want this list to range over any features of belief that could be claimed, with some considerable plausibility, to be desiderata from the epistemic point of view. Some will perhaps be eliminated or marginalized in the course of further discussion. In Chapter 2 I briefly defended the epistemic desirability of some directly TC properties of belief, and I need not repeat that here, though I will add some other alleged examples of TC desiderata and indicate how they fit into the overall organization when we get to that topic. And there are a number of other candidates that remain to be treated and given their place.

Here then is a preliminary list of features of beliefs or systems thereof that may be desirable from the epistemic point of view.

I. *Truth*

This item will, no doubt, be surprising to many readers. It is the most shocking exception to the generalization that my ED are taken from features that are claimed by some to be necessary or sufficient for justification. As I pointed out earlier, one of the very few things on which practically all epistemologists who are concerned with justification agree is that truth is neither necessary nor sufficient for justification. But now that I am no longer constrained by what it takes for a belief to be "justified", I find that I cannot deny that a belief's being true is a very good thing from the epistemic point of view that is defined by the aim at true beliefs on matters of interest or importance. Indeed, how could any property of a belief be better from that point of view?

But why, then, do justificationist epistemologists take the truth of a belief not to count at all in favor of its being justified? I need to understand the source of this intuition, especially since it seems to carry over to a like reluctance to think of truth as an *epistemic* desideratum of belief. My sense is that it has something to do with the fact that truth—in contrast to having strong evidence or reasons, being based on an adequate ground, being generated by a reliable process, having direct accessibility to the ground of one's belief, and so on—is too external to the process of acquiring, retaining, and using beliefs, that is, their involvement in cognitive activity.[1] This

---

[1] In this connection, note that it is universal among those who take knowledge to be a belief that satisfies further conditions to take one of those conditions to be truth. But this has to do with knowledge, and in this book I am in the same territory as epistemic justification theory in concentrating on epistemic features of belief that fall short of all that is required for knowledge.

ties in with the point that it could be sheer luck for a given belief of a subject to be true and have no discernible connection with the subject's contribution to the belief generation. If this is on the right track, we need to ask the question, "Why is the epistemology of belief, including the ED approach, specifically concerned with the subject's contribution to the cognitive process?" If we could answer that question, we would have uncovered some deep insight into what the epistemology of belief is all about.

Before trying to answer this question I want to guard against possible misunderstandings of what I am seeking to explain. When I say that epistemologists generally do not take truth to be either necessary or sufficient for a belief to be justified and, more generally, that they are or would be reluctant to treat it as an *epistemic* desideratum, I don't mean to deny, of course, that they consider justification to be related in important ways to truth and/or consider epistemic desiderata to be so related. This is obviously the case for all those who construe the epistemic point of view in the way I have explained it. Not all contemporary epistemologists do so; and those who do not, think of the relation of epistemic desiderata to truth in different ways. But for those epistemologists who take the basic goal of cognition to be something like what I have claimed, there is the perhaps puzzling combination of (1) regarding justification and other ED to have that status by virtue of, shall we say, tending toward true belief and (2) not regarding truth itself as an epistemic desideratum, or would if they were to use my terminology. And that is what I feel the need to understand.

I find an important clue to this in a passage from BonJour 1985.

> What makes us cognitive beings at all is our capacity for belief, and the goal of our distinctively cognitive endeavors is *truth*; we want our beliefs to correctly and accurately depict the world. If truth were somehow immediately and unproblematically accessible (as it is, on some accounts, for God) so that one could in all cases opt simply to believe the truth, then the concept of justification would be of little significance and would play no independent role in cognition. But this epistemically ideal situation is quite obviously not the one in which we find ourselves. We have no such immediate and unproblematic access to truth, and it is for this reason that justification comes into the picture. The basic role of justification is that of a *means* to truth, a more directly attainable mediating link between our subjective starting point and our objective goal. We cannot, in most cases at least, bring it about directly that our beliefs are true, but we can presumably bring it about directly (though perhaps only in the long run) that they are epistemically justified. (7–8)

When this is translated into my ED approach, the point is that the epistemology of belief is concerned with what we can do, what we have effective control over, to maximize the chances of our beliefs being true rather than false. If we had "immediate and unproblematic access to truth", that is, an effective capacity to discern whether any possible belief would be true, then we could make use of that to ensure that what we believe is true, insofar as truth value would (at least sufficiently often) move us to form or abstain from belief depending on that value. In that case we would have little or no use for these intermediate truth-conducive desiderata. We could effectively aim at the ultimate goal of truth itself. It is because we lack those powers that in our cognitive activity we need to be concerned with belief properties that, though distinct from truth, are both sufficiently apparent to us and sufficiently conducive to truth. Note that the concern with what we can do about seeing that our beliefs are mostly true holds steady over the contrast between the ideal and the actual human situation. It is what is open to us along that line that implies that the desiderata of direct concern are steps along the road to truth rather than truth itself.

BonJour no doubt overstates the relative accessibility of truth value and the justification-related properties of beliefs. I would say that in many cases, such as simple everyday perceptual and introspective beliefs, it is much more unproblematically obvious which ones are true than it is how adequate their grounds are or how reliably they are formed. But, nevertheless, it remains the case that in many matters of great concern to us, truth value is not obvious on simple inspection. And here, as BonJour points out, we are forced to concentrate on doing what we can to see to it that our grounds of belief are adequate, our ways of forming beliefs are reliable, and our beliefs enjoy other "intermediate" desiderata, if we are concerned, as we all are, to maximize the ratio of true to false beliefs. And that, I believe, is the best way to understand why truth itself is not necessary for justification, or, in my terms, seems out of place as an *epistemic* desideratum for belief. It is the aspiration of epistemology to be practical, to have a role in shaping our efforts toward true belief, which is responsible.

What bearing does this have on the issue that gave rise to this discussion, whether truth can be counted as an epistemic desideratum? It does, as I have been saying, explain why that intuitively seems wrong. But it does nothing to shake the reasons I gave for regarding truth as an epistemic desideratum, indeed the master epistemic desideratum for belief. What we are left with is that in my radically pluralistic approach to the epistemology of belief, we can recognize both desiderata like truth that (in many cases) are not suitable for proximate goals of cognitive endeavor, as well as those that are suitable in those cases. In other terms, and overstating the relative inaccessibility of truth value, we can recognize both proximate and ultimate goals of cognition as possessing distinctive epistemic value. Here as elsewhere the motto of pluralistic views, "Let a thousand flowers bloom", holds sway.

After this long excursus we can turn to listing the epistemic desiderata with which we will be mostly concerned, each of which would be recognized by one or another group of epistemologists as genuinely epistemic desiderata (if they were to use that conceptual framework).

II. *Truth-conducive desiderata*

1. The subject (S) has adequate evidence (reasons, grounds . . .) for the belief (B).
2. B is based on adequate evidence (reasons, grounds . . .).
   If 1 and 2 are to be *epistemic* desiderata, *adequacy* must be so construed that adequate evidence, and so on, for B entails the probable truth of B.
3. B was formed by a sufficiently reliable belief-forming process.
4. B was formed by the proper functioning of S's cognitive faculties.
5. B was formed by the exercise of an intellectual virtue.
   As with 1 and 2, 4 and 5 are assumed to be so construed that they entail that B is probably true. This will be explained when we go into more detail about these desiderata in Chapter 6.

III. *Desiderata that are thought to be favorable to the discrimination and formation of true beliefs*

6. S has some high-grade cognitive access to the evidence, and so on, for B (and perhaps to its sufficiency).
7. S has higher-level knowledge, or well-grounded belief, that B has a certain positive epistemic status and/or that such-and-such is responsible for that.
8. S can carry out a successful defense of the probability of truth for B.

Since facts of none of these sorts *render* B true or likely to be true, they do not count as TC desiderata, as I have defined 'truth-conducive'. Of course, knowing that B is probably true entails that B is probably true just because of the truth condition for knowledge. But this entails the probable truth of B in a very different way from B's being based on an adequate ground. For the latter is what *renders* B probably true and in *that* way entails its probable truth whereas knowing that it is probably true *presupposes* its probable truth rather than being responsible for it. S knows that B is probably true because (in part) it is; whereas B's being based on an adequate ground is what makes B probably true. We have opposite relations of priority in the two cases. For a similar point about 8, see below. It was primarily in order to underline this difference that I defined 'directly TC' not simply in terms of entailing truth or the likelihood of truth but rather in terms of a certain way of entailing that, namely, rendering the belief probably true.

Nevertheless, although 6–8 fail to count as directly TC, they contribute to S's being in a position to arrange things in a way that is favorable to acquiring true rather than false beliefs. As for 6 and 7, the basic point is that the more we know, or are able to know, about the epistemic status of various beliefs or kinds of beliefs, the better position we are in to encourage true beliefs and discourage false beliefs. For example, I might know that my belief that Jim is in Los Angeles is well grounded because he has just called me from there. If the well-groundedness of the lower-level belief that Jim is in Los Angeles is a TC feature of that belief, my knowing that it has that feature does not do anything further to make that belief likely to be true. Nevertheless, the possession of such knowledge, or the capacity for it, will increase my capacity to form a true belief about this matter and others. For in this and in other situations it brings with it the ability to distinguish between beliefs that are likely to be true and those that are not and to encourage the development of those that satisfy the former description. Note that the possession of such knowledge and the capacity to acquire it has this indirect connection to the goal of true belief as a general capacity, not limited to the instances in which the epistemic features of the lower-level belief are themselves TC. If it were *limited* to *non-truth-conducive* epistemic features, then it would not enjoy the right kind of connection with the goal of true belief to render it epistemically desirable. But the *general* capacity to acquire such higher-level knowledge, one that ranges over all sorts of cases, does contribute to the ability to acquire true rather than false beliefs just because it increases one's ability to discriminate those epistemic features of belief that are TC from those that are not, and hence it increases one's ability to so arrange matters as to favor the former over the latter.

As for 8, the verdict depends on the criteria for a successful defense of the attribution of probable truth to B. In the strongest sense a successful defense of p involves *showing* that p in a strong sense of 'show' in which it requires that p be true. In that sense a successful defense presupposes that it is true that p rather than renders p true. This would put 8 in basically the same situation as 6 and 7. Where one is able to mount such a defense, one is in a good position to discriminate between beliefs on the subject that are true and those that are not. But there are various weaker criteria for a successful defense of p that require only making a strong case for p, on various conceptions of what that would take. But here too 8 is not directly TC, for it still does not count as rendering p likely to be true. At most the capacity would be rather to make a strong case for supposing p likely to be true. Again, the relation of the capacity and the likelihood of truth for the target of the defense is in the wrong direction for truth-conducivity.

We might also consider adding to our list of epistemic desiderata:

On adequate reflection S would believe that B has a positive epistemic status.

The idea for this sort of desideratum is taken from Foley 1987, where what one would believe on adequate reflection figures prominently in his account of "epistemic rationality". Whether B's satisfying this description would significantly increase the chances of its being true depends on (a) how we construe '*adequate* reflection' and (b) how likely we take it to be that reflection that is adequate in that sense would eventuate in true beliefs. Foley himself disavows any logical connection with even the probability of truth. Because of these doubts I will not include this item in my list of epistemic desiderata.

IV. *Deontological features of belief*

9. B is held *permissibly* (one is not subject to blame for doing so).
10. B is formed and held *responsibly*.
11. The causal ancestry of B does not contain violations of intellectual obligations.

The question of the relation of these belief features to the goal of truth is a complex and tortuous one. As for 9, there is a serious problem as to whether the formation and retention of beliefs can be thought of as required, forbidden, or permitted. Thinking of it in these ways presupposes that beliefs are under effective voluntary control, and in Chapter 4 I will argue that they are not. If 10 has the same presupposition, the same problem arises, and if it does not, it is not clear how it is to be understood. That leaves 11, and there we are faced with the question whether the absence of violations of intellectual obligations in the causal ancestry of a belief correlates significantly with truth. That depends, inter alia, on just what intellectual obligations we have and how they are related to truth. I won't try to go into all that here; I will put this group of candidates on the shelf for the moment and postpone consideration of these issues until Chapter 4.

V. *Features of systems of beliefs that are among the goals of cognition*

12. Explanation
13. Understanding
14. Coherence
15. Systematicity

It is reasonable to take these as being goals of cognition that are partly independent of any connection with the goal of truth. Consider a set of mostly true beliefs that contain little or nothing in the way of explanation and other forms of understanding. Let's say it is all or mostly an assortment of true beliefs that one or another kind of phenomenon occurs, but without much of anything by way of an explanation of these occurrences. Its intellectual value, its value vis-à-vis our cognitive aims, would be greatly increased by the acquisition of explanations of all or many of these facts, an increase far beyond any that is due to the acquisition of additional true beliefs. And something similar can be said for 14 and 15. A set of true beliefs that is a heterogeneous assortment or heap with little or no systematization or mutual support of its constituents would be greatly increased in intellectual value by being put into some sort of coherent, systematic order, again well out of proportion to the number of additional true beliefs this would involve.

But since their intrinsic value as aims of cognition is independent of the aim at true belief, why should we count these items as *epistemic* desiderata on the criteria I have been using for that? If we have a reason for doing so, it is that they also have an essential relation to true belief, though it differs from the relations we found for the desiderata in either Group II or Group III. Coherence, despite BonJour's strenuous efforts in his 1985 to establish the contrary, is not necessarily TC. And, as the possibility of highly coherent systems of belief that are all or mostly false shows, it cannot reasonably be claimed that the coherence of a system is a good contingent indication of the proportion of true beliefs it contains.[2] The relation is of another sort. It consists of their cognitive desirability *depending* on being associated with true belief rather than their providing resources for *producing* beliefs that are true rather than false. Explanations that do not provide the *true* reason why something happened are of no cognitive value qua explanations. In seeking to explain an occurrence, we want to find out what was in fact responsible for it, not just what might conceivably have produced it. And a coherent or otherwise systematic body of beliefs that are all or mostly false would lack what we are after in seeking to render belief systems more coherent or systematic. So unless by and large truth can be assumed, these features of belief systems would fail to exhibit the intrinsic cognitive desirability that would otherwise attach to them. So the question is whether we

---

[2] It was suggested to me by a reader of the manuscript that one might well suppose that most belief systems actually held by human beings contain mostly true beliefs, and hence that it is a contingent fact that membership in a coherent system is a good indication of truth. I agree that this is possible, but a consideration of how likely it is would take me too far afield for this book.

want to loosen up the requirements of *epistemic* desirability to include items the intrinsic desirability of which is over and above that of the true-false balance but which presupposes such a balance as a necessary condition of that desirability. In the absence of any sufficient reason for being hard-nosed on this issue, I will allow the realization of these cognitive goals to count as epistemic desiderata.

Continuing a line of argument begun in the previous chapter, this discussion shows that although the formation of true rather than false beliefs about matters of interest and/or concern is the most basic goal of cognition, and hence is the most fundamental epistemically desirable feature of belief, it is not by any means the only epistemic desideratum. The features of beliefs in Groups II, III, and V can also lay claim to that title through their several relations to the most fundamental goal. Having recognized features of beliefs that render them true or likely to be true (Group II), and other features that though not necessarily connected with truth or likelihood of truth of their possessors, are such that their possession is favorable to the acquisition of true beliefs in general (Group III) and important features that presuppose mostly true belief but add something of their own to its value (Group V), we see that we cannot reasonably claim that true belief is the only important goal of cognition. Nevertheless, its basic status is shown by the fact that the other important goals are connected with it in one or another way and depend, in part, for their status as important goals on that connection. So we may continue to say, keeping these complications in mind, that ED are those features of beliefs or bodies thereof that are valuable from the epistemic point of view, defined in terms of the aim at acquiring true rather than false beliefs about matters that are of interest or importance to us.

ii. An Outline of the Epistemic Desiderata Approach

Now for a brief outline of the ED approach to the epistemology of belief. The general idea has already been adumbrated. Instead of assuming one unique central repository of positive epistemic status of beliefs, "being justified", we recognize an irreducible plurality of positive epistemic statuses—epistemic desiderata—of beliefs, each of which defines a distinctive dimension of epistemic evaluation. We then conduct the epistemology of belief by studying these several ED, their *nature*, their *interrelations*, their *viability*, and their *importance* for the success of the cognitive enterprise. As foreshadowed in Alston 1993b, this enterprise will be carried out under the four headings just indicated.

1. *Nature.* Here the main task is the elucidation of each of the desiderata, with attention to the different forms each one can take. For each variant there are sometimes difficult questions that arise as to how it is to be understood. What is it for the grounds of (or evidence or reasons for) a belief to be more or less adequate? What contributes to this and in what proportions? What principles govern the support a body of evidence gives a particular belief? If it is a matter of rendering the belief more or less probable, in terms of what concept of probability should this be understood? What is it for a belief to be *based on* certain grounds? Is it just a matter of the latter causing the former, or is something more or something other involved? How are we to understand the reliability of a way of forming beliefs? And how do we determine what (general) way of forming beliefs to evaluate when investigating whether a particular belief was formed reliably? How is the coherence of a system of belief to be understood? All these old friends and many more will still be with us in the new dispensation.

2. *Viability.* Here we have the questions of the extent to which various states of affairs that would be epistemically desirable are realizable by human beings. One issue of this sort already touched on concerns the alleged epistemic desideratum of the permissibility of belief. If, as seems clear, beliefs can be thought of as permitted, required, or forbidden only if they are, or can be, under effective voluntary control, the viability of this alleged desideratum hangs on that issue. For another example, consider strong cognitive access to evidence and/or to the degree of support it provides and to other matters that are relevant to the epistemic status of a belief. No doubt, it would be highly desirable if we could determine just on reflection, as Chisholm supposes, everything that is relevant to the epistemic evaluation of beliefs. But to what extent is this possible? In particular, how can we determine just by asking ourselves the extent to which a given body of evidence makes it objectively probable that a belief is true? Doesn't that depend on a variety of factors that we have to go beyond mere armchair reflection to determine? Extreme internalists tend to respond to this point by denying the relevance of the *objective* probability of truth to epistemic evaluation. But then that calls into question whether what they do recognize as relevant has distinctively epistemic value. But even with respect to what evidence one has for a belief, and setting aside the question of access to the support it gives, the generally accepted principle of total evidence seems to require that one be able to survey one's complete body of beliefs in order to be sure that one has a complete grasp of the evidence for a given target belief. And that seems to go well beyond what anyone can do on reflection.

3. *Importance*. Under this heading we investigate the importance, both theoretical and practical, that the realization of one or another desideratum has for human life. We have already touched on the most basic consideration concerning this in Chapter 2 when treating the importance of truth for human theoretical and practical affairs, and the way in which the importance of truth trickles down to directly truth-conducive desiderata. And in the discussion of the interrelations of ED to which we will come shortly, other ways in which one or another desideratum is important in relation to the basic aim of cognition will be brought out. What remains to be done is to explore the contexts, conditions, or assumptions relative to which one or another desideratum assumes a greater or larger importance. In that inquiry we shall see additional reasons for not conducting the epistemology of belief in terms of one master epistemic desideratum, "justification". For if, as I shall show, different contexts and conditions render quite different desiderata most salient, that is a powerful reason for the pluralistic character of the ED approach.

4. *Interrelations*. Are we to think of the various epistemic desiderata as simply forming a heap, or are they systematically connected in an organized whole? This is obviously a rhetorical question leading up to an answer in favor of the latter alternative. And I will not keep the reader waiting for that answer but provide what I have to say on the subject here and now. You may think that I should undertake the elucidation of the various desiderata, answering salient questions as to how each should be construed, before embarking on an account of their interrelations. And that would indeed be the logical order of presentation. But since I can present what I have to say about the interrelations of desiderata in a relatively short compass, whereas a proper treatment of the nature of each will require several chapters, I shall reverse the order, taking it that our intuitive understanding of the various desiderata will be sufficient for an appreciation of what I have to say about their interrelations.

iii. Interrelations of Desiderata

The main questions about interrelations concern which desiderata are most basic, which depend on others for their status, and what sorts of dependence are involved. I can be brief about this because the fundamental points have already been made in Chapter 2 and earlier in this chapter in the discussion of the way in which each desideratum can lay claim to being an *epistemic* desideratum, where that involves being desirable from the standpoint of the primary aim of cognition at acquiring and retaining true rather than false beliefs on matters of interest and/or importance. It remains only to place those points in the context of our present concern with the relations of dependence between particular desiderata. I will order the presentation in terms of the list of epistemic desiderata other than truth, arranged in four groups, presented in section i of this chapter, remembering that Group IV is reserved for separate treatment in Chapter 4.

There can be no doubt but that the directly TC desiderata in Group II are the most basic from the epistemic point of view as I have explained that. For that point of view is defined in terms of the aim of cognition at true rather than false beliefs. And since Group II desiderata are all TC, in the sense of being ways in which a belief is rendered true or likely to be true and in that way entails truth or likelihood of truth for a belief that has it, this gives them the most direct and unmistakable claim to be valuable from the epistemic point of view. For short of truth itself, no status of a belief can be more favorable vis-à-vis the goal of truth than a status that renders the belief true or likely to be true. And, as we shall see in a moment, the desiderata in the other two groups can be viewed as dependent for their epistemic desirability on their relation to the items in the first group. Later I will be suggesting that some members of Group II are more basic than others. In particular, I will be suggesting that being based on adequate evidence is more fundamental than simply having adequate evidence. And there will be questions about the relations of both of these to 3, being acquired in a reliable way. Moreover, I have still said nothing about 4 and 5. For now, it suffices to say that in order to count as TC, they must be so construed that their realization renders or tends to render beliefs that have them probably true. All these points will be dealt with in Chapters 5 and 6.

Turning to Group III, we see that these desiderata are not directly TC themselves. They do not consist of ways in which a belief is rendered true or likely to be true. But, as I brought out earlier, they earn the title of ED in an indirect way by contributing to S's being in a position to arrange things in a way that is favorable to acquiring true rather than false beliefs. To repeat the basic point for 6 and 7, the more we know, or are able to know, about the epistemic status of various beliefs or kinds of beliefs, the better position we are in to encourage true beliefs and discourage false beliefs. As for 8, if S is capable of successfully defending a positive epistemic status (of a truth-conducive sort) for B where B has such a status, then, again, S is in a position to recognize when B does or does not have such a status and so, again, is in a position to encourage such beliefs and to discourage the opposite. Thus what is epistemically desirable about them is not the possession of them by a particular belief but rather the general capacities, and their exercise, that are presupposed by that possession.

Group V presents a quite different picture. As pointed out earlier, it is reasonable to take the members of this group as having the title of goals of cognition in a way that is independent of the goal of true belief. Of two bodies of belief that are ranked as equivalent in terms of the proportion of true to false beliefs on matters of interest and/or importance, if one contains much more than the other in the way of explanations and other forms of understanding or in the way of coherence or other forms of systematicity, then the former system ranks higher in terms of the goals of cognition than the latter just on that basis. Nevertheless, there is a clear connection of these desiderata to truth. It consists of their cognitive desirability depending on their being associated with a favorable balance of truth over falsity in the body of beliefs to which they apply, rather than their having a tendency to produce such a balance, much less entailing such a balance. Since their cognitive desirability depends on the beliefs, or bodies thereof, which have them being mostly true, this connection suffices to render them desirable from the epistemic point of view as I have explained that.

Let me sum up the ways in which ED are interrelated and hence are organized. What we have seen is that of the desiderata short of truth itself, the directly TC desiderata in Group II are clearly the most basic since they are most closely related to true belief itself, by virtue of being ways of rendering beliefs true or likely to be true. The items in Groups III and V have a more derivative status as desiderata through more indirect connections with true belief or the likelihood of such. One way this indirectness shows itself is by the fact that the epistemic desirability of items in Groups III and V could be exhibited either by their relations to the most basic goal of true belief, as I have been doing, or by their relations to Group I desiderata and through them to the fundamental truth goal of cognition. These ways of putting the matter will be equally applicable wherever true belief functions as a goal of cognitive activity, including, as pointed out in section i, cases in which the function of the activity is to produce true belief even though the agent is not consciously aiming at it. In all these cases true belief is realized through the possession of one of the Group I desiderata. And the basic status of Group I desiderata is shown by the fact that its relation to the fundamental truth goal is not mediated by its relation to Group III or V desiderata.

iv. Internalism and Externalism

It will not have escaped the reader's notice that I have written a substantial number of pages without mentioning the controversy between *internalism* and *externalism* that has been so prominent in recent epistemology. This contrast is usually construed as one between different views as to the nature and conditions of epistemic justification, and I have turned my back on that. But we can preserve an internalism-externalism contrast by reinterpreting it as a contrast between different ED, as I shall now proceed to do.

'Internalism' and 'externalism' are used in different ways. (See Alston 1986b for a discussion of the most important of these differences). Here I will take the crucial difference to be whether the desideratum in question involves S's grasp of the epistemic status of belief B. Distinctively internalist desiderata do, and distinctively externalist desiderata do not. Thus 6–8 are paradigm internalist desiderata whereas 3 is a paradigm externalist desideratum since B can be formed in a reliable way without S's knowing, or being able to know, that this is the case. The other items on the list fall into an internalist or externalist grouping depending on whether they are or are not held in conjunction with a commitment to S's knowing, or being able to know, that they hold. Thus 1 is regarded as internalist where it is assumed that S has direct access to what evidence S has for S's beliefs. But there are serious questions as to whether this is always, or even generally, the case. They will be discussed in Chapter 7. Moreover, it is not always noticed that 1 embodies two different possible objects of cognitive access: (a) what evidence (reasons, grounds . . .) one has for the belief and (b) the degree of adequacy or conclusiveness of the support it gives. Object (a) is a much more plausible candidate for ready cognitive accessibility than (b). It is much more likely that I can easily know what my evidence is for a perceptual or a testimonial belief than that I can easily know the extent to which it makes the belief probably true. Desideratum 2 is less plausibly treated as internalist. In any event, it is clear that people are sometimes mistaken about the grounds on which their beliefs are based, depending on how we explicate the notion of the basing of beliefs. This will be taken up in Chapter 5. And it is even more obvious that people are sometimes ignorant of, or mistaken about, the degree of adequacy of the grounds of their beliefs. This will be gone over in Chapter 7. Desiderata 14 and 15 can be held in either an internalist or an externalist way, though the former is more common. A system might have a certain degree of systematicity or coherence without the subject's realizing that it did possess that merit. If coherence is understood so as not to imply the subject's realizing that coherence, or being able to readily do so, coherence is an externalist criterion. It is internalist only if it is so construed that it is not realized unless the subject does have full cognitive access to it. The same point holds for explanation and other forms of understanding. It seem clear to me that it is much more obviously possible for a certain kind and degree of coherence to attach to a system of beliefs without the subject's realizing this than it is for a subject to have arrived at an explanation of a fact without realizing it.

At least it would be strange to have arrived at a putative explanation without realizing that, though it is not at all strange to have taken oneself to have successfully explained something though the real explanation lies elsewhere. Here too the desideratum can be construed with or without the internalist rider of high-grade cognitive access.

In this connection it is interesting that BonJour, in his coherentist days, was driven to admit that his coherentist conditions for justification were seldom or never fully satisfied because they put too much of a burden on S's knowledge of S's system of beliefs. This shows that BonJour was more strongly committed to internalism than to coherentism. Rather than take our general failure to have, or be able to have, a complete grasp of one's total system of belief with the details of how it enjoys the degree of coherence it does to show that coherentism must be held in an externalist form, he abandons the coherentism (eventually) and earlier, at the conclusion of BonJour 1985, admits that the coherentist requirements for justification are rarely, if ever, satisfied.

v. Internalism and Externalism on Justificationism and on the Epistemic Desiderata Approach

I will conclude this chapter by contrasting the ED approach to some controversies between internalism and externalism with the more familiar justificationist approach. I will show how different these controversies look on my ED approach, and how this standpoint enables us to avoid the dead ends we run into when seeking to determine the nature of the supposed objective status of beliefs termed 'justified'.

I begin with a group of putative counterexamples, presented in chapter 3 of BonJour 1985, to the supposition that reliable belief formation is *sufficient* for justification. These involve four imaginary cases of individuals who possess reliable clairvoyant powers. In each case the person comes to believe, truly, that the president is currently in New York City, without having any of the usual reasons for such a belief. In each case the belief results from the exercise of a reliable clairvoyant power. The cases differ in what other relevant beliefs or knowledge the person has or lacks—reasons of the ordinary sort for or against the president's being in New York, reasons for or against the possession of reliable clairvoyance, and so on. In none of the cases does the person have strong evidence that he or she is a reliable clairvoyant or that there is any such power. I will focus on the fourth case, that of Norman. Norman "possesses no evidence or reasons of any kind for or against the general possibility of such a cognitive power or for or against the thesis that he possesses it" (41). BonJour alleges that since this is the case, Norman is "highly irrational and irresponsible in accepting" the belief that the president is in New York, given that from his own subjective conception of the situation he has no grounds for accepting it, and hence is not justified in doing so (38).

I am particularly interested in Norman because, unlike some of the other cases, Norman has no reasons for supposing that he lacks a reliable clairvoyant power and no reason for supposing that the president is *not* in New York. The lack that leads BonJour to deem him unjustified is the lack of sufficient reasons for supposing that the source of the belief in question is a reliable one. And one might well wonder whether the great mass of unsophisticated sense perceivers are not in the same situation. Dolan visually detects a truck coming down the street and thereupon believes that there is a truck coming down the street. But he has no independent reason for or against this belief, nor does he have reasons for supposing visual perception to be a generally reliable source of belief. BonJour's line of argument would seem to brand a large proportion of human perceptual beliefs unjustified as well.

But my concern here is not to get into the controversy between BonJour and reliabilists but to look at that controversy from the standpoint of my ED approach. There the crucial point is that BonJour's judgment on these cases depends on his assumption that one necessary condition for a justified belief is that the subject is "responsible" in holding it, which in turn requires that the belief be supported by the subject's "own subjective conception of the situation". The reliabilism he is attacking, in particular that of David Armstrong (1973), does not recognize any such requirement. The disputants do not completely disagree on requirements for justification. They both hold that a belief is justified only if it is held in such a way that it is likely to be true.[3] But BonJour differs from Armstrong and some other reliabilists in endorsing the requirement just mentioned. What are we to say about this difference? To be sure, there might be a negotiated settlement. It is noteworthy that in the literature spawned by BonJour's cases, it is rare to find an externalist taking the hard line that if someone does possess reliable clairvoyant powers, beliefs acquired by exercising those powers would, just by that fact, count as justified. Goldman, for example, in his 1992b, attempts to defuse BonJour's cases as objections to reliabilism without according justification to any of the clairvoyants in question. But for present purposes I am interested in the standoff between BonJour and a more hard-nosed reliabilist, like Armstrong, who takes reliability of belief formation to be sufficient for at least prima facie justification (justification

---

[3] Here BonJour departs from some of his fellow internalists. See Alston 1996a, chap. 8, for a survey of internalists on this point.

in the absence of sufficient overriders within the subject's knowledge or justified beliefs). If both stick to their guns, and we cannot find any neutral ground on which to resolve the difference, what should we say about the situation? From my antijustification perspective, we should say that, unlike his opponent, BonJour is *emphasizing* the desideratum of one's beliefs being supported by "one's epistemic perspective", one's current body of knowledge and well-supported belief. And, presumably, the reliabilist will not deny that this is something valuable for the cognitive enterprise. How could one deny that it is better to have good reasons for a belief than not? The dispute *only* concerns whether the absence of this prevents a belief from being *justified*. And if we were to forget "justification" and what it takes for that, and concentrate on the desiderata that are driving the argument, we would save ourselves a great deal of futile controversy. Norman exhibits one epistemically important desideratum—a belief formed in a reliable way—and lacks another. We can then discuss what the further implications are of the possession or lack of each of these desiderata.

My next exhibit concerns an internalist argument that reliability is not *necessary* for justification. Here is a statement of the argument by Richard Foley.

> Consider a world in which S believes, seems to remember, experiences, etc., just what he in this world believes, seems to remember, experiences, etc., but in which his beliefs are often false. Suppose further that in this other world the confidence with which he believes, and the clarity with which he seems to remember, and the intensity with which he experiences is identical with the actual world. Suppose even that what he would believe on reflection (about, e.g., what arguments are likely to be truth preserving) is identical with what he would believe on reflection in this world. So if S somehow were to be switched instantaneously from his actual situation to the corresponding situation in the other world, he would not distinguish any difference, regardless of how hard he tried. To use the familiar example, suppose that a demon insures that this is the case. Call such a demon world "w" and then consider this question. Could some of the propositions which a person S believes in w be epistemically rational for him? For example, could some of the propositions which S perceptually believes be epistemically rational? The answer is "yes". If we are willing to grant that in our world some of the propositions S perceptually believes are epistemically rational, then these same propositions would be epistemically rational for S in w as well. After all, world w by hypothesis is one which from S's viewpoint is indistinguishable from this world. So, if given S's situation in this world his perceptual belief p is rational, his belief p would be rational in w as well. (1985, 189–190)

In this argument Foley obviously assumes that where two worlds are indistinguishable *from S's viewpoint,* they are thereby epistemically indistinguishable for S. More specifically, whatever justifies ("makes it rational", in

Foley's terminology) a certain belief in the one world will ipso facto do so in the other. But this is just what a reliabilist will (should) deny. For the reliabilist the question whether the way a belief is formed is a generally reliable one is crucial to its justificatory status. Here too we find some reliabilists, Goldman in particular, trying various maneuvers to accommodate Foley's intuitions without giving up reliabilism. At one point he suggests that what is crucial for justification is reliability in normal worlds, "worlds consistent with our general beliefs about the actual world" (Goldman 1986, 107). This would allow the beliefs in the demon world to be justified on a reliabilist account. In a later publication (1988), reprinted in Goldman 1992a, he distinguishes strong and weak justification, the former being reliabilist justification and the latter amounting to something like one's being nonculpable in forming the belief. The beliefs in the demon world would be weakly but not strongly justified. But, again, I am interested in the controversy between Foley and a hard-nosed reliabilist, or, alternatively, between Foley's view and the "strong justification" view.

What are we to say about the standoff concerning whether what we ordinarily take to be adequate evidence (grounds, reasons ...) for a belief is sufficient for justification, even if the process engendering it is markedly unreliable? Again, it seems impossible to find any neutral ground on which to resolve the dispute. Are we then to throw up our hands and say that we are faced with irresolvably divergent intuitions? An alternative is to accept the thesis that 'epistemic justification' picks out no objective status about which the parties are disagreeing. Instead, one party is much more impressed with the importance for epistemic evaluation of a certain obvious desideratum, reliability of belief formation, than the other. If we put aside the supposition that we have to decide whether that is necessary for "epistemic justification", we can proceed to the more fruitful task of determining what importance this and other desiderata have for the cognitive enterprise, for inquiry and for the assessment of the results thereof.

My last case involves a reliabilist, Alvin Goldman, taking the offensive against internalism. In his 1999b Goldman presents some alleged counterexamples to an accessibility form of an internalist view of justification. He distinguishes different versions of his target. I will restrict myself to what he calls "weak internalism":

> (WI) Only facts concerning what conscious and/or stored mental states an agent is in at time t are justifiers of the agent's beliefs at t. (279)

The rationale for this restriction would be that only such mental states are cognitively accessible to the subject in a relatively direct fashion.

Against the supposition that only such facts contribute to the justification of a belief, Goldman proffers alleged cases of justified beliefs that are not justified by facts like these. I will mention two.

1. *Forgotten evidence.* Sally received adequate evidence for the beneficial effects of broccoli in a *New York Times* article. She still believes this but has forgotten what her evidence was and cannot directly access it.

Nevertheless, Goldman supposes, her belief is still justified (280–281).

2. *Logical or probabilistic relations.* Sally's belief about broccoli cannot be justified by any old conscious or stored mental state. The content of such a state or states must bear the appropriate logical or probabilistic relation of support to the broccoli belief. But such relations are not themselves conscious or stored mental states (282).

If we look at internalist rejoinders, we again find various kinds of weaving and bobbing. For example, Feldman and Conee (2001) discuss a number of attacks in Goldman's "Internalism Exposed", but for the most part they confine themselves to pointing out other forms of internalism that are immune to his criticisms. For example, as for 2 above, it is common for internalists to claim that logical and probabilistic relations are as directly knowable as conscious mental states. But, again, I am concerned here not to enter into the dispute but to look at it from my nonjustification perspective. From that vantage point the crucial question is why the disputants make the judgments they do as to when we do and do not have justified belief and as to what is required for this. And, I suggest, hard thinking about those issues will give rise to the more basic question how, if at all, one can identify what it is about which they take themselves to be disagreeing. Assuming, as I argued in Chapter 1, that there is no satisfactory way to provide such an identification, the way is open to the further realization that what is really driving the argument on both sides are the conditions the relation of which to "justification" is supposed to be the heart of the matter. Put in those terms, Goldman is bringing out the fact that having acquired a belief in a truth-conducive way is an epistemically favorable feature of a belief, even if one can no longer remember that way. Whereas internalists tend to be more impressed by the importance of current access to what supports the belief. Again, both sides will presumably recognize that both these features are desirable for the cognitive enterprise. Unless and until it becomes clear that 'justified' picks out a feature of beliefs about which internalists and externalists are disagreeing *and* which is of crucial importance for the epistemic assessment of beliefs, we will do much better to stick with the various epistemic desiderata the alleged relevance of which to "justification" occupies so much of epistemologists' attention.

CHAPTER 4

DEONTOLOGICAL DESIDERATA

i. Preliminaries

I now begin the detailed treatment of the items on my initial list of alleged epistemic desiderata. I will be concerned with clarification of the nature of each desideratum, how it should be construed. Where there are serious questions as to the viability of an item, those will be addressed. I discuss the deontological group first because it gives rise to crucial problems about viability, as a result of which I postponed consideration of it in Chapter 3 until and unless they can be resolved.

Here are the deontological candidates for epistemic desiderata of belief (B) that were listed in Chapter 3.

9. B is held *permissibly* (one is not subject to blame for doing so).
10. B is formed and held *responsibly*.
11. The causal ancestry of B does not contain violations of intellectual obligations.

First a word about my terminology. 'Deontology' and 'deontological' come from the Greek *deon*—'what is binding' or 'duty'. In ethics, deontology is the study of duty or obligation, and a deontological theory of ethics is one that takes duty or obligation to be the most basic ethical concept and treats it as an intrinsic ethical value of an act rather than in terms of the consequences of the act. My use is broader. I use it to range over any kind of requirement, not restricted to moral obligation, and not excluding requirements that are based on consequences of what is required. And I identify deontological considerations as having to do with the triad of statuses—*required*, *forbidden*, and *permitted*. Thus any way in which it would be epistemically desirable (desirable from the standpoint of an aim at true belief) for a belief to be required or permitted (i.e., not forbidden) would count as a deontological desideratum in my terminology.

Back to the above list, I think it will suffice to concentrate on 9 and 11. Each of these can be construed as focusing on something's being permitted, not being in violation of any intellectual requirements. Desideratum 9 is matter of the having or the acquiring of the belief being permitted. Desideratum 11 is a matter of the permissibility or lack thereof of what one did that led to the acquisition of the belief. Although 10, the formation in terms of responsibility, is familiar in the literature, I think it is ambiguous between 9 and 11 and so does not require separate treatment. The basic difference between 9 and 11 is what is said to be permitted—either the believing itself or what led up to it. Thus, to foreshadow a major point in the ensuing discussion, 9 gives rise to problems about voluntary control of belief whereas 11 does not.

I have already pointed out in Chapter 1 that it is plausible to suppose that 'justified' came into epistemology from its more unproblematic use with respect to voluntary action. I am justified in doing something, for example, appointing someone to a Teaching Assistantship on my own, provided my doing so is in accordance with the relevant rules and regulations, provided it is *permitted* by those rules and hence that I could not rightfully be *blamed* or *held to account* for it, and was acting *responsibly* in doing so.[1] The rules could be institutional, as in the above example, or legal or moral. Thus I would be morally justified in failing to make a contribution to a certain organization provided my doing so doesn't violate any moral rule. Because of this provenance it is natural to think of believing, when taken to be subject to being justified or unjustified, as subject to requirement, prohibition, and permission. We say things like "You shouldn't have supposed so readily that he would not return", "You have no right to assume that", "You shouldn't jump to conclusions", and "I ought to have trusted him more than I did". Locutions like these seem to be interchangeable with speaking of a belief as being, or not being, justified. These considerations

---

[1] I don't suggest that doing what is not permitted by the rules is coextensive with being subject to blame for doing it. One might have a valid excuse for doing it despite the rules. When I speak of violating a rule as being blameworthy, it is presupposed that there is no such excuse.

were introduced in this book prior to the abandonment of a justification-based epistemology of belief, and in the new dispensation they have no force. Since we are thinking of 9 and 11 simply as states of affairs that are, or may be thought to be, important goals of cognition, the fact that they have often been thought to constitute a belief's being justified, with all the associations that brings from talk of the justification of actions, has lost whatever meta-epistemological significance it had under the old dispensation. The idea of a belief's being required, permitted, or forbidden will have to swim or sink on its own, without support from the etymology of 'justified'. I will now enter onto the elucidation of 9 and a critical discussion of its credentials as an epistemic desideratum. The criticism will mostly hinge on whether we have effective voluntary control of believings. I will argue that we do not.

It seems clear that the terms of the deontological triad, *permitted*, *required*, and *forbidden*, apply to something only if it is under effective voluntary control. By the time-honored principle "Ought implies can", one can be obliged to do A only if one has an effective choice as to whether to do A. It is equally obvious that it makes no sense to speak of S's being permitted or forbidden to do A if S lacks an effective choice as to whether to do so. Therefore, the most fundamental issue raised by the claim of 9 to be an epistemic desideratum is whether believings are under effective voluntary control. If they are not and hence if deontological terms do not apply to them, alleged epistemic desiderata like 9 do not get so far as to be a candidate for an epistemic desideratum. It suffers shipwreck before leaving port. I will argue that believings are not subject to voluntary control. But before that, there are some preliminary points to be made.

First, if I considered the possibility of deontological ED for beliefs to be a live one, I would need to consider a belief's enjoying the stronger deontological status of being a case of complying with an epistemic obligation, doing what is required, as well as the weaker status of merely being something that is epistemically permitted. But since I hold that no deontological status is possible for beliefs, I will not need to go into the different statuses separately. And since justificationists of a deontological bent have concentrated on a belief's being epistemically permitted, I will go along with that focus.

Second, although the discussion in the book thus far has been solely in terms of belief, we need to include consideration of other propositional attitudes that are contrary to belief. Chisholm (1977, chap. 1) speaks in terms of a trichotomy of 'believe' (or 'accept'), 'reject', and 'withhold' that p. Since rejecting p is identified with believing some contrary of p, at least not-p, it brings in no new kind of propositional attitude, but withholding p, believing neither it nor any contrary, does. The basic point here is that one has control over a given type of propositional attitude only if one also has control over some field of incompatible alternatives. To have effective control over believing that p is to have control over whether one believes that p or takes on some alternative thereto. Therefore, to be strictly accurate we should say that our problem about 9 concerns voluntary control over intellectual propositional attitudes generally. Though my formulations will mostly be in terms of belief, they should be understood as having this more general bearing.

Third, something must be said about the relation between the voluntary control of actions and of states of affairs. Thus far I have been oscillating between the two. A belief is a more or less long-lived state of the psyche that can influence actions and reactions of the subject so long as it persists. And the same holds for other propositional attitudes. Thus, in speaking of voluntary control of beliefs, we have been speaking of the control of states. But couldn't we just as well speak of the voluntary control of the action of bringing about such states: accepting, rejecting, or withholding a proposition? If the two are strictly correlative, we could equally well conduct the discussion in terms of either. Whenever we are responsible for a state of affairs by virtue of having brought it about, we may just as well speak of being responsible for the action of bringing it about. There are reasons, however, for proceeding in terms of states.

The main reason is this. If we hold that beliefs are subject to deontological evaluation because they are under voluntary control, we need not restrict ourselves to beliefs that are formed intentionally by a voluntary act. I could be blamed for believing that p in the absence of adequate evidence, even if the belief was formed automatically, not by voluntarily carrying out an intention to do so. Provided believing in general is under voluntary control, it is enough that I could have rejected or withheld the proposition by a voluntary act had I chosen to do so.

The final preliminary note is this. Our issue does not concern free will or freedom of action, at least in any sense in which that goes beyond one's action being under the control of the will. On a "libertarian" conception of free will this is not sufficient; it is required also that both A and non-A be causally possible, given all the causal influences on the agent. A libertarian will, no doubt, maintain that if deontological concepts are to apply to believings in the same sense in which they apply to overt actions, then all the libertarian conditions will have to apply to believings. Here, however, I am concerned only with whether believings are under voluntary control.

ii. Basic Voluntary Control of Believing

Locutions like the ones cited earlier as encouraging the application of deontological terms to believing—"You shouldn't jump to conclusions", "I had to accept his testimony; I had no choice"—also strongly suggest that belief is under voluntary control. Else why could we speak of what beliefs one should or shouldn't form, or that one did or did not have a choice as to whether one forms a certain belief? Though this view is distinctly out of favor today, it still has its defenders.[2] Such locutions also naturally suggest not only that believing is under voluntary control but that this control is of the maximally direct sort that we have over the motions of our limbs, the voluntary movements of which constitute *basic* actions. A basic action is one that we perform "at will", just by an intention, volition, choice, or decision to do so. It is something we "just do", not by doing something else. Let's call the kind of control we have over states of affairs we can bring about by basic actions *basic voluntary control*. If we do have voluntary control of beliefs, we have the same reason for supposing it to be basic control that we have for supposing ourselves to have basic control over movements of our limbs, namely, that we are hard pressed to specify any action by doing which we get the limbs moved or the beliefs acquired. Hence it is not surprising that the basic voluntary control thesis has had distinguished proponents throughout the history of philosophy. Augustine, Aquinas, Descartes, Kierkegaard, and many others have usually been read this way.[3] And discussions pro and con of the voluntary control of beliefs have mostly focused on the basic control version. Nevertheless, as the subsequent discussion will show, there are other forms of voluntarism about belief that need to be taken into account in a complete treatment.

But for now I am concerned to give a critical examination of the basic voluntary control thesis. Those who have attacked it are divided between those who hold that believing at will is logically impossible and those who hold that it is only psychologically impossible, a capacity that we in fact lack though one we conceivably could have had.[4] I cannot see any sufficient reason for the stronger claim, and I shall merely contend that we are not so constituted as to be able to take propositional attitudes at will. My argument

---

[2] See, e.g., Ginet 1985 and Meiland 1980.

[3] On the basis of a distinction between believing that p and "accepting" that p, according to which the latter but not the former is a voluntary action, I have argued that these philosophers and others are best construed as ascribing voluntary control to accepting, not believing. See Alston 1996b.

[4] The best-known defense of the logical impossibility is Bernard Williams's "Deciding to Believe", in Williams 1972. It has been criticized in, inter alia, Govier 1976 and Winters 1979.

for this, if it can be called that, simply consists in asking you to consider whether you have any such power. Can you, at this moment, start to believe that the Roman Empire is still in control of western Europe, just by deciding to do so? If you find it incredible that you should be sufficiently motivated to even try to believe this, suppose that someone offers you $500 million to believe it, and that you are much more interested in the money than in believing the truth. Could you do what it takes to get that reward? Remember that we are speaking of believing *at will*. No doubt, there are things you could do that would increase the probability of your believing this, but we will get to that later. Can you switch propositional attitudes toward that proposition just by deciding to do so? It seems clear to me that I have no such power. Volitions, decisions, or choosings don't hook up with propositional attitude inaugurations, just as they don't hook up with the secretion of gastric juices or with metabolism. There could conceivably be individual differences in this regard. Some people can wiggle their ears at will, but most of us cannot. However, I very much doubt that any of us are endowed with the power of believing that p, for any given p, at will. The temptation to suppose otherwise may stem from conflating that power with others that are clearly distinct. If I were to set out to bring myself into a state of belief that p, just by an act of will, I might assert that p with what sounds like conviction, or dwell favorably on the idea that p, or imagine a sentence expressing p emblazoned in the heavens with an angelic chorus in the background intoning the Gloria of Bach's Mass in B Minor. All this I can do at will, but none of it amounts to forming a belief that p. It is all show, an elaborate pretense of believing. Having gone through all this, my propositional attitudes will remain just as they were before; or if there is any change, it will be as a *result* of these gyrations.[5]

Don't suppose that our inability to believe at will is restricted to what is obviously false. It also extends to beliefs that are obviously true. I have already made the point that voluntary control attaches to sets of contraries. To take the simplest case, if the sphere of my voluntary control does not extend both to A and to not-A, then it attaches to neither. If I don't have the power to choose between A and not-A, then we are in no position to say that I did A at will, rather than just did it, accompanied perhaps by a volition. Thus, even if I willingly, or not unwillingly, form perceptual beliefs in the way I do, it by no means follows that I form those beliefs *at will*, or that I have voluntary control over such belief formation. It would have to be true that I have voluntary control over whether I *do or do not* believe that the tree has leaves on it when I see a tree with leaves on it just before me in

---

[5] A bit later in the discussion I will present other tempting conflations.

broad daylight with my eyesight working normally. And it is perfectly clear that in this situation I have no power at all to refrain from that belief. So it is with everything that seems obvious to us. We have just as little voluntary control over ordinary beliefs formed by introspection, memory, and simple uncontroversial inferences from uncontroversial premises.

The above discussion may suggest to the voluntarist that he can still make a stand on propositions that do not seem clearly true or false and hold that there one often has the capacity to adopt whatever propositional attitude one chooses. In religion, philosophy, history, and high-level scientific inquiry it is often the case that, so far as one can see, the relevant arguments do not definitively settle the matter one way or the other. I engage in a prolonged study of free will or causality. I carefully consider arguments for and against various positions. It seems to me that none of the positions have been decisively established, though there are weighty considerations that can be urged in support of each. There are serious difficulties with all the positions, though, so far as I can see, more than one contender is left in the field. So what am I to do? I could just abandon the question. But, alternatively, I could, so it seems, simply *decide* to adopt one of the positions. Is that not what I must do if I am to make any judgment on the matter?

There are also practical situations in which we are confronted with incompatible answers to a certain question, none of which we see to be clearly true or false. Here we often do not have the luxury of leaving the field; since we must act in one way rather than another, we are forced to form and act on some belief about the matter. It would be a good idea for me to plant these flowers today *iff* it will rain tomorrow. But it is not at all clear to me whether tomorrow will be rainy. I must either plant the flowers today or not, and if I just ignore the issue, that will be equivalent to assuming that it will not rain tomorrow. Hence the better part of wisdom would be to make a choice between the alternative predictions. On a larger scale, a field commander in wartime is often faced with questions about the current disposition of enemy forces. But often such information as he has does not tell him just what that disposition is. In disposing his own forces he must act on some assumption about the enemy's forces. Hence he is forced to decide on a hypothesis as to that disposition and act on that basis. What else can he do?[6]

---

[6] Even if beliefs can be formed at will in these kinds of cases, there still remain vast stretches of our belief, including all the cases discussed above, where it seems obvious what is the case, where we have already seen believing at will not to be a possible move. And so it would still be true that believing permissibly would not be generally viable as an epistemic desideratum.

Despite the intuitive appeal of the idea that beliefs are formed at will in these cases, there are several alternative construals, one or another of which is a better reading of each. Begin with the philosopher who really does come to believe the libertarian account of free will or the epiphenomenalist position on the mind-body question. Where that happens it is presumably because at least for the moment the considerations in favor of the position seem to be conclusive, even though previously they did not. And at that time the belief follows automatically from that momentary seeming of conclusiveness, just as it does in cases where it always seems obvious what the truth of the matter is whenever one turns one's attention to it. At that moment, S is no more able to accept a compatibilist account of free will or a hard-nosed materialism on the mind-body problem than he would be if the positions he comes to believe had seemed obviously true from his first consideration of the problem. If, at a given time, it still seemed to the philosopher that libertarianism and compatibilism were approximately equally well supported, how could she simply decide to believe one rather than another? How could we do that any more than, lacking any reasons at all for one alternative rather than the other, we decide to believe that the number of ultimate particles in the universe is even rather than odd?

The above account in terms of a momentary sense of conclusive support for one alternative could also apply to our practical cases. It could be that the military commander, at a certain point in his deliberations, comes to think the reasons for a particular hypothesis concerning the disposition of enemy forces are conclusive. But I believe that there are other construals for both the theoretical and practical cases. For one thing, the subject may be *resolving to act as though it is true that p*, adopting it as a basis for action without actually believing it. This could well be a correct description of the military commander. He may have said to himself: "I don't know what the disposition of enemy forces is. I don't even have enough evidence to consider one hypothesis much more likely than any other. But I have to proceed on some basis or other, so I'll just assume that it is H and make my plans accordingly". If that's the way the land lies, it would be incorrect to describe the commander as believing that the disposition of enemy forces is H or having any other belief about the matter. He is, self-consciously, proceeding on an assumption concerning the truth of which he has no belief at all. One may also make an assumption for theoretical purposes, in order to see how it "pans out" in the hope that one will thereby obtain some additional reasons for believing it to be true or false. A scientist can adopt "as a working hypothesis" the proposition that the atomic nucleus is positively charged, draw various consequences from it, and proceed to test those consequences. He need not believe that the atomic nucleus is positively charged in order to carry out this operation. Indeed, he would be doing this because he does not yet know what to believe about the matter. Likewise a philosopher might take materialism as a working hypothesis to see how it works out in application to various problems.

Working hypotheses may also be involved in activities that are a blend of the theoretical and the practical. One may accept the existence of God, or some more robust set of religious doctrines, as a guide to life, trying to live in accordance with them, seeking to act and feel one's way into a religious community, in order to determine how the doctrines work out in the living of them, both in terms of how satisfactory and fulfilling a life they enable one to live and in terms of what evidence for or against them one acquires. Again, at least in early stages of this process, one does not yet believe the doctrines in question.

There are other possibilities as well. S may be seeking, for whatever reason, to bring herself into a position of believing p, and she, or others, may confuse this activity, which can be undertaken voluntarily, with believing the proposition to be true. Or S may align herself with some group—a church, a political party, a group of thinkers—that is committed to certain doctrines, and this, which can be done voluntarily, may be confused with coming to believe those doctrines. Finally, there is the distinction between *acceptance* and *belief* that was briefly mentioned earlier. The basic distinction is that belief is something that one *finds* oneself with, something that springs into consciousness spontaneously when the question is raised. Whereas acceptance of a proposition is, at least in the first instance, a deliberate voluntary act of accepting a proposition as true. It differs from the "working hypothesis" or "assuming that p as a basis for action" in that, unlike these cases, S does commit himself to p's being true. He "takes it on board" as one of the things he acts on and draws consequences from. It is, we might say, just like belief except that the commitment to p's being true doesn't arise spontaneously but, at least at the outset, has to be kept in activation by a deliberate voluntary act. Thus the philosopher and the religious seeker might accept, in this sense, a position on the free-will issue or the mind-body problem or various religious doctrines. The philosopher, even though libertarianism does not seem to him to be conclusively established, might accept it—take it as his position on the issue, defend it, draw various consequences for it, while seeking for conclusive evidence pro or con, and not yet finding himself believing it. And there is an analogous possibility for religious doctrines.[7]

---

[7] The latter application is explored in detail in Alston 1996b.

Thus I take it that the analysis of a wide variety of supposed cases of believing at will reveals that in each case coming to believe that p may well have been confused with something else. Hence I think that there is a considerable case for the position that no one ever acquires a belief at will.

iii. Other Modes of Voluntary Control of Believing

The demise of basic control of belief is by no means the end of voluntarism about belief. Many deontologists, after avoiding any commitment to what they call "direct voluntary control of belief" (what I have called "basic voluntary control"), insist that beliefs are subject to what they term "indirect voluntary control".[8] They generally use this term in an undiscriminating fashion to cover any sort of voluntary control that is not basic. Hence they fail to distinguish the three kinds of nonbasic control I will proceed to enumerate.[9] Some of their examples fit one of my three types and some another.

First, note that we take many nonbasic overt actions and their upshots to be under voluntary control in a way that is sufficient for their being required, permitted, or prohibited. Consider opening a door, turning on a light, and informing someone that p. Succeeding in any of these requires more than a volition; in each case I must make one or more bodily movements, and these movements must have certain consequences. In order for me to open a door, I must pull it, push it, kick it, or put some other part of my body into suitable contact with it (assuming that I lack telekinetic powers), and this must result in the door's coming to be open. In order to inform H that p, I must produce various sounds, marks, or other perceivable products, and the product in question must fall under linguistic rules in such a way as to constitute a vehicle for asserting that p. Thus actions like these are not immediately consequent on a volition and are not strictly done "at will". Nevertheless, I might be blamed for my failure to open the door when it was my obligation to do so and I was not prevented from performing basic bodily movements sufficient to bring it about that the door was open. In typical cases we take the extra conditions for success for granted. We suppose that if the agent will just voluntarily exert herself in a way that is open to her, the act will be done. Here we can say that the action and its upshot are subject to the *immediate voluntary control* of the agent

---

[8] See, e.g., Alvin Goldman 1980, Plantinga 1983, Wolterstorff 1983, Moser 1985, Steup 1988.
[9] Even the extended treatment in Pojman 1986 fails to make any distinctions within "indirect control".

(more strictly, *nonbasic* immediate voluntary control), even though more than an act of will is required. I call this control "immediate" since the agent is able to carry out the intention right away, in one uninterrupted intentional act, without having to return to the attempt a number of times.[10] I will use the term 'direct control' for both basic and nonbasic immediate control. If beliefs were subject to one's direct control in either way, that would suffice to render them susceptible to deontological evaluation.

But are beliefs always, or ever, within our immediate nonbasic voluntary control? As in the discussion of basic control we can first exempt most beliefs from consideration. Where it is perfectly clear that a certain proposition is true or false, as with typical perceptual, introspective, memory, and simple inferential beliefs, it is absurd to think that one has any such control over whether one accepts, rejects, or withholds the proposition. When I look out my window and see rain falling, water dripping off the trees, and cars passing by, I no more have immediate nonbasic control over whether I accept those propositions than I have basic control. I form the belief that rain is falling willy-nilly. There is no way I can inhibit this belief or acquire a contrary belief. At least there is no way I can do so on the spot, in carrying out an uninterrupted intention to do so. What button would I push? I could try asserting the contrary in a confident tone of voice. I could rehearse some skeptical arguments. I could invoke the Vedantic doctrine of *Maya*. I could grit my teeth and command myself to withhold the proposition. But none of these will have the least effect on my doxastic condition. Since cases in which it seems obvious to the subject what is the case constitute an enormously large proportion of propositional attitudes, the above considerations show that immediate nonbasic voluntary control cannot be the basis for the application of deontological concepts to most of our beliefs and withholdings.

But what about situations in which it is not clear whether a proposition is true or false? Here I can simply refer the reader back to the last section, in which I argued with respect to basic control that the cases in which it may look as if one comes to believe a proposition at will are best construed in other ways. In those cases involving the philosopher, the general, and the gardener, it is, I claim, implausible to suppose that the subject acquired a belief voluntarily, whether by a mere act of will or by a series of basic or more nearly basic actions that led right away to the intended result. Here, as with the obviously true or false cases, we are at a loss to think what button to push, what bodily movements to make so

---

[10] Of course, opening a door or turning on a light may, in special cases, require repeated attempts with intervals between. In the above I was speaking of the simple unimpeded cases.

as to bring about the formation of an intended belief. Until some plausible story can be told as to what one can do voluntarily to result in a belief's being formed immediately, we can ignore the possibility of treating voluntary control of beliefs on the model of nonbasic but immediate voluntary control of doors being open and lights being on.

This brings us to a second grade of what is commonly called "indirect voluntary control", what I will call *long-range voluntary control*. It will be noted that the types of voluntary control I am considering are arranged in an order of increasing indirectness, increasing distance from the most immediate control. Here, as with immediate nonbasic voluntary control, we think of the belief as being produced by the carrying out of an intention by one or more actions that are designed to produce the belief rather than as being produced by a mere act of will, choice, or decision. But unlike the last case, the belief production is not carried out in one uninterrupted action. It involves a series of actions spread out over a greater or smaller period of time, the smallest period of which is too extended to accommodate a single uninterrupted act.[11] A number of voluntarists seem to be thinking in these terms of the cases in which it is not immediately obvious whether a given proposition is true or false. After all, they say, that is what inquiry is for, to resolve such issues. One certainly has voluntary control over whether to keep looking for evidence or reasons, and voluntary control over where to look, what steps to take to find relevant considerations, and so on. It is suggested, in effect, that since we have voluntary control over these intermediate steps, this amounts to what I call *long-range voluntary control* of a propositional attitude. Chisholm, for example, says:

> If self-control is what is essential to activity, some of our beliefs, our believings, would seem to be acts. When a man deliberates and comes finally to a conclusion, his decision is as much within his control as is any other deed we attribute to him. If his conclusion was unreasonable, a conclusion he should not have accepted, we may plead with him: "But you needn't have supposed that so-and-so was true. Why didn't you take account of these other facts?" We assume that his decision is one he could have avoided and that, had he only chosen to do so, he could have made a more reasonable inference. Or, if his conclusion is not the result of a deliberate inference, we may say, "But if you had only stopped to think", implying that, had he chosen, he could have stopped to think. We suppose, as we do whenever we apply our ethical or moral predicates, that there was something else the agent could have done instead. (1968, 224)

---

[11] Obviously, there is no precise boundary between a "single uninterrupted act" and a "series of temporally extended acts" where the temporal extension is small. But there are enough clear cases on either side of the distinction to make it usable.

To be sure, the mere fact that one often looks for evidence to decide an unresolved issue does not show that one has voluntary control over one's propositional attitudes. That would also depend, at least, on the incidence of success in these enterprises. And sometimes one finds decisive evidence and sometimes one doesn't. But let's ignore that complexity and just consider whether there is a case for long-range voluntary control of belief in the successful cases.

No, there is not, and primarily for the following reason. Claims like those in the quote from Chisholm ignore the difference between doing A in order to bring about E, for some definite E, and doing A so that some effect within a certain range will ensue. In order that the phenomenon of looking for more evidence would show that we have voluntary control over propositional attitudes, it would have to be the case that the search for evidence was undertaken with the intention of taking up a *certain* attitude toward a *specific* proposition. For only in that case would it have any tendency to show that we have exercised voluntary control over *what* propositional attitude we come to have. Suppose that I can't remember Al Kaline's lifetime batting average, and I look it up in the baseball almanac. I read there the figure .320, and I thereby accept it. Does that show that I have voluntary control (of any sort) over my belief that Kaline's lifetime batting average was .320? Not at all. At most it shows that I have long-range voluntary control over whether I take up *some* propositional attitude toward *some* proposition ascribing a lifetime batting average to Kaline. So this is not at all parallel to cases where we definitely do have some (albeit fallible) long-range voluntary control over other sorts of affairs. Suppose that I can perform voluntary actions that will result, subject to the usual chances that infect all human endeavor, in my losing twenty pounds. Here there is a completely definite and unique result toward which my voluntary efforts are directed, and success, or at least repeated success, will show that I do have long-range voluntary control (within limits) of my weight.

What the situation described by Chisholm is closely analogous to is the following. I am a servant, and I am motivated to bring the door into whatever position my employer chooses. He has an elaborate electronic system that involves automatic control of many aspects of the household, including doors. Each morning he leaves detailed instructions on household operations in a computer. Doors can be operated only through the computer in accordance with his instructions. There is no way I can carry out an intention of my own, no matter how long range, to open or to close a particular door at a particular time. All I can is to actuate the relevant program and let things take their course. Since the employer's instructions will be carried out only if I actuate the program, I am responsible for the doors' assuming positions he specified, just as in the Kaline case I was responsible for taking up some attitude or other toward some proposition within a given range. But I definitely am not responsible for the front door's being open rather than closed at a particular time, nor can I be said to have voluntary control over its specific position. Hence it would be idle to apply deontological concepts vis-à-vis the specific position of the door: to forbid me or require me to open it, or to blame or reproach me for its being open. I had no control over that; it was not subject to my will. And that's the way it is where the only voluntary control I have over my propositional attitudes is to enter onto an investigation that will eventuate in some propositional attitude or other on what is being considered.

Or consider propositions concerning what is visible. I have the power to voluntarily open my eyes and look about me, thereby putting myself in a position, when conditions are favorable, to reliably form propositions about the visible environment. Again, with respect to past experiences, I can "search my memory" for the details of my experiences of the middle of yesterday, thereby usually putting myself in a good position to form beliefs reliably about my experiences at that time. No one, I suppose, would take these facts to show that I have voluntary control over what I believe about the visible environment or about my remembered experiences. What I can control voluntarily is whether I form (or am in a position to form) some accurate beliefs or other about my current visible environment or about my experiences of yesterday. And yet this is the same sort of thing as the search for additional evidence of which Chisholm speaks, differing only in the type of belief-forming mechanisms involved.

I suspect that those who take positions like the one in the passage just quoted from Chisholm secretly suppose that the additional evidence, rather than "automatically" determining the propositional attitude, simply puts the subject in a position to make an informed choice of an attitude. That is, they really locate the voluntary control in the moment of attitude formation rather than in the preliminary investigation, thereby in effect taking the (basic or nonbasic) immediate-control position. But then, faced with the implausibility of those positions, they think to save the application of deontological concepts to beliefs by pushing the voluntary control back to the preliminary search for decisive considerations. But their undercover attachment to the immediate-control thesis prevents them from seeing that voluntary control of the investigative phase has no tendency to ground the deontological treatment of propositional attitudes themselves.

Despite the above arguments against false pretensions to the title of "long-range voluntary control of belief", I have no intention of suggesting that there could not be legitimate claimants. Let's take a fresh start and lay out what it takes for a genuine case of such control in general (not restricted to beliefs). It requires the capacity to bring about a state of affairs, C, by voluntarily doing a number of different things over a considerable period of time, typically interrupted by activity directed to other goals. One has this sort of control, to a greater or lesser degree, over many things: one's weight, cholesterol concentration, blood pressure, and disposition; the actions of one's spouse or one's offspring. One can, with some hope of success, set out on a long-range project to reduce one's weight, improve one's disposition, or get one's spouse to be more friendly to the neighbors. The degree of control one is likely to have varies markedly among these examples. But all these examples and many more illustrate the point that one can have long-range control over many things over which one lacks immediate control. I cannot markedly reduce my weight right away by the uninterrupted carrying out of an intention to—by taking a pill, running around the block, or saying 'Abracadabra'. But that doesn't nullify the fact that I have some degree of long-range control.

To return to our main concern, it does seem that we have some degree of long-range voluntary control over at least some of our beliefs. People do set out on long-range projects to get themselves to believe a certain proposition, and sometimes they succeed in this. Devices employed include selective exposure to evidence and deliberate attention to supporting considerations, seeking the company of believers and avoiding nonbelievers, self-suggestion, and more bizarre methods like hypnotism. By such devices people sometimes induce themselves to believe in God, in materialism, in communism, in the proposition that they are loved by X, and so on. Why doesn't this constitute a kind of voluntary control that grounds deontological treatment of beliefs?

Well, it would if we *do* have sufficient control of this sort. People could properly be held responsible for their attitudes toward propositions in a certain range only if those who set out to intentionally produce a certain attitude toward such a proposition and made sufficient efforts were frequently successful. For only if we were generally successful in bringing about goal G when we try hard enough to do so, do we have effective control over whether G obtains. And if I don't have effective control over G, I can hardly be held to blame for its nonoccurrence. This is a generally applicable principle, by no means restricted to beliefs. If I am so constituted that the most I can do with respect to my irritability is to make it slightly less likely that it will exceed a certain high average threshold, I can hardly be blamed for being irritable.

It is very dubious that we have a reliable long-range voluntary control over any of our beliefs, even in the most favorable cases, such as beliefs about religious and philosophical matters and about personal relationships. *Sometimes* people succeed in getting themselves to believe (disbelieve) something. But I doubt that the success rate is substantial. I know of no statistics on this, but I would be very much surprised if attempts of this sort bore fruit in more than a small proportion of the cases. In thinking about this, let's first set aside cases in which the attempt succeeds because the subject happens onto conclusive evidence that would have produced the belief anyway without deliberate effort on his part to produce that belief. Thus we need to consider cases in which the subject is swimming against either a preponderance of contrary evidence or a lack of sufficient evidence either way. That is, S is fighting very strong tendencies to believe when and only when something seems true to her. Whether these tendencies are innate, or engendered and reinforced by socialization, they are deeply rooted and of great strength. To combat them one must exercise considerable ingenuity in monitoring the input of information and in exposing oneself to nonrational influences. These are tricky operations, and it would be very surprising if they were successful in a significant proportion of cases. I am not suggesting that it is unusual for people to form and retain beliefs without adequate grounds. That is all too common. But in most such cases the proposition in question seems clearly true to the person, however ill supported. The typical case of prejudice, for example, is not one in which S manages to believe something contrary to what seems to him to be the case or something concerning which he has no definite impression of truth or falsity. It is a case in which his socialization has led it to seem clearly true to him that, for example, blacks are innately inferior.

Thus the possibility of long-range voluntary control of beliefs does not provide significant grounding for deontologism, even for the sorts of propositions people do sometimes try to get themselves to believe or disbelieve. Much less is there any such support for deontologism for those propositions with respect to which people don't normally even try to manipulate their attitudes. We have already noted that most of our beliefs spring from doxastic tendencies that are too deeply rooted to permit of modification by deliberate effort. In such cases the project of deliberately producing belief or disbelief is one that is never seriously envisaged. Thus, even if we were usually successful when we set out to produce a propositional attitude, the voluntary control thus manifested would not ground the application of deontological concepts to beliefs generally.

iv. Indirect Voluntary Influence on Believing

Up to this point I have been considering various ways in which believing, rejecting, and withholding propositions might be themselves under effective voluntary control. We have seen that for most of our beliefs we have no such control and that for the others we have at most some spotty and unreliable control of the long-range sort. But this is not the end of the line for the prospects of an epistemic desideratum of the deontological kind. There is still one more way in which subjects might be held responsible for their believings, for believings to be required, forbidden, or permitted, even though they themselves are not under effective voluntary control. To see this, consider the general point that we can be blamed for a state of affairs F, provided something we voluntarily did (didn't do) and should have not done (done) was a necessary condition (in the circumstances) of the realization of F. That is, F would not have obtained had we done (not done) something we should have done (not done). If my cholesterol buildup would have been prevented had I regulated my diet in the way I should have done, but didn't, I can be blamed for that buildup, whether or not I have direct effective voluntary control of my cholesterol level.

Applying this general point to beliefs, we can say that even though believings are not under effective voluntary control, we can be blamed for holding a certain belief, B, if there are things we can voluntarily do such that we should have done (not done) them and if we had done (not done) them we would not have held that belief. Suppose that I accept some idle gossip to the effect that Jim is trying to undermine Susie's position as departmental chair. If I had done what I should have done by way of checking into this matter, I would not have formed that belief or would not have retained it for as long as I did. Hence I could be blamed for holding the belief. To take a case where I am blameless in holding a belief, consider a visual belief where my vision and my belief-forming mechanisms are working normally. There is nothing relevant to that belief formation that I should have done but didn't, and so I am not subject to blame in forming the belief. Note that other deontological terms like 'ought' and 'should' are also applicable to states of affairs not themselves under direct voluntary control in this derivative way. Thus we can say that I *ought* to have a lower cholesterol count and that I *should* not have believed that he did it.

Note that this kind of application of the deontological categories of blameworthiness or the reverse to believings is a derivative one. It is the (actual or possible) voluntary acts in the causal ancestry of the belief to which blameworthiness and other deontological terms of evaluation apply in a primary way. My checking, or failing to check, on the accuracy of the gossip is something that is directly, underivatively blameworthy or the reverse. The propositional attitude that eventuates is blameworthy or the reverse only by derivation from the voluntary acts that give rise to it. Strictly speaking, in thinking of the matter in this way we should not think of the forming of the propositional attitude itself as required, forbidden, or permitted since it itself is not under effective voluntary control. Its blameworthiness or blamelessness stems from the required, forbidden, or permitted voluntary acts in its causal ancestry. Harking back to the initial list of candidate deontological desiderata, we have now moved from

9. B is held permissibly (one is not subject to blame for doing so).

to

11. The causal ancestry of B does not contain violations of intellectual obligations.

I will call this kind of impingement of the voluntary on belief *indirect voluntary influence*.[12]

I will now proceed to put a bit of flesh on the idea of an indirect influence of voluntary actions on propositional attitudes. First, let's note that we do have voluntary control over many actions that can influence our believings, rejectings, and withholdings. These can be divided into two groups: (a) activities that bring influences to bear, or withhold influences from, a particular candidate, or field of candidates, for belief, and (b) activities that affect our general belief-forming habits or tendencies. There are many examples of (a). With respect to a particular issue, I have voluntary control over whether and how long I consider the matter, over whether and where I look for relevant evidence or reasons, reflect on a particular argument, seek input from other people, search my memory for analogous cases, and so on. Here we come back to the activities we saw Chisholm wrongly classifying as the intentional inauguration of an attitude toward a specific proposition. Group (b) includes such activities as training myself to be more critical of gossip, instilling in myself a stronger disposition to reflect carefully before making a judgment on highly controversial matters, talking myself into being less (more) subservient to authority, and practicing

---

[12] This kind of relation of voluntary action to belief is given much less attention in the literature than the kinds I have judged to lack viability. Nevertheless, as an important aspect of cognitive endeavors, it deserves more attention than it receives. I should also mention that in Alston 1988a I argue that a concept of epistemic justification based on this kind of voluntary influence on belief is not adequate, not because there is no such influence but rather because it is not closely enough related to the goal of true belief. Though I am not concerned here with how to construe epistemic justification, I will make a similar point about treating 11 as an *epistemic* desideratum.

greater sensitivity to the condition of other people. It is within my power to do things like this or not, and when I do them with sufficient assiduity I make some difference to my propositional attitude tendencies, and thus indirectly to the formation of such attitudes.

There would be no harm in including in (a) attempts to bring about a particular attitude to a specific proposition. For these too would be things that influence our propositional attitudes and over which we have voluntary control. The point of stressing other things is that since the earlier discussion provided reason for thinking such attempts are rarely successful, I want here to emphasize the point that even if we are never successful in voluntarily bringing about a belief that p, there are still many things we can do voluntarily that do have a bearing on what propositional attitudes are engendered.

The next question is whether the deontological triad of concepts applies to activities like those canvassed in the next-to-last paragraph. Is it ever the case that we ought or ought not to engage in an activity of these sorts, such as searching for new evidence or critically examining the credentials of gossip? Is it ever the case that we ought or ought not to strive to make ourselves more (less) sensitive to contrary evidence? Deontologists typically hold that we have intellectual obligations in such matters, obligations rooted in our basic intellectual obligation to seek the true and avoid the false in belief. I accept this view, which seems eminently plausible.

Thus it will sometimes be the case when I believe that p that I would not have done so had I done various things in the past that I could and should have done but failed to do, and it will sometimes be the case that I would not have believed that p had I not done various things in the past that I could and should not have done but did. In either of these cases there is a failure of obligations in the causal ancestry of the belief that renders me blameworthy for having the belief. And if neither of these is the case, then I am blameless, not properly held to blame for the belief. (All this applies equally to rejectings and withholdings). Hence the indirect voluntary influence on the formation of propositional attitudes does have an evaluative bearing on those attitudes, either positive or negative.

I must pause to refine the above formulation. There are certain ways in which dereliction of intellectual duty can contribute to belief formation without rendering S blameworthy for forming that belief. Suppose that I fail to carry out an obligation to spend a certain period in training myself to look for counterevidence. I use the time thus freed up to take a walk around the neighborhood. In the course of doing so I see two dogs fighting, thereby acquiring the belief that they are fighting. There was a relevant intellectual obligation I didn't fulfill, which is such that if I had fulfilled it I wouldn't have acquired that belief. But if that is a perfectly normal perceptual belief, I am obviously not to blame for having formed it.[13]

Here the dereliction of duty contributed to belief formation simply by facilitating access to data. That is not the kind of contribution we had in mind in the above formulations. The sorts of cases we had in mind were those most directly suggested by the two sorts of voluntary activities that affect belief formation: (a) those that involve looking for considerations relevant to the belief in question, or not doing so, and (b) those that affect our general belief-forming habits or tendencies. By revising 11 so as to make this explicit, we can avoid counterexamples like the above.

11A. S is intellectually to blame for believing that p *iff* if S had fulfilled all her intellectual obligations, then S's access to relevant considerations, or S's belief-forming habits or tendencies, would have changed in such a way that S would not have believed that p.[14]

It follows from the above that 11A is a genuine intellectual desideratum, a desirable feature of belief outputs of cognition. And it also follows from the above discussion that, unlike 9, 11A does not fail to qualify as an epistemic desideratum because it is not a real possibility for human beings. But though it is a cognitive desideratum, it will still not be an *epistemic* desideratum if it is not connected in the right way with the truth goal. And how do we determine whether it is? Since we have identified three groups of cognitive desiderata that are, in their several ways, related to the truth goal so as to qualify as epistemic desiderata, an obvious way to proceed is to consider whether 11 is related to the truth goal in one of those ways.

I think we can straightaway eliminate the Group III and the Group V ways from consideration. As for III, it is obvious that where there are no violations of intellectual obligations in the ancestry of a considerable number of S's beliefs, this in no way provides S with resources for determining under what conditions a belief is likely to be true and thereby putting S in a good position to restrict belief formation to true beliefs, in the way higher-level epistemic knowledge or the capacity for such does. Nor does 11A presuppose such a capacity as 8 does. As for Group V, although it could

---

[13] I am indebted to Emily Robertson for calling this problem to my attention.

[14] Another fine-tuning point has to do with the "absoluteness" of the counterfactual involved. Desideratum 11A says S *would not have believed that p* under these conditions. But perhaps S is also blameworthy for believing that p even if it is only much less likely that S would have believed that p under these conditions. I am inclined to accept this weaker interpretation, but I will not press the matter here since I will go on to reject 11 as an epistemic desideratum anyway.

be argued that fulfillment of intellectual obligations has an intrinsic cognitive value that is independent of truth, as 12–15 do, that value is in no way dependent on being associated with a preponderance of true beliefs, as is the case with the Group V desiderata. Even if S's beliefs are preponderantly false, it is a good thing for S to fulfill her intellectual obligations, insofar as this is possible in the face of something less than an outstanding record of achieving the truth.

So this leaves us with Group II, the directly truth-conducive desiderata. Though I will argue that 11A is not related to the truth goal in this way either, I do not think that this is obvious on the face of it, as is the case with the Group III and Group V desiderata. Hence this suggestion deserves more serious consideration. It is prima facie conceivable that being formed in a way that does not depend on violations of intellectual obligations should be a way of rendering a belief probably true. Nevertheless, there are many counterexamples to such a claim, some of which I shall now make explicit.

Before we embark on this, something needs to be said about what would constitute failure to fulfill an intellectual obligation. What makes this difficult is that attempts to conform to an obligation might or might not be successful, and where they are not they might be more or less close to achieving it. On a sufficiently rigorous interpretation we are almost always failing in some intellectual obligation or other. This in turn depends on just how it is specified what one is intellectually obliged to do. Consider the obligation to look for relevant considerations pro and con when it is not clear whether the proposition in question in true. How long and how assiduously does one have to look to fulfill the obligation? To require that every conceivably relevant consideration must be taken into account would be a counsel of perfection that is beyond any of our powers, not to mention the fact that we couldn't know whether that limit had been reached. It seems that to make the notion of fulfilling intellectual obligations usable we have to build in a limitation to what could reasonably be expected of a subject, and that is itself is a very imprecise notion and one that is subject to varying interpretations. Moreover, there is the point that what could be reasonably expected along this line will vary for different people in accordance with their abilities, experience, education, propensities, and so on. So the question whether a given subject has done as much as could be expected of him or her is beset with uncertainties, imprecision, and disagreements.

Keeping all this in mind, let's do the best we can by proceeding on the basis of some sense of what could be expected of a given subject and on the basis of some plausible construal of the content of intellectual obligations. I now want to suggest that there are very many sorts of cases in which one does as much as could be reasonably expected of one in the way of voluntary acts leading up to a given belief without the belief's thereby acquiring any considerable likelihood of truth.

First, there are cases of cognitive deficiency. Consider one who forms the belief that socialism is contrary to Christianity for the reasons that are often given for this view by the Christian Right, and is intellectually incapable of figuring out how bad these reasons are, cases that I fear are all too common. Such a person may have done as well as could be expected of him in coming to this belief, but that fact does nothing to make the belief likely to be true. (Thoroughly bad reasons are not truth-conducive). Or consider a college student who doesn't have what it takes to follow abstract philosophical exposition or reasoning. Having read parts of Bk. IV of Locke's *Essay Concerning Human Understanding*, he takes it that Locke's view is that everything is a matter of opinion. He is simply incapable of distinguishing between that view and Locke's view that one's knowledge is restricted to one's own ideas. There is nothing he could do that would lead him to appreciate the difference. Hence he cannot be blamed for interpreting Locke as he does; he is doing the best he can to fulfill his intellectual obligations. But his belief about Locke's view is outrageously ill-grounded, based as it is on his dim-witted impression of Bk. IV of the *Essay*.

Second, consider the innumerable beliefs each of us forms on testimony or authority. Practically everything we believe about science, history, geography, and current affairs is taken on authority. Ideally, we would check out each source to make sure that it is reliable before accepting the testimony. But who has time for that? We can do it in special cases where the matter is of special importance, but it is not a real option for such beliefs generally. If we tried to do so, our doxastic structure would be so impoverished that we would not be able to function in society. Moreover, even if we had time to check up on each authority, in most cases we lack the resources for making an informed judgment. Thus in most cases in which I uncritically accept testimony I have done as much as could reasonably be expected of me. Now consider those cases in which the authority is incompetent or the witness is unreliable. There we are forming a belief on an objectively unreliable basis and hence the belief is not probably true, even though no dereliction of intellectual duty is in the background.

Next consider irresistible beliefs and belief tendencies. If it is impossible for me to alter a certain belief or belief tendency, I can hardly be expected to do so. But some irresistible beliefs are formed in an unreliable fashion in such a way as not to make them likely to be true. The most obvious examples concern strong emotional attachments that are unshakable. For many people their religious or irreligious beliefs have this status, as do beliefs concerning one's country, one's close relations, or one's political party. Such beliefs are often not formed in a truth-conducive way that would render them likely to be true. But S cannot be blamed for doing or having something she can't help doing or having. Here too the believing's not depending on any violation of intellectual obligations is no (even fallible) guarantee of the belief's likelihood of being true.

Of course, showing that 11A is not related to the truth goal in any of the ways the desiderata already approved as epistemic are is not a proof that it is not an epistemic desideratum. Perhaps it is related to the truth goal in some other way that qualifies it as epistemically desirable. That is an abstract possibility. Why shouldn't there be a fourth way, as different from the first three as they are from each other? But I must confess that I have found no fourth way. And until I do, I must rest with the conclusion that 11A does not qualify as an epistemic desideratum.

Thus none of the deontological candidates makes the grade. The first three (alternative versions of 9) fail through the failure of the version of voluntary control of belief presupposed by each to be a real possibility for human beings. And the last (11A) fails through not being connected with the truth goal in the right kind of way. Thus they will receive no further attention in the development of the ED approach to the epistemology of belief.

CHAPTER 5

ADEQUACY OF GROUNDS OF BELIEF

i. Grounds and the Basing Relation

I will now devote three chapters to raising and answering various questions that arise when we seek to be as explicit as possible about the constitution of the various epistemic desiderata that we are taking seriously when they are suitably construed. This chapter and the next will be devoted to Group II desiderata, the most fundamental ones, the ones that are, in some versions at least, "truth-conducive" in the strong sense that by their very nature they provide strong support for the truth of the beliefs that enjoy them. These include the first five items on the list at the beginning of Chapter 3.

1. The subject (S) has adequate evidence (reasons, grounds . . .) for the belief (B).
2. B is based on adequate evidence (reasons, grounds . . .).
3. B was formed by a sufficiently reliable belief-forming process.
4. B was formed by the proper functioning of S's cognitive faculties.
5. B was formed by the exercise of an intellectual virtue.

Looking at 1 and 2, I need to say something about the open-ended disjunction that includes evidence, reasons, and grounds. I am going to take 'ground' as the most basic of these notions and will treat evidence and reasons as items that can figure as grounds. 'Ground' is a functional term; a ground for a belief is something that fulfills a certain function in the formation and/or sustenance of the belief. More specifically, it is what the belief is *based on*. And so the basing relation is really the key notion here, and this section will be devoted to explicating 'based on' and 'ground', and answering questions about them.

But first I should note that taking the basing relation as fundamental contrasts with another possibility for organizing this discussion, namely, taking logical (including probabilistic) relations between *propositions* as basic. My choice is a natural one, given that my concern is with epistemically desirable properties of *beliefs*. A consideration of how what a *belief* is based on can make it likely to be true and hence figure as an epistemic desideratum is a more direct route to that concern than is a detour through logical relations between propositions, from which epistemically desirable properties of beliefs with certain propositional content would then have to be derived. But that more indirect procedure would seem to be a possibility. If we could specify how one proposition, P, gives adequate support to another proposition, Q, by virtue of Q's enjoying a high conditional probability on P, that might give us a handle on how a belief that Q's being based on a belief that P could render the former belief probably true and hence be an epistemically desirable property of the belief that Q. There are more solid reasons than greater directness for the other choice, but they will appear only in the course of the discussion in this chapter and the next. As another quick preview, note that the propositional approach is more directly suggested by 1, in which nothing is said explicitly about basing. As things will turn out, my choice of 2 as the more fundamental desideratum will also be a reason for organizing the discussion in terms of bases of beliefs rather than in terms of logical relations between propositions.

Next I will say something about evidence and reasons, and other ways of designating what can perform the function of grounds. 'Evidence' is a term used variously, at least by philosophers. In ordinary language the tendency is to think of it as consisting of *facts* the subject knows to obtain, "factual evidence". Thus the evidence the detective has collected includes the fact that suspect A was in the vicinity at the time of the murder, the fact that his fingerprints were on the murder weapon, and so on. But there is more than one reason why this is too narrow for an absolutely general account of evidence. For one thing, what if the detective has strong reasons (testimony of alleged witnesses, apparent locus from which the suspect made a telephone call) for believing that A was in the vicinity at the time but in fact he was not? In that case, prior to the discovery of his real location, we would count this as part of his evidence; and even having discovered the truth about his location, we might still say that it was misleading evidence rather than not evidence at all. Hence for complete generality we need to speak of evidence as consisting of beliefs rather than facts.[1] Second, when we are seeking a maximally general notion of evidence, there is some reason to include experience, particularly sensory experience, under that heading. We speak of the "evidence of the senses". This is further supported by a natural tendency to use 'evidence' to cover every ground that contributes to the positive epistemic status of a belief. At least a good part of what gives positive epistemic status to perceptual beliefs is the sensory experience on which they are based. I cannot give a comprehensive account of what makes my belief that it is raining at my residence now well supported without including my visual experience of rain falling when I look out the window.

'Reasons', on the other hand, are naturally restricted to propositionally structured entities, either facts or, because of considerations brought out above, pieces of knowledge or well-supported beliefs, both of which have a propositional structure. So the main reason for including both 'reasons' and 'evidence' in the disjunction is that, depending on the details of the explication of each of these, they will not wholly overlap.

For these and for other reasons, 'evidence' and 'reasons' are terms that are too squishy to mark precisely the most important distinctions between items that can function as grounds of beliefs. They are useful for giving an initial idea of what gives more or less support to taking a belief to be true, but for a more fine-grained account sharper terms are needed. Let me first nail down the point illustrated above by the detective case and say that the grounds in which we are interested for epistemological purposes, the grounds that most crucially affect the epistemic status of a belief, are the proximate inputs to the belief formation.[2] And since belief formation is a psychological process, what immediately triggers it must also be something psychological—some psychological state or process. Extra-psychological facts or objects can affect belief formation only through affecting, and/or being represented by, psychological states. It seems clear that the only possibilities for this office are beliefs (treating pieces of knowledge as special instances of beliefs) and experiences, including sensory experiences, feelings of various kinds, and perhaps others. Hence the main division in grounds of beliefs is between the *doxastic* (grounds that are themselves beliefs) and the *nondoxastic* (primarily if not exclusively experiences). We shall see that this distinction is of crucial importance for the epistemology of belief.

---

[1] For the contrary view that evidence is restricted to what we know, see Williamson 2000, sec. 9.5.

[2] Later, in Chapter 6, section vii, I will introduce some qualifications to this flat restriction to *proximate* inputs. But they will still be in the center of the picture in this book.

Here I must pause to introduce a complication. The previous paragraph might well give the impression that I take each belief to be based only on the ground that led to its initial acquisition. But this is false to the facts. For beliefs that go beyond the most simple and elementary ones derived from such basic sources as perception, introspection, memory, and the simplest forms of inference, it is the rule rather than the exception that they continue to receive support or the reverse from further doxastic and nondoxastic inputs after their initial formation. Just think of the way in which a fairly complicated hypothesis is sometimes strengthened by further considerations well after it was originally formed, and sometimes weakened instead or also as time goes on. For such cases we must think in terms of not one but a series of basings and weakenings. But by a process of analysis we can think of each basing in the series as exhibiting the same generic features as one that inaugurates a new belief. In particular, it will be true of each that the crucial input is the terminal one that results in the inauguration, strengthening, or preservation of the belief. Still, in thinking of the basing relation we must be careful to recognize it in the sustenance and preservation of beliefs as well as in their inauguration.

But having put this complication on record, I shall feel free to leave it implicit in further discussions of basing beliefs on grounds and the bearings of this on the epistemology of beliefs. To avoid undue prolixity I will usually speak as if the only concern is with the initial basing that leads to the initial formation of the belief, and leave it to the reader to regard this, where it is, as only one of a series of basings responsible for the acquisition, sustenance, strengthening, and preservation of the belief.

Now I turn to the explication of the basing relation. There are various views on this in the field.[3] My preference is to think of what a belief is based on as *what gives rise* to the belief, what *leads* S to form the belief. Or, keeping the complexity just expounded in mind, as what strengthened or preserves the belief. If you want to think of this as what *causes* the belief, or *causal* influences on it, my only reservation is that this is not just any form of causality. It is the kind involved in the operation of input-output mechanisms that form and sustain, and so on, beliefs in a way that is characteristic of human beings. The detailed description of such a mechanism and how it differs from other modes of psychological causation is a task for cognitive psychology, or the philosophy thereof, and I will not attempt to enter onto it here, though I will stick my toes in the water in the next chapter. Suffice it to say that it is the sort of belief-forming and strengthening process that, when the subject reflects on it, is naturally thought of as

---

[3] For an extensive survey, see Radcliffe 1996.

coming to believe something or to believe it more confidently because of some sort of *cognition* of something that supports it, that renders it probable, credible, or possessing some other kind of positive epistemic status (PES). I am not saying that for a belief to be based on a ground, S has to reflect on what is going on, or *take* the ground to be giving rise to or influencing the belief in this kind of way. That view will be discussed shortly and rejected. I am only alluding to how S *would* typically view the proceeding *if* S came to reflect on it, and using this hypothetical as a way of distinguishing this kind of causation of belief from other kinds. That should be sufficient to distinguish it, for example, from the kind of causal influence that is involved when a bout of indigestion leads one to believe that an interlocutor is unfavorably disposed toward one. I will have more to say about typical human belief-forming mechanisms in the next chapter.

Now for some other ways of characterizing the *based on* relation and what motivates it. We have already seen that it is typical of internalists in epistemology to hold that nothing can contribute to the PES of a belief unless its subject has direct knowledge of this, or at least can acquire such knowledge at will, by reflection. (Call this the *accessibility principle*).[4] It is generally agreed that what actually gives rise to a belief, or otherwise causally influences it, is not accessible to its possessor directly on reflection. Hence according to internalism, if a belief's being based on a certain ground is to endow it with a PES, basing must be construed in some other way, some way that makes it directly accessible to the subject. The most common internalist choice here is to explain basing in terms of S's *taking* something as supporting the belief or as conferring or strengthening some other PES. On this reading, S's belief, B, being based on a certain ground, G, requires S to have a higher-level belief about the relation of G and B. The trouble with this is that it seems that normal mature human subjects do not have such higher-level knowledge whenever they form a belief on a certain basis. To do so they would have to have some conceptual grasp of PES and would have to identify the ground sufficiently to take it to be what is conferring that status. And not all human believers generally are cognitively sophisticated enough to satisfy these requirements. Internalists aware of this problem sometimes have recourse to supposing the "taking" in question to be more or less implicit, but it is rarely if ever made sufficiently clear

---

[4] As was pointed out near the beginning of Chapter 3, section v, internalism in epistemology is construed in various ways. The kind I am concerned with in this book I have called "accessibility internalism", which can be thought of as defined by the accessibility principle just formulated in the text. Another kind, found, for example, in Pollock 1986, simply takes internalism to restrict what bears on epistemic status to internal psychological states of the subject with no additional requirement of accessibility.

just what this amounts to. If it is an unarticulated sense of something's being O.K., going along as it should, or the like, then the more inarticulate this is, the less meat there is on the bones of the internalist higher-level epistemic belief requirement. And if, as is sometimes said, this "taking" is "exhibited" by the fact that S unhesitatingly forms the belief on being presented with the ground, then the higher-level knowledge requirement seems to have disappeared altogether.[5] We must not forget, of course, that the internalist has an alternative to the actual possession of such knowledge, namely, the capacity to acquire it at will. But, obviously, any difficulties that attach to the attribution of the knowledge will, ipso facto, attach to the attribution of the capacity to attain it. If the possession is out of our reach, there can hardly be the capacity to attain it!

There are other suggested alternatives to the causal account of basing. For example, it is sometimes said that B's being based on ground G simply consists in S's disposition to defend the belief against objections by citing G. This cannot help the internalist preserve the accessibility principle, for one cannot always tell just by reflection how one would defend a belief if it is challenged. But the most serious problem with this account is that it misses the target by a wide margin. It is perfectly clear that what a belief is based on, in any reasonable sense of that term, and what one would cite in its defense do not necessarily coincide. I might come to a belief that someone was blocking my driveway because of what I saw, but I might defend the charge by calling on other witnesses. In many cases the two do coincide, but the fact that they often diverge shows that what the belief is based on can't *consist* in what one cites in defense of it.

Another and perhaps more influential source of the identification of what the belief is based on with how it would be defended is the conflation, in justification theory, of the *state* of a belief's *being justified* and the *activity* of *justifying*. If our thought on the subject is dominated by the latter, we are likely to look for what the belief is based on in the activity of justifying the belief, of showing it to be true or justified.

Another problem about basing is whether it must be conscious. It often is. When I consciously perceive an object and on the basis of that perception come to believe that it is a beech tree, both the perceptual experience and its functioning as a basis of the belief is something I am conscious of. The same can be said of the ground and the grounded belief when I consciously infer p from q. But is this necessarily the case? Can a belief be formed unconsciously on the basis of a certain ground? We might be tempted to divide this question into several, dealing with whether each part

---

[5] For this reading, see Dretske 1971.

of the basing could be unconscious—the ground, the belief, and the belief's being based on the ground. But I will resist the temptation, partly because it is not clear that one of these "parts" could be unconscious while the others are conscious but also because I am concerned here only with the possibility of a (completely) unconscious basing. And if actual examples of that can be exhibited, that will settle the matter. It's reasonably clear that there are such examples. The phenomenon of subliminal cues is sufficient to establish this. It took the experimental psychology of perception to reveal that our depth perception is dependent on various cues of which we are blissfully unaware. If we accept that "depth perception" involves judgments (beliefs) of distance, size, spatial relations of items in the visual field, and so on, then there are innumerable examples of belief formation in which we not only are not aware of the inputs, the belief outputs, and the relation between them but are incapable of being aware of them. There are also cases in which the basing process, though not conscious, is of a type other examples of which are conscious. Consider the favorite stock example of driving with one's mind on something other than one's immediate environment. The driver makes adjustments to the distances from other vehicles, where it is and isn't safe to change lanes, where it is necessary to slow down, and so on without being conscious either of the beliefs guiding all this or the visual inputs on which the beliefs are based. Either type of case is sufficient to show the possibility of unconscious basing of a belief on a ground, though only the first type exhibits a type of basing process of which the subject could not be conscious.

The most important remaining issue concerning grounds is whether every belief has a ground. Can we suppose that whenever a belief is formed there is something distinguishable from the belief on which it is based, or do some beliefs simply appear "out of the blue"? When I was engaged in justification theory, my favored account of what it is for a belief to be justified was in terms of being based on an adequate ground. An objection leveled by Plantinga (1993a, 190) to this was that not all beliefs have grounds distinct from themselves. For example, not all memory beliefs are based on memory experiences. And what about self-evident truths?

The first thing to notice about this issue is that since I am no longer seeking to give an account of a unique, central positive epistemic status called 'being justified', I don't have to worry about whether all beliefs have grounds. Obviously, most of them do. For them it can still be the case that having adequate grounds is an important epistemic desideratum even if there are other beliefs that lack this particular desideratum. But it is still an interesting question whether there are exceptions. Let's consider it.

Since I have recognized unconscious as well as conscious belief formation, the mere absence of any conscious ground in a certain belief formation is not a conclusive reason for denying that the belief is based on something other than itself. And I think that there are very general considerations that strongly suggest that either there are no groundless beliefs or if there are they are markedly unusual and even degenerate cases. The point is that there must be some explanation of the fact that S forms a belief at a certain time and forms a belief with one propositional content rather than some other. The obvious explanation is that an input-output mechanism of the sort characteristic of normal human belief formation was activated. And whatever the input was that triggered the generation of a belief output, it is functioning as a ground whether S is conscious of it as such or not. I don't deny that it is conceivable that some beliefs simply happen either in a chance fashion or by some causal mechanism other than the normal human belief-forming mechanism. But if so, it would not fit any well-established mode of belief formation in cognitive psychology, and for the purposes of epistemology we can neglect that possibility.

But leaving aside speculations about the abnormal, let's consider familiar kinds of belief formation of the sort mentioned above in connection with Plantinga's criticisms. Is it true that when I form a memory belief not on the basis of a memory image, when I simply find myself remembering that I heard a recital by Artur Schnabel in San Francisco in 1944, my belief that I heard this is based on nothing distinguishable from the belief itself? It must be admitted that there is no ground that is as external to the belief as a sensory experience is to a perceptual belief that it grounds or as a set of premises is from the belief inferred from it. Nevertheless, I think that there is something about my state of consciousness that leads me to be sure that I was at that recital then. We lack any established terminology for this, but, as we might say, the thought of that recital comes to me with a sense of "pastness", a sense that what I am believing to have occurred is an experience I really had in the past. This is a feature of my state of consciousness when forming the belief, but it is at least a limiting case of a ground for the belief. It is the input to the belief-forming mechanism of which the belief in question is the output.[6] And something similar, I believe, can be said about the apprehension of self-evident truths, or of propositions that seem to be self-evident. The phenomenology of this kind of belief formation includes a certain kind of clarity, luminosity, a sense of ineluctable rightness and certainty.

[6] This discussion of memory is restricted to memories of past experience or actions, as contrasted with remembering other sorts of facts, e.g., the number of U.S. senators. In those cases, provided a ground is not also remembered, the ground for the belief is the ground it had when first acquired.

Again, what functions as a ground, what triggers the belief output, is a feature of the total consciousness involved in the belief formation rather than anything more external to the belief. So I think that so long as we recognize unconscious belief formation and recognize grounds that consist in a feature of the current state of consciousness, it is only in the unlikely event that a belief just pops into existence without having been triggered by anything that we have a belief without some ground.

So we may as well take it that all beliefs are based on grounds. But, as I pointed out earlier, since we are not in the quest of necessary and sufficient conditions for epistemic justification, desideratum 2, which is in terms of being based on an adequate ground, can count as an epistemic desideratum even if not all beliefs enjoy it.

ii. Having Evidence and Basing a Belief on It

Now we need to take a harder look at 1. Desideratum 2, as we have pointed out repeatedly, is obviously an epistemic desideratum, assuming that 'adequate' is so construed that a belief's being based on an adequate ground provides strong support for taking the belief to be true. Most of the rest of this chapter will be devoted to how to understand 'adequate' in 'adequate ground'. But is 1 an epistemic desideratum? If it is, of what is it a property and how does having this property render some belief or other probably true? No answers to these questions appear from the above formulation of 1.

First, some clarification of the notion of having evidence is called for. (I will let 'evidence' stand for evidence and reasons). It is clear that 'having evidence' is some sort of dispositional notion. If one has a certain piece of evidence, this is a state one can be in continuously, including times at which one is wholly attending to other things. In this it is like belief and other attitudes, propositional and otherwise. A first shot might be that having in one's possession the evidence that *Smith's fingerprints were on the gun* (G) is simply believing that. But if having that and other evidence that *Smith murdered Robinson* (R) simply amounted to having certain beliefs, whatever their epistemic status, then that will not render R probably true or confer any other PES on it. Hence it is not a concept that is epistemologically interesting. To get that, we must add that the belief that G itself has a sufficient PES. (It is not necessary for my present purposes to say just what degree of what kind of PES is required). Since what is naturally called my beliefs may range over all degrees of ready accessibility, we should also add the requirement that the belief that G be fairly readily accessible, again without attempting to spell out exactly what this amounts to. That should give us an intuitive grasp of *having evidence* that is sufficient for discussing the question whether 1 is an epistemic desideratum.[7]

Now 1 as stated differs from 2 in that it does not specify that the belief in question is based on the evidence in question. (It doesn't deny that it is either; the issue is left open). The case for 1's being an epistemic desideratum is basically this. The evidence S has for B, E, is said to be adequate. Assuming this implies that if S based B on that evidence, the belief would be rendered probably true, then there would be, in a sense, the same reason for regarding 1 as an epistemic desideratum as for so regarding 2. But 1, unlike 2, does not make explicit anything about the way B was formed that renders it probably true. What we have instead is, so to say, a shadow of that. According to 1, S has resources such that if she uses them in a certain way (bases B on them), B will thereby be rendered probably true. But if all that is required beyond what is stated in 1 is for S to do something, something that is well within her capacity, then as far as the content of E and the content of B is concerned, there is, we might say, a guarantee of probable truth for B. It is just that S has not yet taken advantage of this guarantee.

Here is another way of putting it. Desideratum 2 is the actualization of the possibility provided by 1. For 1 is equivalent to saying that if S were to base B on E, then B would be rendered probably true. Now it seems clear from all this that (a) 1 is an epistemic desideratum and (b) it is less epistemically desirable than 2. I have been presenting an argument for (a). The argument for (b) is simply that the possibility of something desirable is less desirable than its realization. Being in possession of the funds and other requirements to take a vacation in the Greek Isles is a good thing, but only because it is the possibility of something actual that is a good thing. And sitting at home realizing that I could visit the Greek Isles if I chose is obviously not as good (with respect to what is good about experiencing being there) as actually being there. For purposes of this illustration I ignore complications such as the possibility of an actual trip being very disappointing.

But if 1 specifies an epistemically desirable property, what or who is the subject of that property? It would seem to be S, the one who has the adequate evidence for a belief. We will encounter another case of this kind of

---

[7] For a more extended discussion of the problem, see Feldman 1988. Among the fine-grained issues is whether we wish to say that S has all the evidence that is entailed by any evidence which S has. Since there can be propositions entailed by propositions that embody evidence which S has but which S could not recognize as being entailed, we should not embrace any such principle in an unrestricted form. But we might choose to include in the body of one's evidence anything that one would recognize as entailed by evidence one has if the question arose.

possession of an epistemic desideratum when we look at intellectual virtues in Chapter 6, sections ix–xi.

The conclusion that 1 is an epistemic desideratum though of lesser magnitude than 2 parallels a conclusion that many justification theorists hold with respect to whether 1 is sufficient for B's being justified, or whether it is justified only if it is beefed up as in 2. Gilbert Harman (1973) argues for the latter as follows. Consider a student in an introductory philosophy course who has excellent evidence that he will fail the course. He has received failing grades on all the tests and papers thus far, he misses class a good deal of the time, and he has no interest in the course. And indeed he believes that he will fail, not for those reasons but because he thinks the instructor is prejudiced against him because he is an existentialist. The student satisfies 1 vis-à-vis the belief that he will fail but not 2. This is another case in which the abandonment of epistemic justification saves us a lot of bother. We can recognize that both 1 and 2 are ED. It is a good thing from the standpoint of the truth goal to have strong evidence for a proposition, at least if it is of interest or importance, whether or not it is exploited as a basis for belief in that proposition. And, obviously, it is a good thing from the standpoint of the truth goal to hold beliefs on the basis of strong evidence. So from my antijustificationist perspective we are not forced to choose between these desiderata and to eliminate the loser in the competition. Nevertheless, I can ask the question which is more epistemically desirable. And it seems clear that the palm goes to 2. If, like Harman's student, I believe something for which I have strong evidence but on some misguided basis, something is lacking in the values we seek in our cognitive endeavors, something that is present if 2 is the case. For it is important to the aim at believing what is true rather than false about important and/or interesting matters to form beliefs on the basis of adequate grounds, and not *just* form beliefs for which we have adequate (potential) grounds. Although there will be cases in which we form true beliefs when 1 but not 2 holds, those will be lucky accidents. It is clear that if, or to the extent that, we believe that p only on the basis of adequate grounds, we will be much more likely to realize a high proportion of true over false beliefs in our total belief corpus than if we significantly often believe that p where 1 but not 2 holds. Desideratum 2 is clearly a more epistemically valuable and more basic desideratum than 1.

But perhaps putting it that way is giving too much to 1. We could also look at the situation this way. Remember that 1 implies that S has what it takes to base belief B on an adequate ground but, where 2 is not realized, fails to take advantage of this. It would seem that everything epistemically desirable about 1 comes from S's possession of adequate evidence for B. S's failure to base B on that evidence certainly does not contribute anything to its epistemic desirability. Quite the contrary. Thus we may say that everything epistemically desirable about 1 is found in 2 plus something that makes it still more desirable. The epistemic value of 1 comes, as we might say, from its being part way toward the value of 2. But, then, since 2 contains all the epistemic value to be found in 1, with some additional value as well, we can just as well forget about 1 and concentrate our attention on 2. We can forget the potentiality and focus on the full actualization. It still remains true that when some subject realizes 1 but not 2 vis-à-vis some belief B, some epistemic value is realized. But it also remains true that in treating the main *kinds* of epistemic value we will lose nothing by highlighting 2 and ignoring 1.

iii. Adequacy of Grounds and Truth

The above section is only a clearing of the decks for the really difficult and thorny question about 2, namely, how to understand the 'adequate' qualifier, and in particular how to understand it in such a way that 2 is clearly a desideratum from the epistemic point of view, construed in terms of the truth goal. This issue will get us into internalism-externalism contrasts as well as lingering echoes of deontological epistemology.

I take it that a ground for a belief could not be called 'adequate' in any natural sense unless it does have some bearing on the truth of the belief. But some epistemologists of an internalist bent hold that a ground for a belief could confer a PES on the belief without being adequate in this truth-conducive sense. So before exploring the ways in which a ground could be adequate in the truth-conducive sense, I must take a brief look at positions that would turn their back on truth conducivity for grounds and consider whether, or to what extent, they envisage conditions that make being based on such grounds epistemically desirable. These non-truth-conducive positions are generally advocated in the context of looking for an account of "justification of belief" or the "epistemic rationality of belief". And so we will have to presuppose a translation of that into my "positive epistemic status" idiom.

Here are a couple of denials of a truth-conducive conception of PES of beliefs.

> According to this traditional conception of "internal" epistemic justification, there is no logical connection between epistemic justification and truth. (Chisholm 1989, 76)

The context makes it clear that this is intended to rule out even a logical connection between justification and the *probability* of being true. This is closer to being explicit in the next quotation.

> ... to say that the goal that helps distinguish epistemic rationality from other kinds of rationality is a truth-directed goal is not to say that truth is a prerequisite of epistemic rationality. In particular, it is not to say that it is impossible for what is epistemically rational to be false, and likewise it is not even to say that it is impossible for most of what is epistemically rational to be false. (Foley 1987, 156)

The denial of any logical connection with the probability of truth comes in the last clause, assuming that Foley would endorse some kind of frequency conception of the probability of truth.

Since I take a status of a belief to be an *epistemic* desideratum only if it is desirable from the point of view of the aim at having true rather than false beliefs on matters of importance and/or interest, I do not recognize being justified or epistemically rational in these senses as distinctively *epistemic* desiderata. Then how are such theorists thinking of the PES of beliefs? Chisholm thinks in terms of epistemic principles that lay down conditions for a belief's being *justified*. He sometimes suggests that they are synthetic a priori principles we know by rational intuition. And sometimes he takes it that we arrive at them by induction from reflective, intuitive knowledge we have of the justified or unjustified status of particular beliefs. He also explains various degrees of being justified in a propositional attitude in terms of a basic undefined notion of one propositional attitude (accepting, rejecting, or withholding) toward a given proposition being "more reasonable" for a person at a time than others. And "more reasonable than" is itself informally explained in terms of a certain "intellectual requirement"—trying one's best to bring it about that, for every proposition h that he considers, he accepts h *iff* h is true. So one propositional attitude is more reasonable for S at t than another *iff* this intellectual requirement is better fulfilled by the former than by the latter. Note that this makes a logical connection between 'reasonable' and trying one's best to restrict oneself to true beliefs rather than between reasonableness and truth or high probability of truth.

As for Foley, he has a complicated view according to which it is epistemically rational to believe that p at t *iff* "S has an uncontroversial argument for p, an argument that he would regard as likely to be truth preserving were he to be appropriately reflective, and an argument whose premises he would uncover no good reasons to be suspicious of were he to be appropriately reflective" (Foley 1987, 66). Assuming that Foley's talk of an argument could be restated in terms of a type of argument, it could just as well be put, with Chisholm, in terms of principles.

There are various difficulties with these positions. Chisholm's supposition that we have the intellectual obligation he mentions would seem to presuppose that we have effective voluntary control over what propositional attitudes we take on, a presupposition that we saw in Chapter 4 that Chisholm accepts and that is not viable. Foley's position raises difficult questions as to what counts as being "appropriately reflective", as well as doubts about the advisability of leaving epistemic status up to what a particular individual would accept, even on considerable reflection. But the main point I want to make at present is the one foreshadowed above. Since being "justified" or "epistemically rational" as these philosophers construe them does not endow a belief with even a probability of being true, it cannot lay claim to being an epistemic desideratum, whether or not it is desirable in some other way. I refer the reader back to the long quotation from BonJour in Chapter 2 for a convincing argument against the significance of a non-truth-conducive version of a PES for beliefs.

iv. Adequacy of Grounds—Preliminaries

Now we can proceed to explore ways of thinking of a ground of a belief as significantly adequate in a truth-conducive sense. The initial intuitive idea is that the ground is an indication that the belief is true, not necessarily a conclusive indication for that, but at least something that provides significant support for taking it to be true. Thus it is natural to think of an adequate ground of a belief B as something such that basing B on it confers a significant probability of truth on B. Sections v through vii will be devoted to identifying the sense of probability that is suitable in this context, as well as considering how to understand formulations like the one in the last sentence.

To dig a bit deeper, the reason we seek a TC sense of adequacy is that we want to construe 2 in such a way that it is a fundamental epistemic desideratum. The earlier treatment of the epistemic point of view implies that the possession of one of the most basic epistemic desiderata by a belief is such as to be favorable to the belief's being true. The only reason this doesn't suffice as an initial intuitive idea of what it is for a ground of belief to be adequate is that it doesn't spell out enough of what kind of feature of a belief is such as to be favorable to the belief's being true. That will be spelled out as we go along in the next few sections.

The first thing to notice about adequacy of ground—like other epistemic notions such as reliability of ways of forming belief, coherence, cognitive accessibility, strength of evidential support, and likelihood of truth—is that it is a degree notion. A ground of belief can be more or less adequate, as evidential support can be more or less strong. Nevertheless, we often speak in apparently absolute terms of an adequate ground or strong evidential support, as well as in rough terms such as 'high probability' or 'sufficient evidence' or 'significant support'. When we say such things, we have in mind some more or less rough standard of adequacy of ground, such as *sufficient for rational acceptance*, or, less ambitiously, *sufficient for prima facie credibility*, and some rough standard of high probability, such as a range something like .85 to .95, or some smaller portion thereof. Speaking in such rough and relatively indeterminate ways of these matters is less disreputable than it would otherwise be because of the fact that it is unrealistic to expect the assignment of anything other than rough numerical estimates of the probability of a belief on the basis of a certain support, and as for adequacy of ground or strength of evidence, in most cases numerical assignments can be given no well-developed interpretation.

At this point I turn to developing an understanding of probability of belief that is suitable for explicating degrees of the adequacy of grounds and other notions that are of importance for the epistemology of belief. This will be done in several stages.

The three most basic points are (a) that the probability that is of interest to the epistemology of belief is, of course, the probability of beliefs, (b) that 'probability of X', whether X is a belief or a proposition or whatever, is to be understood as a probability that X is true, though this is often not made explicit, and (c) that we need to think in terms of conditional probability, the probability enjoyed by a proposition or a belief "on" a certain condition. Probability that is subject to these three constraints I will call 'epistemic conditional probability' or, for short, 'epistemic probability'.[8]

I will begin the discussion of these points with (c). It is clear on the face of it that a given belief may have widely different probabilities on different grounds. The probability that it rained last night around here is fairly high given the puddles in the driveway across the street that I saw early in the morning. It is still higher given the fact that all the pavement in the vicinity is wet. And it is less high on the fact that my lawn is wet. (That could be from dew.) There is, so far as I can see, no epistemologically usable notion of an intrinsic, nonrelative probability of a belief. And so conditional probabilities are in the center of the picture for the epistemology of belief.

---

[8] This term is defined in a variety of ways. See Plantinga 1993b, chaps. 8 and 9, for his own account and a discussion of various others.

Before dealing any further with conditional probability I need to align my discussion with the literature on probability theory, and to do that I must make explicit how conditional probability is generally treated there. It is presented not by thinking of a belief as having a certain probability on a ground, as I am doing here, but more abstractly as a relation between propositions. When a given proposition, h, is said to have a certain probability on another, e, e is assumed for this purpose to be true. And so the claim is that, given e (i.e., given that it is true that e), that makes it likely to a certain degree that h is true. Or, to give it a more epistemological flavor, it is reasonable, given e, to take it that h is likely to a certain degree to be true. It is important that for purposes of assessing the conditional probability of h on e, we artificially abstract from the bearing of any other considerations, from the subject's repertoire or more widely, on the overall probability of h. For this purpose we must assume that e is the only thing relevant to h's likelihood of truth, and on that assumption determine the probability of h.[9] Different conceptions of probability yield different positions on what it takes for h to have a certain degree of probability on e. We will have to settle on one of these for our purposes, but all in good time.

The reader may have noticed a connection of the difference between treating conditional probability as a relation between propositions and treating it as a relation between a belief and its ground, and the difference between desiderata 1 and 2 that was discussed in section ii. Though 1 was stated in terms of having adequate evidence for a belief, since it carries no implications for the belief's being based on that evidence the belief is an extra wheel that is not playing any essential role, and 1 might as well be stated in terms of a proposition that could be the content of a certain belief if it were formed. That is, 1 could just as well be 1A.

1A. S has adequate evidence or reasons for the proposition p.

This makes 1 amenable to the kind of treatment I said above that probability theorists typically give of conditional probability, as a relation between propositions. But 2 resists that treatment because it is crucial to its epistemic desirability that a belief is *based* on adequate evidence; and it is this state of affairs that makes it the distinctive sort of epistemic desideratum it is. Another way of putting the contrast here is to say that 2 is essentially about the epistemology of belief whereas, as we saw in section ii, 1 is more indirectly related to that. In fact, we saw in ii that everything that is epistemically desirable in 1 is simply a potentiality for 2, so that in surveying

---

[9] Compare the definition of 'tends to make probable' in Chisholm 1989, 55.

truth-conducive desiderata we could omit 1 from the list without losing anything of epistemic importance. Thus we would expect conditional probability to work differently when the condition is a fact of basing from the way it does when the condition is a piece of evidence or a reason. And so it will turn out.

Now I turn to ways in which epistemic conditional probability fails to coincide with conditional probability as typically treated in probability theory. The first way has to do with the difference between doxastic and nondoxastic (primarily experiential) grounds of belief.

First look at doxastic grounds. Suppose S's belief that *Susie is planning to leave her husband* (P) is based on S's belief *that Susie told her close friend, Joy, that she was* (J). To decide how strong an indication the belief that J is of the truth of the belief that P, we have to look at two things. First, if we stick for the moment as long as possible with the treatment in terms of propositions, the relation between the propositions that are the contents of these beliefs, J and P, is one factor that influences the conditional probability of P on J. But, second, we have to look at the epistemic status of the belief that J. For even if the conditional probability of P on J is high, that won't put S in a strong epistemic position in believing that P on the basis of J if S had no good reason, or not a good enough reason, to believe that J. This consideration is sufficient to show that where the ground is doxastic the adequacy of the ground is not identical with the conditional probability of the propositional content of the target belief on the propositional content of the grounding belief.

With nondoxastic grounds, on the other hand, we are not faced with this second factor. Where my ground is a certain visual experience rather than, for example, a belief that I have that experience, the ground is a fact rather than a belief in a fact. Hence no problem can arise with respect to the epistemic status of the ground since that ground is not the sort of thing that can have an epistemic status. And so the adequacy of a nondoxastic ground coincides exactly with the conditional probability of the propositional content of the belief on that fact, construed as a true proposition. Here conditional probability as treated in probability theory can translate directly into an epistemic status.

The second way in which the coincidence fails has to do with the fact that standard probability theory is committed to the standard probability calculus, and in particular to the way in which necessarily true or false propositions are treated there. In the standard probability calculus the probability of every necessary truth is 1 and the probability of every necessary falsehood is 0. This makes it impossible to use conditional probabilities in assessing the adequacy of grounds for necessarily true or false beliefs.

Since every necessary truth has a probability of 1, no matter what else is the case, its conditional probability on any proposition whatever is 1. This "rigidity" of the probability of necessary truths prevents it from capturing what we after in thinking of the adequacy of grounds. One who supposes that a person who believes that 2 + 2 = 4 on the basis of the belief that all crows are black, thereby believes the former on the basis of a significantly adequate ground, is missing the epistemological boat. In thinking of a ground as adequate to some considerable degree, we take it to *render* what it grounds more or less probable. It must make a significant difference to the probability of the grounded belief. That is not to say that a belief could not be based on more than one ground and could not acquire a certain probability from more than one ground. But it is to say that when the adequacy of a particular ground of a particular belief is assessed, in order for that ground to be deemed significantly adequate it has to make a contribution to the conditional probability of the belief. It can't be an empty cipher as is the case when the grounded belief enjoys a high probability just because it is a necessary truth. This is another important respect in which *epistemic probability* fails to conform to the standard probability calculus. Clearly, there are distinctions to be drawn between adequate and inadequate, relevant and irrelevant grounds for beliefs in necessary truths. The axioms of arithmetic are adequate grounds for 2 + 2 = 4, unlike the proposition that all crows are black. But this will have to be explained on some basis other than the probability calculus. I will shortly be concerned with explicating the notion of a ground's "*rendering* a belief probable to a certain degree", and that will give us what is needed for handling the adequacy of grounds of necessarily true beliefs, as well as grounds of others.

v. Adequacy of Grounds and Epistemic Probability

Having partially located epistemic probability on the map, I can turn to a fuller statement of how it is related to the degree of adequacy of a ground of belief. The rough statement at the beginning of section iv, that an adequate ground of a belief G is one that renders B probably true, is misleading not only in ignoring the degree character of both adequacy and probability but also, and this is my special concern at the moment, in giving the impression that the probability conferred is some kind of "absolute" or "intrinsic" probability rather than a conditional probability. To obviate this impression I must alter the formulation to make explicit that the basing of the belief on the ground in question is the condition on which on which the probability of the belief is conditional. So let's put it this way, also making the formulation take account of the degree character of adequacy and probability.

I. When a belief B is based on a ground that is significantly adequate, that gives B a significantly high probability on the condition of being based on that ground.[10]

There are several things to note about I. (1) The condition on which it makes the probability of B conditional is not the ground on which it is based but its being based on that ground. B will also have a certain probability on the condition of the ground, but since we are concerned with desideratum 2, which is in terms of a belief's being based on a ground, it is that fact of basing's being the condition of a high conditional probability with which we are concerned. The ground itself will consist of beliefs and/or experiences. The propositional content of B will have a certain conditional probability on the propositional content of any belief in the ground, taken as true, and a proposition according to which the subject has the experience(s) in question, if any, again taken as true. That would be the standard probability theory reading of the situation. But since we are concerned with epistemic probability, we want to know how probable the belief, B, is on the condition that it is based on a ground with a certain degree of adequacy. And that brings in the influence of the epistemic status of any beliefs in the ground, as well as features of any experiences in the ground.

Thus we have, as it were, stumbled on a third way in which epistemic conditional probability fails to coincide with conditional probability as typically treated in probability theory. Concisely put, that on which the probability of the target belief, B, is conditional differs in the two cases. For the latter, it is the conditioning propositions, taken as true. For the former, it is the basing of B on a ground of a certain degree of adequacy. And that degree of adequacy is a function of more than the relation of propositional contents. As we have seen, it is also a function of the epistemic status of any beliefs in the ground. So in addition to the difference between a proposition-proposition(s) relationship and a belief-ground relationship, even the factors relevant to the status of the conditioning item(s) do not exactly match.

So the epistemic probability of B that is involved in desideratum 2 will be some sort of function of the degree of adequacy of the ground on which

---

[10] In the ensuing discussion, primarily but not exclusively in this and the following chapter, I will often be speaking of the way in which a belief's being based on a certain ground (or, to anticipate, a belief's being the output of a certain belief-forming process) affects the probability status of that belief. To avoid undue prolixity I will sometimes not make it explicit that the probability in question is *conditional* on the belief's being generated in the way specified. But that will be tacitly understood.

it is based. I don't have anything to offer by way of a formula for computing the degree of conditional probability of B from the degree of adequacy of its ground. To have such a formula I would have to have a workable method for assessing at least rough degrees of each of these variables, and I don't have that. So far as I can see, intuitive estimates in terms of such categories as *very high, moderately high, significantly high, rather low*, and so on are the best that we can reasonably expect. Further light will be thrown on what it takes for a ground to have a certain degree of adequacy when I come to make a decision on which of the competing accounts of probability to choose for epistemic conditional probability. But, I fear, that will not satisfy demands for a way of making precise assignments of degree.

Prior to that development I do have one further contribution to offer, a suggestion as to how to construe what we might think of as a maximal degree of adequacy of a ground. 'Maximal" here is to be understood as *maximal for human capacities*, not as *the greatest degree conceivable*. The suggestion is that a ground for B is maximally adequate *iff* it engenders *a prima facie (PF) credibility of assigning a high probability of truth to B, all things considered*. Note that according to this idea, a maximal degree of adequacy is not construed in terms of engendering a certain degree of probability for the grounded belief, B. What is conferred is indeed a status that has to do with probability, but it is not exactly B's possessing a high probability. It is, so to say, a higher-level status that bears on the assignment of probability. To explain what this amounts to I must say a word about 'PF' and associated terms. No doubt these are familiar to most readers of this book, but here is a quick reminder.

The crucial distinction is that between a *prima facie* status and one that holds *all (relevant) things considered*. This distinction is familiar from ethics, where we often speak of being PF obliged to, for example, keep a promise, and in epistemology in connection with justification, where it is often said that one's visual experience justifies one PF in believing, for example, that a car is passing by the house. In both contexts the notion of a PF status is intimately connected with the notions of overriders and defeaters. The point of calling a status PF is that it is inherently subject to being canceled, failing to progress into a correlated *all things considered* status. Among these possible contrary considerations I distinguish between *overriders* and *defeaters*. The former are drawn from the subject's repertoire of beliefs and knowledge whereas the latter are contrary considerations that are outside the subject's ken.[11] Though, as just pointed out, these distinctions are most familiar in epistemology in connection with epistemic justification, which

---

[11] 'Defeater' is most commonly used for items on both sides of this distinction.

I have foresworn, they are by no means restricted to that. They can equally be applied to ED that I recognize, and in particular to the directly TC ones currently under consideration—a belief's being based on an adequate ground, and a belief's being acquired by a generally reliable process.

One more important distinction is this. In speaking of what is relevant to the estimate of the probability of the belief's (or proposition's) being true, there are various possible choices as to the territory over which this ranges. It is common to think of this in terms of what is cognitively "available" to a given individual or group. We say things like "As far as I know, or taking into account all the considerations of which I'm aware, it's very likely that Hampson will seek the Democratic nomination for president". That invokes the relativity to a single subject. We also say things like "Given what *we* now know, it is likely that the general theory of relativity is true" or "The evidence *available to us* puts it beyond question that smoking contributes to the development of lung cancer". Often the explicit reference to the group is missing but tacitly assumed, as when one says, "It is very likely that it will rain here tomorrow". But in contrast to this one *could* claim that a proposition is very probably true relative to all the relevant considerations that are "out there", or at least all those that are within human powers to ascertain, whether anyone has done so or not. This, needless to say, would often be an extravagant claim but sometimes not. If our grounds for ascribing a high probability to a proposition like *The sun will rise tomorrow* are strong enough, it might not be unreasonable to make this "Nothing out there could shake this" sort of claim. Our concern with probability here is subject-based, what is probable to a certain degree for a given cognitive subject. Hence the relevant scope for this purpose is what is within that subject's cognitive repertoire. In terms of my distinction between overriders and defeaters, that means that I will be restricting attention to overriders.

Though the claim that B's being based on a maximally adequate ground engenders a PF credibility for an assignment of a high probability to B all things considered is less strong than a claim that it engenders such a high probability of B, it is still of considerable strength. For, as we might say, this specification of what is engendered amounts to a qualified endorsement of B's being highly probable all things considered. Again, it is not that very strong claim itself, but it comes close to that by involving a commitment to that status, so long as there are not sufficient overriders. The approximation to *high probability all things considered* is close enough that no further *supporting* considerations are needed. (That is not to say that there are none.) The only consideration relevant to a final decision on a claim of high probability all things considered is whether there are sufficient overriders to cancel the credibility conferred by the adequate basing.

Let's bring conditional probability into the picture. Granted that what a maximally adequate ground of B ipso facto produces vis-à-vis B is a PF credibility of assigning to B a high probability all things considered, we still need to specify what the probability thus assigned is conditional on. Well, since it is a probability all things considered, it is, of course, a probability conditional on all (relevant) considerations available to the subject. Again, we must not suppose that all things have been considered, as they would have to be to ideally support the assignment. It is just that the maximally adequate ground renders it PF credible that an exhaustive survey of all relevant considerations within the subject's ken would leave unshaken an assignment of such a high probability to B.

The next question is why we should suppose that B's being based on a maximally adequate ground engenders a PF credibility for assigning such a probability to B. The answer lies in how maximal adequacy for a ground is conceived or defined. Since I introduced the term 'maximally adequate ground', I can stipulate a definition for it. And the one I stipulate is that a maximally adequate ground is one such that when *a belief, B, is formed on its basis, B will thereby enjoy a PF credibility of being probably true all things considered.* Since an adequate ground is so *defined*, there is no way in which such basing can fail to engender that status. To suppose that it could would be to suppose that a maximally adequate ground of the belief could be something other than a maximally adequate ground.

Since this is rather tricky, I had better stress the point that what engenders the PF credibility of belief B's having a high probability all things considered is not the ground of B, even if the ground is maximally adequate, but rather *B's being based on an adequate ground*. If you are inclined to think that this is a distinction without a difference, consider the following. Since the *maximal adequacy* of a ground vis-à-vis belief B is *defined* as (or if you prefer, has as its *essential nature*) being such that if B is based on it, it is thereby PF credible that B has a high probability of being true all things considered, this implies that it is a logical (analytic) truth that B's being based on an adequate ground engenders that status. But the ground in question will typically consist of certain beliefs and/or experiences. And it will certainly not be a logical truth that B's being based on them renders its being PF credible that B has a high probability of being true all things considered. Indeed, apart from what is or isn't a logical truth, it is very difficult to find any belief and/or experience ground of a belief such that it is even contingently true that so long as a belief is based on them, it is PF credible that it is extremely likely to be true, taking into account everything in the subject's ken. Suppose that B is the belief that Richard III had the Princes in the Tower murdered, and that the ground for this belief on the part of a certain historian consists in contemporary documents in addition to plausible suppositions about Richard's aims and scruples or the lack thereof. It would be a rash hypothesis to claim that this evidence by itself renders it PF credible that the belief is so likely to be true that no further positive support is needed for that.

Remembering that adequacy comes in various degrees, let me make it explicit that it is not only such a high degree of adequacy as I have been characterizing that is an epistemic desideratum. Lower degrees, all the way to the lower limit below which any lower degree would not count to any extent for the truth of the belief, will constitute lesser epistemic desiderata. Parallel points apply to any epistemic desideratum that comes in degrees.

One may well object that in securing the result that being based on a maximally adequate ground has the effect specified, I am simply pushing the problem back one stage. Granted that given my concept of a maximally adequate ground, it is a logical truth that the specified result is forthcoming, that simply means that we are faced with the problem of how we can be sure that a particular ground is adequate in this sense. If, as I contended in the last paragraph, it is dubious that the content of most plausible grounds is not sufficient to engender all by itself a PF credibility for the grounded belief having a high probability of truth all things considered, why should we suppose that any, or almost any, ground on which beliefs are based is adequate in this sense? Without strong reasons for this in particular cases, the claim that as 'adequate ground' is defined it is a logical truth that the specified effect is forthcoming is at best an empty gesture.

In response I agree that it is difficult to be sure that a particular ground of a belief is an adequate one, as I have defined 'adequate ground'. But what takes the sting out of this confession for my present project is that I am concerned not with how we can tell whether a certain epistemic desideratum is realized in a certain case but only with what it would be for it to be realized, what its realization would consist in. No doubt the "how can we tell?" problem is an important and even crucial one. But I can't handle everything in one book, much less in one chapter. What little I have to say about how we ascertain epistemological facts, including what grounds are adequate to a certain degree, will be found in Part II, particularly in Chapter 10. I am afraid that will leave my critic far from completely satisfied, and with good reason. But a thorough assault on the problem must await another occasion.

For now I will make just one point that is relevant to the above complaint. Because PF credibility is essentially vulnerable to being overridden or defeated, this reduces to a significant extent what an investigator is committing herself to in attributing maximal adequacy to a certain ground of a certain belief. In this way, as pointed out earlier, it is a considerably weaker commitment than was suggested by the earlier formulation in terms of engendering a high probability of truth for the grounded beliefs. But, no doubt, it is still a claim of significant strength and hence one that poses serious problems as to how it can be sufficiently supported.

vi. The Logical Construal of Epistemic Probability

I now come to the long-postponed question how to understand conditional probability in the present context. The specific form this takes at this point is how to understand the notion of a belief's having a certain degree of probability (roughly indicated) on the condition of having been based on a certain ground. The question can be put this way. In making such an attribution, we are thinking of the belief's being related to the ground in a certain way. What way?

Probability is a fearsomely difficult and complex topic, and one in which my expertise, I fear, leaves something to be desired. I shall be seeking to sketch the main outlines of a solution but without going into all the details that would be necessary for a comprehensive treatment. Nevertheless, I feel that what I will present is sufficient for bringing out the main epistemological points with which I am concerned.

The most fundamental divide between alternative positions is between *objective* and *subjective* construals. Depending on just how we think of "subjective", there is more than one subjective concept, but since it is clear on the face of it that what we want for epistemological purposes is something objective, I will not spend time surveying the subjective candidates. As an example, take the idea that the probability of a belief consists in the degree of confidence with which it is held. It is clear that a high degree of confidence in itself has no epistemological value. Clearly, and unhappily, many people not infrequently very confidently hold beliefs on the most outrageous and irrational bases. We need something much more objective than this.

Objective concepts of probability earn that title by thinking of the conditional probability of P on Q as a fact of the matter that is not dependent on what S believes or how strongly S believes it. The main construals that meet this condition are (a) a priori or "*logical*", (b) *propensity*, and (c) *frequency*. I will consider them in that order.

The logical conception of probability treats conditional probability on the model of logical implication. Just as it is an a priori matter whether P logically implies Q, so it is an a priori matter whether the probability of Q on P is of a certain degree (more realistically, within a certain range itself not precisely bounded).[12] And just as in simple enough cases one can intuitively grasp that P logically implies Q, so, according to the logical theory, it is with conditional probability. The relations in the two cases are equally "logical". Just as in the logical implication case it is logically impossible that P be true and Q false, so in the conditional probability case it is logically impossible that P be true and Q lack a certain degree of probability. The fountainhead of the logical conception of probability in the twentieth century is Keynes's magisterial *A Treatise on Probability* (1921). Other versions are found in Jeffreys 1939, Carnap 1950, Stove 1986, and elsewhere.

It seems clear that a logical theory of conditional probability will be concerned initially with propositions, since they are the primary terms of logical relations. The application to conditional probabilities of beliefs on grounds will have to be derived from this. I will assume that this can be done and will feel free to oscillate in this discussion between speaking of propositions and of the beliefs and experiences that are suitably related thereto.

At this point in the discussion I will borrow, not unacknowledgingly, from Plantinga's superb treatment in Chapters 8 and 9 of Plantinga 1993b:

> Wherein lies the appeal of the logical theory? Chiefly in the fact that for a significant range of pairs of propositions <A,B>, it seems to be no more than the sober truth; there *does* seem to be a relationship of probability between the propositions in question, and it also seems to be *necessary* that there is the relation in question. Principal among the logical theorist's exhibits would be statistical syllogisms; it seems intuitively obvious that the proposition *Feike can swim* is probable with respect to the proposition *9 of 10 Frisians can swim and Feike is a Frisian*. Furthermore, *that* this relation obtains between them does indeed seem necessarily true; it is at best extremely hard to see how it could be that the first should fail to be probable with respect to the second. (145)

But, as Plantinga goes on to point out, there are many pairs of propositions such that it does not seem that one has a certain degree of probability on the other, much less one that holds necessarily. What is the probability of *It will rain here tomorrow* on the proposition *The Roman Empire extended to the Rhine?* One would be hard put to say. But though the idea that every pair of propositions has a certain logical probability relationship is often associated with the logical theory of probability, it is not necessarily so. One could give a logical construal of conditional probability relations where they exist without supposing that they exist everywhere. But a more fatal

---

[12] To avoid intolerable circumlocution I shall usually omit this parenthetical qualification, but it is to be understood whenever I speak of a "certain degree" of probability.

difficulty concerns the point that probability relations often depend on empirical, contingent facts of various sorts.

Consider a typical case of interpreting signs or symptoms. A certain look and bearing of my wife leads me to believe that she is worried or upset about something. When we make such inferences, it is often difficult or impossible to give an adequate specification of just what kind of look and bearing it is that one is taking to indicate worry, but let's suppose that I and many others have the capacity to identify looks and bearings of the appropriate sort for such inferences without being able to be fully explicit about the type in question. Now how probable does that make the proposition that she is worried? If the proposition ascribing the look in question to her were combined with a general proposition to the effect that a look of this sort is generally, or almost always, indicative of worry, then we have a "statistical syllogism" of the sort mentioned by Plantinga in the above quotation. But suppose that we do not spell this out, as we ordinarily don't. In any event, we ordinarily are unable to specify the sort of look in a way that would make this possible. So let's take it that we suppose *looking like that* to give a considerable probability to the proposition that *she is worried*. Is this a logical relation that necessarily holds between two propositions, or does its holding depend on certain contingent states of affairs obtaining? It seems that the latter is the case. After all, people differ a lot in the way in which their thoughts and feelings are mirrored in their outward appearance. If I haven't had much acquaintance with a person, a certain kind of look is going to give much less probability, for me, to beliefs about what the person is feeling or thinking than if I am intimately acquainted with the person over a long time. The kind of familiarity that I have with my wife involves, inter alia, my acquiring a lot of empirical knowledge over the years about what various looks of hers strongly indicate, knowledge I lack for strangers or casual acquaintances. In cases like this the conditional probability can't be known a priori.

It may be thought that I get this result only by trading on special features of beliefs about other persons, a notoriously complex and delicate matter. But that would be a mistake. The same points could be made about inferring that there is probably oil underground here from the way the terrain looks or inferring that it will probably rain tomorrow from the look of the sky.

Partisans of the logical construal often respond to such criticisms by saying that if we were to put all the relevant a posteriori considerations in that on which the target belief is conditional, the statement of conditional probability would be logically true. It is somewhere between difficult and impossible to put this claim to the test just because it is somewhere between difficult and impossible to make sure that we have included all the relevant a posteriori considerations. I am not aware of any serious attempt to give an example that involves anything more complicated than the statistical syllogisms cited by Plantinga. At least this seems clear. In ever so many cases like the ones just cited where a conditional probability is claimed and where it seems plausible, it is not a logical truth that the conditional probability obtains. It is noteworthy in this connection that when Plantinga in Chapter 9 of his 1993b propounds a logical account of what he calls the "objective" component of what he calls "epistemic probability", this is what he has to say.

> ... the objective probability in question is indeed a logical probability, but it isn't one conditional just on the evidence. It is also conditional on other propositions: such propositions, perhaps, as that *The future will relevantly resemble the past* (the world is not, for example, a grue world) and perhaps *Simpler theories are more likely to be true than complex ones*. Alternatively, the relevant set of possible worlds is not just the worlds in which the evidence is true, but some narrower class of worlds, perhaps specifiable in part in terms of similarity to what we think the actual world is like. This problem of saying precisely what it is that the relevant objective probability is conditional upon is both tantalizing and difficult (and perhaps it is relative to context); I shall leave it to the reader and hurry on. (162)

Plantinga was well advised to make the last move. In any event, even if we were to add his suggestions of very general assumptions to the stated evidence in examples like the ones I cited above, we would still be far away from anything that could plausibly be thought to be a logically necessary truth.

Richard Fumerton (1995, chap. 7) has an interesting argument for the necessity of some "epistemic principles" (defined as propositions asserting a probabilistic connection between propositions) being known to hold by direct acquaintance with their holding. The argument requires accepting the "internalist inferential" principle that an inferential justification of a belief requires that one "be aware" (i.e., knows) that the evidence from which the belief is inferred makes probable the target belief. Given that principle, it is easy to show that not all epistemic principles we accept and use can be inferentially shown to hold. For if each case of inferential justification requires that we know that the relevant epistemic principle holds, we are faced with an infinite regress if we suppose that all known epistemic principles are known by inference. Hence some must be known noninferentially. And Fumerton holds, quite reasonably, that the logical account of probability provides the only intelligible model of a noninferential knowledge of inferential principles: " ... you must hold that in the sense relevant to epistemology, making probable is an internal relation holding between propositions, and that one can be directly and immediately acquainted with facts of the form 'E makes probable P'. Otherwise, you must embrace massive skepticism with respect to the past, the external world, the future, and other minds". (200). The reason for this last claim is that the only way to gain knowledge in these areas is to engage in justified probabilistic reasoning. Fumerton then goes on to draw the unwelcome conclusion that if probabilistic connections are internal relations between propositions (i.e., derivative from intrinsic features of those propositions), there is no reason to suppose that beliefs arrived at by such probabilistic reasoning are likely to be mostly true. And hence such reasoning does not give us what we are looking for epistemologically.

I have myself argued back in my justificationist day, in Alston 1988b and 1991b, that Fumerton's principle of inferential internalism leads to a vicious infinite regress. But, lacking Fumerton's attachment to this strong an epistemological internalism, I took this as a conclusive reason for rejecting the satisfaction of this principle as a necessary condition for what he calls "inferential" justification of a belief. And, projecting myself back into the role of a justification theorist, I certainly think that the principle is much less compelling than the rejection of a massive skepticism. Hence, even playing the epistemic justification game, I am not convinced by Fumerton's argument for the need for a logical account of epistemic probability. Nevertheless, I find Fumerton's argument instructive for our present concerns. For even though he is convinced that being directly acquainted with probabilistic connections of the sort that will ensure at least by and large truth in the most crucial areas would enable us to avoid skepticism, he despairs of the possibility of there being such direct acquaintance. Thus his endorsement of a logical construal of epistemic probability is even less wholehearted than Plantinga's.[13] And so we are still without a good reason for supposing that the logical concept of probability will fit our needs.

There is another consideration that I believe to be a powerful influence in adopting a logical concept of probability for epistemological purposes, namely, the difficulties attaching to other candidates. It cannot be denied that there are such difficulties, and we will survey them shortly. But we have also found difficulties aplenty in the use of the logical concept, and so in the end the choice will boil down to which candidate has not been thoroughly discredited.

---

[13] I should make clear that Fumerton's discussion in chap. 7 of his book is much richer than my brief sketch thereof. I have simply mined his discussion for those parts that are of use at the present stage of my argument.

vii. A Frequency Construal of Epistemic Probability

I take the upshot of the last section to be that a logical construal of conditional probability does not give us what we need for an explication of the adequacy of a ground. I turn to its main rivals for an objective probability—propensity and frequency. Propensity would be just right for our purposes if there were only a sufficiently developed concept of this sort that applied to our subject. Unfortunately, the only well-worked-out concept of propensity has to do with the physical chances of an event in a situation of physical indeterminacy (not complete physical determinism) such as we have in quantum mechanics. But the propensity that is relevant to the explication of adequacy of grounds is the propensity of a ground to yield true rather than false beliefs. Another way to put it is to say that it is the propensity of a ground to yield a belief if and only if the belief is true. Because of the fallibility of human belief-forming processes, this area is tailor-made for a notion of propensity. Practically all grounds of human beliefs will yield some false beliefs in a large enough number of trials. This is clear for perceptual and memory beliefs and for beliefs based on most forms of inference. Sometimes we are fooled by perceptual appearances. Sometimes it seems for all the world that we remember doing or experiencing something when in fact we didn't. Prediction based on induction from prior cases is notoriously fallible, as is inference to (what seems to be) the best explanation. Even where the inference is deductively valid, so that it is impossible that the premises should be true and the conclusion false, the truth of the conclusion will be guaranteed only if the premises are all true, and there is usually no guarantee of that. And so in general the most we can hope for in the way of a truth conducivity of a ground is a *propensity* to produce true rather than false beliefs. But how is such a propensity to be conceived? It is clearly not an intrinsic property of the ground. No scrutiny of it by itself will reveal how likely it is to generate true beliefs when it functions as a ground of belief. It has something to do with the relation between the ground and what it grounds. But just what?

I must confess that I can think of nothing that would constitute such a propensity except something in the area of the *frequency* with which grounds relevantly like the one in question would give rise to true beliefs relevantly like the one in question within a very large set of groundings that satisfy relevant sampling principles. If that is the case, then the attempt to find the desired objective probability in the *propensity* neighborhood irresistibly leads us to the third type of objective probability—*frequency*. That is because propensity, like all dispositional notions, requires us to look beyond the particular case to some suitable generalization of which it is an instance. A certain visual appearance has a propensity to yield true beliefs about what is presenting the appearance *iff* it is generally the case that visual appearances like that would give rise to true beliefs about what is appearing in a sufficiently large and varied number of cases of such appearances generating beliefs about what is appearing. And, as always with frequency statements in application to a particular instance, we are faced with the problem of deciding which of the many ways of generalizing from the particular case to make use of in deciding how likely it is to generate true beliefs. It is important to realize that we cannot shirk the task of applying a general statement of frequency to the particular case. We can of course consider, use, and evaluate general frequency statements. The frequency with which American teenage boys born between 1970 and 1985 have been charged with a crime is, say, 18 percent. But if we consider a particular such boy who is currently a teenager and ask what is the likelihood of his being charged with a crime, what is his "propensity" for being so charged, then we have to ask which general frequency or frequencies to consult. For this individual boy not only belongs to the class just specified but also to many others—American, American male, resident of North Dakota, over six feet tall, and so on. Suppose we are interested in the question whether a particular belief by a particular subject that is acquired at a particular time has an adequate ground, as we are in this book. And suppose further that we try to tackle this question by asking whether grounds like this usually lead to true beliefs where the beliefs are like this. Then we have to decide which of many similarities of this ground and belief to other grounds and beliefs to use in determining the class of grounds and class of beliefs to be investigated for the relative frequency of true beliefs in that class when formed on grounds of that class. And that is not the end of what has to be decided. After picking the relevant classes we must decide what range of ground-belief pairs belonging to the relevant classes to examine for the relative frequency of true beliefs. Again, there are many candidates here from which to choose. Having settled on a class of grounds, say visual appearances that are qualitatively like this one in such-and-such respects, and a class of beliefs, say beliefs that the seen object is a Victorian house, we must decide what run of cases in which a belief belonging to the second class is formed on the basis of a ground belonging to the first class to examine for the frequency of true beliefs in it. The point is that the frequency can vary markedly depending on what constraints we put on the selection of cases. To take an extreme example, if the cases were restricted to those in which the subjects are under the influence of a certain drug, we would get very different results from the ones that resulted from a restriction to more normal cases. Or, again, take the class of grounds to be those in which someone purports to give information that P about a certain topic, and the class of beliefs are S's beliefs that are formed on grounds of that sort. Depending on the population of informers we pick, the frequency of true beliefs might be higher or lower, higher if the proportion of extremely scrupulous and careful informers is high, lower if the proportion of uncritical gossipers is high. Let's call the two decisions we are required to make the *decision on the reference classes* and the *decision on the range of cases*.

Rather than enter at this point on how to pick out the relevant reference classes and how to decide on the range of cases, I will postpone that discussion until after the extended discussion in the next chapter of the next item on the list of truth-conducive epistemic desiderata, 3—*reliability*. For the question how to determine whether a particular belief-forming process was a reliable one raises closely analogous issues. Reliability is a notion that is applied to something general, something that has (at least potentially) many different cases or instances. If you ask whether a computer is reliable, you must want to know about the frequency with which it works or would work as it is supposed to in a large number of uses. If you ask whether a gun is reliable, you want to know whether in a large number of cases it fires a bullet when loaded and the trigger is pulled. It makes no sense to ask of a particular use of the computer to do a particular job at a particular time whether that is reliable unless there is at least a tacit generalization over many such uses. And so it is here. When we ask whether a belief was reliably formed, that is, formed in such a way as to be likely to be true (on condition of being so formed), there is no way to seek an answer except by considering whether the way in which this particular belief was formed is an instance of a general way of forming beliefs that would yield mostly true beliefs. Again, once we have picked out a certain general way of forming beliefs of which this particular belief formation was an instance, our results are sensitive to the range of cases we examine. They will vary, for example, with the attention our subjects give to whether there are strong reasons against a belief they are on the verge of accepting.

We have just uncovered an exact parallel between the task of determining whether a belief is based on an adequate ground and the task of determining whether the way in which it was formed was a reliable one. In both cases we have to fasten on something general (class of grounds and class of belief contents—class of ways of forming beliefs and class of belief contents) such that the particular (ground and belief—process of formation and belief) in question are members of those classes. And it is those classes that have to be examined for the proportion of true belief outputs. And so here too we need a way of picking one out of the indefinitely many classes to which this particular process belongs as the one that is crucial for the question at issue. Moreover, in each case the range of ground-belief pairs (cases of belief formation) that we examine will have to be chosen in such a way that it satisfies appropriate criteria of numerosity, representativeness, typicality, and others. Thus the tasks look remarkably similar. In the next chapter I will further explore this similarity and determine what it implies. My expectation is that it will turn out that the two sets of tasks are much closer than would appear at first sight, and that they may even turn out to be two sides of the same coin.

Here is another point that needs emphasis with respect to the frequency conception of probability that we are proposing to use to develop the idea that an adequate ground of belief is one such that it is PF credible that a belief based on that ground will enjoy a high probability of truth all things considered on the condition of being so based. I have just been suggesting that the relevant frequency of truth is that of beliefs belonging to an appropriately chosen class when based on grounds of an appropriately chosen class in an appropriate range of cases. But there is still a choice to be made between a "track record" frequency, the frequency in which such beliefs *actually* based on such grounds are true, and what we might call a "subjunctive" frequency, the frequency with which such beliefs based on such grounds *would* be true if they were so based. It is not difficult to see that it is the latter notion that we want for epistemology. This can be most easily seen by reflecting that a ground of a certain sort could be an adequate (possible) basis for a belief with a certain kind of content even if such a belief is never in fact based on it. And opting for a de facto, "track record" frequency would freeze out examples like this. This point too will be developed more fully in Chapter 6 in connection with the discussion of the notion of a reliable belief-forming process.

Here is one more bit of evidence for the intimate relationship of desiderata 2 and 3. We have seen that where the ground of a belief is doxastic, there are two contributors to the epistemic probability of the grounded belief—(a) the conditional probability of the propositional content of the belief on the propositional content of the ground, and (b) the truth status or epistemic status of the ground. We will see that a similar distinction is involved in treating the reliability of belief-forming processes, one formulated by Goldman as a distinction between "conditional" and "unconditional" reliability.

By way of further preview I will mention one basis for the opposing view that adequacy of grounds is something quite different from the reliability of ways of forming beliefs. I will not attempt to refute this view here; that will come in the next chapter. But I will briefly set out the view and give a hint as to how it will be refuted. The basis in question is a distinction between the reliability of a *process* of belief formation and the reliability of an *indication* or ground for taking the belief to be true. The claim is that since these are fundamentally different kinds of items that can be said to be more or less reliable, and since the notion of adequacy of grounds obviously concerns the reliability of *indicators* if it has to do with any kind of reliability at all, whereas the reliability of a way of forming beliefs is the reliability of a certain kind of *process*, the two concerns are poles apart and never the twain shall meet. In opposition to this I will seek to show in the next chapter that once we find a satisfactory way of construing the reliability of a process of belief formation, the notion of the reliability of an indicator of the truth of a belief will occupy a central place in that construal. So far from being unrelated epistemological concerns, the one essentially depends on the other.

CHAPTER 6

RELIABILITY AND OTHER TRUTH-CONDUCIVE DESIDERATA

i. The Problem of Generality

I now turn to number 3 on the list of epistemic desiderata: a belief's being acquired in a reliable way, by a reliable belief-forming process. As foreshadowed in the previous chapter, this discussion will lead us back to the adequacy of grounds of belief.

Theories of epistemic justification and of knowledge, in terms of the reliability of ways of forming belief, have been prominent in epistemology for several decades.[1] Since I have abandoned justification theory and since knowledge is off limits for this book, I will be treating reliability not with those interests in mind but instead as one among other epistemic desiderata for belief. Hence in discussing the literature on this topic I will have to abstract from its concern with those applications. What I will take from these writers is their attempt to explicate the notion of reliable ways of belief formation and their attempt to solve problems that this raises, or, in the case of critics, their attempts to show that the problems cannot be solved. We will find plenty of material of this sort, more than enough to keep us busy.

The main difficulty posed by the notion of a belief's being formed in a reliable way is essentially the same as we saw to arise with the notion of the

[1] See especially Goldman 1979 and 1986, Armstrong 1973, and Swain 1981.

ground of a particular belief being adequate.[2] In both cases we want to be able to assess the adequacy of the ground, G, or the reliability of a way of belief formation, W, of a particular belief, B, held by a particular person, S, at a particular time, t. But there is no way to make such assessments except by taking G, W, and B to be instances of some general types of Gs, Ws, and Bs, and investigating the relative frequency of true Bs of that type that are based on Gs of that type or are generated by Ws of that type. And that raises the question how to pick types for this purpose out of the indefinite multiplicity of types of which the G, B, or W in question is an instance. This problem is particularly obvious with respect to reliability since, as I indicated at the end of the last chapter, it makes no sense to ask of the reliability of anything that does not have multiple instances or uses. But we saw there that the same problem arises, though perhaps less obviously, for the adequacy of grounds. I will begin by laying out the problem as it arises for the reliability of ways of belief formation and then return to the adequacy of grounds.

The reference in the last paragraph to the "formation" of a particular belief and to a way of forming beliefs "generating" a particular belief indicates that the reliability of what we might call "doxastic processes" is subject to the same kind of complication that we discussed in connection with grounds on which a belief is based. That is, the psychological processes that have a bearing on the epistemic status of a belief are not limited to those that generate the belief. Where a belief is strengthened or weakened or preserved by processes that occur after initial acquisition, those too enter into what gives the belief a stronger or weaker epistemic status. Most of the discussion of reliability in epistemology has been focused on processes that generate the belief. And, as I am doing with grounds on which a belief is based, I will, for the most part, follow this practice in the treatment of doxastic processes. But here too it must be remembered that significantly often there are post-acquisition processes that significantly affect the belief's epistemic status.[3] Where this point needs to be emphasized, I will speak more generally of "doxastic processes" rather than more narrowly of "generating processes". I should also mention a related point, that in section vii the question is considered whether segments of a doxastic practice that are prior to the final effect on belief have to be recognized as epistemologically relevant.

---

[2] With respect to the latter topic we will restrict ourselves for now, where the ground of the belief is doxastic, to the first contribution to adequacy, namely, the connection between the ground and the grounded belief. Later we will bring in the other consideration, the epistemic status of the ground.

[3] We must remember that what counts as a "favorable outcome" will differ for generating, strengthening, and preservative processes. For the first it is true beliefs; for the second, beliefs with epistemically improved status; and for the third, the retention of the same belief.

A particular belief is generated by a particular psychological process. But a particular process, with a certain spatiotemporal location, is not the sort of thing that can be more or less reliable. Reliability or the reverse attaches only to what is repeatable, to what has, actually or potentially, a number of instances. At least this is true if we are thinking of events or processes, as reliabilists in epistemology typically are. It is more common in ordinary speech to attribute reliability and unreliability to mechanisms like thermometers, carburetors, and clocks, or to medicines or sources of information. 'Repeatability' or 'instances' does not apply directly to them. Nevertheless, repeatability comes in more indirectly. Though a clock or an encyclopedia or a medicine is not "repeatable", it is something that can be operated, consulted, or used many times, and so there is something like repeatability here, namely, repeated employments. So the general point holds that to be assessable as reliable or the reverse, something must, actually or potentially, provide a range of cases of the appropriate sort. For reliability is always a matter of the incidence of favorable outcomes in a multitude of instances or employments of the item in question. What counts as *favorable* differs, of course, from one application to another. With medicines it is a certain kind of improvement in health. With clocks it is registering the correct time. With maps it is accurate representation of location and distance. For the case at hand—belief-forming processes—it is truth. A reliable belief-forming process is one that usually yields, or would yield, true beliefs. To get back to the original point, a particular process that takes place at a particular precise time is not the sort of thing that does or does not enjoy a favorable ratio of true beliefs among its products. It occurs just once; the one belief it produces is either true or false, and there's an end to it. Hence, as is regularly said by both friend and foe, it is a *type* of cognitive process rather than a particular process (a token) that can be assessed for reliability.

The difficulty arises when we ask how to identify the type of process that must be checked for reliability in order to determine whether a particular belief was formed in a reliable way. The problem is that there is no unique type to which the particular belief formation belongs. Any particular process, like any particular anything, is an instance of indefinitely many types. Here is a statement of the problem from an oft-cited article, Feldman 1985.

> The specific process token that leads to any belief will always be an instance of many process types. For example, the process token leading to my current belief that it is sunny today is an instance of all the following types: the perceptual process, the visual process, processes that occur on Wednesday, processes that lead to true beliefs, etc. Note that these process types are not equally reliable. Obviously, then, one of these types must be the one whose

reliability is relevant to the assessment of my belief. Intuitively, it seems clear that the general reliability of processes that occur on Wednesday or processes that lead to true beliefs is not relevant to the assessment. The reliability of the visual process or of the perceptual process may well be important.

Let us say, then, that for each belief-forming process token there is some "relevant" type such that it is the reliability of that type which determines the justifiability of the belief produced by that token. Thus, the reliability theory can be formulated as follows:

> (RT) S's belief that p is justified if and only if the process leading to S's belief that p is a process token whose relevant process type is reliable.

In order to evaluate (RT) we need some account of what the relevant types of belief-forming processes are. Without such an account, we simply have no idea what consequences the proposal has since we have no idea which process types are relevant to the evaluation of particular beliefs. (159–160)

Here is another formulation of the same point in Plantinga 1988.

> The main problem, as I see it, still remains. Note first that any particular token—any relevant sequence of concrete events—will be a token of many different types. Consider a specific visual process in Paul, where the input consists in retinal stimulation, let's say, and the output consists, for some particular scene *s* on his television, in his believing that he sees *s*. The process in question will presumably involve a large number of events: it will no doubt include an event consisting in Paul's being appeared to in a characteristic way. Now this sequence of events will be a token of many different types—*the cognitive process, the visual process, the cognitive process occurring on a Thursday, the visual process occurring in a middle aged man, the visual process occurring in a middle aged man under such and such lighting conditions, the visual process occurring in a middle aged man when his retinas are being stimulated by light of such and such a character*; and many more.
>
> It is these types that are to be evaluated for reliability (since, as we recall, the degree of justification enjoyed by the belief in question is a function of the reliability of the process (type) causing it); but obviously the types may differ wildly among themselves with respect to reliability. Which is the relevant type? Which type is the one such that its reliability determines the justification Paul has for the belief in question? (28–29)

For 'is justified' in the above passages read, for my purposes, 'has a positive epistemic status'.

Since there is no unique type to which a particular belief-forming process belongs, we must find some way to pick, from this multiplicity of types that will typically enjoy different degrees of reliability or unreliability, the one that is to be assessed for reliability in determining whether the particular belief in question was formed in a reliable way. And it has been argued by Feldman, Plantinga, Pollock, and others that there is no nonarbitrary way of making a choice. Here is the beginning of the argument in Feldman 1985.

> In coming up with an account of relevant types, defenders of the reliability theory must be guided by the following point. If relevant types are characterized very narrowly, then the relevant type for some or all process tokens will have only one instance (namely that token itself). If that token leads to a true belief, then its relevant type is completely reliable, and according to (RT) the belief it produces is justified. If that token leads to a false belief, then its relevant type is completely unreliable, and, according to (RT), the belief it produces is unjustified. This is plainly unacceptable, and in the extreme case, where every relevant type has only one instance, (RT) has the absurd consequence that all true beliefs are justified and all false beliefs are unjustified. We can say that characterizing relevant types too narrowly leads to "The Single Case Problem".
>
> A very broad account of relevant types of belief-forming processes leads to what we may call "The No-Distinction Problem". This arises when beliefs of obviously different epistemic status are produced by tokens that are of the same (broad) relevant type. For example, if the relevant type for every case of inferring were the type "inferring", then (RT) would have the unacceptable consequence that the conclusions of all inferences are equally well justified (or unjustified) because they are believed as a result of processes of the same relevant type.
>
> The problem for defenders of the reliability theory, then, is to provide an account of relevant types that is broad enough to avoid The Single Case Problem but not so broad as to encounter The No-Distinction Problem. Let us call the problem of finding such an account "The Problem of Generality". (160–161)

Feldman then goes on to argue at some length that this cannot be done.

Feldman's challenge is to find a way of picking the relevant type that will give us types that are highly reliable when the belief in question appears, to intuition or otherwise, to be highly *justified*. I have already dissociated myself from the pursuit of *that* investigation, though I have also suggested that being formed by a reliable process is an important epistemic desideratum for a belief. And that suggestion will be elaborated in this chapter. But embedded within the challenge Feldman issues to the reliabilist in justification theory is an assumption that I will be concerned with, namely, that there are no objective, psychological facts of the matter that pick out a unique type as the one of which a particular process is a token in some special, privileged sense. It is only if that assumption is true that the reliabilist is faced with the daunting task of providing a principled way of selecting a single winner from a plethora of candidates. And even if she should succeed in that task, the result would be subject to the complaint that the assignment of each token to a unique type has been rigged to fit an antecedent decision as to the epistemic status of the belief, thereby implying that it is not reliability that is calling the shots as to epistemic status. Hence a great deal is riding on the above assumption. I will now seek to discredit it.

Before turning to that, I can use purely conceptual considerations to avoid Feldman's Scylla, the "Single Case Problem". This can be disposed of just by making it explicit that reliability is not a matter of actual track record but rather is a *dispositional* or *propensity* notion. To say that a thermometer, medicine, or atlas is reliable is not to make a report of the relative frequency of favorable outcomes in the cases in which it has been used. It may never have been used, but that doesn't keep it from being reliable or unreliable. We may not be able to tell how reliable it is if it hasn't yet been used, but here as elsewhere it is a great mistake to conflate X's being P with *our ascertaining or being able to ascertain that X is P*. An atlas may be very reliable even though no one ever consults it. In this respect reliability functions like other dispositional properties. A rubber band can be elastic even though it is never stretched and so never has the chance to manifest that disposition. The applicability of a dispositional term depends on whether the appropriate manifestations *would* result from the satisfaction of the relevant antecedent conditions in a suitable range of cases, whether or not such a spread of cases, or any cases at all, are forthcoming. An elastic substance is one that *would* resume its shape *if* deformed. In parallel fashion a reliable type of belief formation is one that *would* generate preponderantly true beliefs in a large run of suitable cases.

In denying that reliability is a matter of actual frequencies, I am not denying that the most direct way of assessing a device or a process type for reliability is to ascertain the frequency of favorable outcomes in a suitable range of actual cases. That is not the only way, but it is the most direct way. And if we couldn't use that approach for many dispositional properties, we would not be in a position to employ less direct procedures for certain cases, procedures that require already knowing how to apply other dispositional predicates. Thus, having ascertained by actual frequency counts that certain human perceptual belief-forming processes are reliable, we thereby have some basis for inferring that processes sufficiently similar to those are likely to be reliable also. But these latter inferences presuppose that we have already done some frequency-count spade work for some processes.

Note that I have said that we need to *make explicit* the point that reliability is a dispositional notion rather than a track-record notion. I did not say that we need to *develop* the notion in this direction or *modify* it so that it takes this shape. It seems perfectly clear to me that as we ordinarily use the term 'reliable', it functions in the way I have just described. Feldman (1985, 168–170) presents the propensity construal as something a reliability theorist might be driven to in order to answer objections. And Goldman is much too permissive on this point.

> I have characterized justification-conferring processes as ones that have a 'tendency' to produce beliefs that are true rather than false. The term 'tendency' could refer either to *actual* long-run frequency, or to a 'propensity', i.e., outcomes that would occur in merely possible realizations of the process. Which of these is intended? Unfortunately, I think our ordinary conception of justifiedness is vague on this dimension. (1979, 11)

But I don't see how anyone could possibly think that 'tendency' might mean 'actual long-run frequency'. Nor do I see how anyone could reasonably suppose that 'reliable' (that's the term we should be discussing rather than 'justified') is vague on the distinction between propensity and actual frequency.

The application of my point that reliability is a propensity notion to Feldman's worries about the "Single Case Problem" is quite straightforward. Since reliability doesn't hang on actual frequency, there is no excuse for supposing that if a belief-forming process is exemplified only once and produces a true belief, it is perfectly reliable whereas if it produces a false belief on its only instantiation, it is perfectly unreliable. Its place on the reliability dimension depends on what proportion of true beliefs *would be* produced in a suitable range of instantiations, not on what actually results when it is instantiated.

ii. Belief-Forming Processes

There are several details concerning belief-forming processes to be cleared up before I can deal with the Problem of Generality.

1. There is the question of the boundaries of the processes the reliability of which we are claiming to have an epistemological bearing. Many discussions of the topic are not very specific about this. Clearly, the causal ancestry of a belief, like anything else, can be traced back indefinitely into the past. To go very far in that direction in the individuation of the process would make it unmanageable. But where should we place the starting point? In particular, should we include events outside the organism or limit it to certain intraorganic or intrapsychic events, perhaps even further limited to those that function as *proximate* causes of the belief? David

Armstrong's formulation is a good example of one that leaves this hazy (see Armstrong 1973, 168). It runs something like this. S's belief that p is reliably formed provided that S has some property, H, such that it is nomologically necessary that if a subject that is H forms a belief that p, that belief is true. This is not explicitly in terms of processes, but it could be rewritten in those terms. "S's belief that p is reliably formed provided the process that generated that belief has some property, H, such that it is nomologically necessary that any belief that is generated by a process with that property is true". This obviously puts no restriction on the extent of the process. Any characterization of the process that will yield the nomological necessity in question will ensure reliability of belief formation.[4]

As for critics of reliabilism, we find Feldman and Pollock considering perceptual processes that include factors outside the subject, such as distance from the object and lighting conditions, but without indicating any definite boundaries for the process. Our paradigm reliabilist, Goldman, is more specific.

> In addition to the problem of 'generality' . . . there is the problem of the '*extent*' of belief-forming processes. Clearly, the causal ancestry of beliefs often includes events outside the organism. Are such events to be included among the 'inputs' of belief-forming processes? Or should we restrict the extent of belief-forming processes to 'cognitive' events? . . . I shall choose the latter course, though with some hesitation. My general grounds for this decision are roughly as follows. Justifiedness seems to be a function of how a cognizer deals with his environmental input, i.e., with the goodness or badness of the operations that register and transform the stimulation that reaches him. . . . A justified belief is, roughly speaking, one that results from cognitive operations that are, generally speaking, good or successful. But 'cognitive' operations are most plausibly construed as operations of the cognitive faculties, i.e., 'information-processing' equipment internal to the organism.[5] (1979, 12–13)

This seems to me just the right thing for a reliabilist to say on this point.[6] But note that although this restricts the epistemically relevant process to psychological operations within the organism, that still leaves a number of factors involved that are prior to the proximate input to the

---

[4] Note that these formulations restrict reliable ways of forming beliefs to *infallible* ways. In the course of his treatment Armstrong makes certain restrictions on H, but they have no effect on this point or on the point that the extent of the process is left undetermined.

[5] By the time Goldman came to write his 1986 he had lost the "hesitation" of which he speaks in this passage. See particularly chapter 5.

[6] In section vii I will give some reasons for this judgment.

belief formation. In visual belief formation there are all the stages of perceptual processing between the retinal stimulation and the conscious perceptual experience that is the final input to the belief formation. It is crucial for the treatment of the reliability of belief-forming, and other doxastic, processes that I will give that the epistemically relevant process be construed in terms of that final stage. This will, by the way, make possible a close parallel between the reliability of a belief-forming process and the adequacy of a ground of belief. That is not my justification for this way of construing such processes; that will come later, in section vii.

2. In his 1979 Goldman distinguishes between "belief-independent" and "belief-dependent" belief-forming processes. The distinction is in terms of the inputs: the former take no doxastic inputs; the latter take at least some. He characterizes reliability differently for the two. The intuitive preliminary characterization given earlier applies without qualification only to the belief-independent type. But where the input is at least partly doxastic, since the epistemic character of the output depends not only on the relation between input and output but also on the epistemic status of the input, we cannot suppose that the excellence of the former factor alone ensures a large proportion of true beliefs among the outputs. For the process might be ever so reliable in transmitting truth from input to output, but if a substantial proportion of its inputs are false, it cannot be depended on to yield mostly true outputs. Whereas with belief-independent processes, where the input is an experience, or something else other than a belief, no question arises as to the truth or the epistemic status of the input since it is not susceptible of such. The contrast of true or false and of lesser or greater PES does not apply to a visual appearance of a red sphere or a feeling of exaltation. Thus belief-dependent processes can, at most, be termed "conditionally reliable", that is, reliable tout court on the condition that the input is true or least has a sufficient PES. Whereas a belief-independent process is susceptible of unconditional reliability since no further condition over and above the character of the input-output relationship is required for its yielding a high proportion of true beliefs.

The reader will remember the similar point about adequacy of grounds. Where the ground of a belief is one or more beliefs, the epistemic status of the latter depends not only on the conditional probability of the latter on the former but also on the epistemic status of the former. But when the ground is an experience, there is no such double dependence since the notion of epistemic status does not apply to that kind of ground. Goldman's "conditional probability" of the belief-belief process parallels the conditional probability of the target belief on the ground-belief. Whereas Goldman's "unconditional probability" of a "belief-independent process" parallels the way in which a nondoxastic experience grounds a belief and yields, without further condition, an epistemic status for it. This is the first connection to be made in this chapter between the reliability of belief-forming processes and the ways in which the ground of a belief is a condition for a conditional probability of truth on that belief. In discussing the reliability of belief-dependent processes, we will treat separately the conditional reliability of the process from the truth or epistemic status of the input, just as in discussing the epistemic bearing of doxastic grounds of belief, we treat separately the epistemic status of the grounding belief from the conditional probability of the target belief on the ground.

3. Finally, I have to deal with a much more complex and difficult piece of the picture. In contrasting a track-record construal of reliability with a propensity construal, I have presented the latter in terms of the frequency of true beliefs that would result from a "suitable" or "appropriate" range of deployments of the process-type. What does it take for a range to be "suitable"? First, it must be sufficiently numerous. What counts as sufficient will vary with different subject matters. We learn from experience how much homogeneity or heterogeneity to expect in cases of a given sort. The more variation we have learned to expect across instances, the larger the sample we need. Since people vary much more than chemical substances, we need a larger sample for opinion or attitude research than for determining atomic weight. Second, the cases must be sufficiently varied along relevant dimensions to rule out, so far as possible, the results being due, to a significant extent, to factors other than the one being tested for. If we are testing for arithmetic ability, we wouldn't want to confine ourselves to very easy or very difficult problems; we would want a spread of difficulty in the test. Similarly, if we are testing a perceptual belief-forming process for reliability, we would want to vary the cases with respect to such factors as distracting "noise" from other psychological inputs and the degree of discrimination required between inputs. These two points are applications to this topic of criteria that are used in any sampling procedure.

But there are other factors to take into account. What the last paragraph suggests is that a belief-forming process will be deemed reliable *iff* its activation in a suitable number and range of cases would result in a high proportion of true beliefs. But this is false for many of the processes we would ordinarily regard as reliable, so long as no further restrictions are put on the circumstances in which the process occurs. Many familiar human belief-forming processes would exhibit sharply different degrees of reliability depending on what is allowed into the set of circumstances of activation. This may not be true of all. Some have supposed that introspection must yield only truths, no matter what, and some have taken the apprehension of propositions as self-evident to enjoy a like immunity to error. Moreover, with respect to the conditional reliability of inferences, it seems that in no possible situation would deductively valid inferences fail to be conditionally reliable. But look at perception and nondeductive reasoning. For any perceptual belief-forming mechanism that produces mostly truths in the situations of the kind in which it is typically exercised, there are possible situations in which that reliability would be sharply reduced. And not just logically possible situations involving Cartesian demons and the like. It is well within our powers to arrange environments in which a normal person, utilizing normal mechanisms of perceptual belief formation that serve us well in run-of-the-mill situations, would usually or always be led astray. We need only manufacture realistic enough look-alikes, or do something more ambitious with holographs or something still more ambitious with direct brain stimulation. If the range of cases included a considerable proportion of situations like these, the process would score rather low, even if the score would be high when tested in more familiar situations. To illustrate the problem with respect to nondeductive reasoning, we must have recourse to more recherché possibilities. Consider induction from simple enumeration. Surely there are possible worlds in which when there is a high proportion of Fs in Gs in what we take to be a properly constituted sample, it is the case that most Gs are not F. If all else fails, we can introduce a Cartesian demon that delights in arranging things so that such inferences are usually or invariably frustrated.

Thus we are faced with a question as to the range of situations in which yielding mostly true beliefs by a process would be necessary and sufficient for its being reliable.[7] If we require reliability over all possible situations, even all situations that are possible in the actual world, we will, at best, be left with a sharply reduced set of reliable belief-forming processes. To avoid that, how shall we demarcate those situations over which the test sample must range in order to give an epistemologically relevant result?

I can't think of any better answer to this question than the following. The requirement is that the process would yield a high proportion of truths over a wide range of situations *of the sort we typically encounter.* Obviously, this is

---

[7] This formulation is for only the belief-independent inputs. For belief-dependent inputs, change 'yielding mostly true beliefs' to 'yielding mostly true outputs from true inputs' and insert 'conditionally' before 'reliable'.

far from precise. It doesn't draw a sharp boundary between typical and atypical. Moreover, it leaves open the possibility that the boundary, such as it is, can shift over time. What was atypical up to now may become typical with cultural, technological, or other changes. But I believe that this suggestion has the right kind and degree of sloppiness for the concept of reliability we want for epistemic purposes. It does unequivocally rule out clearly atypical situations—Cartesian demons, brains in vats, and the like. And it makes a judgment of reliability dependent on our situations as human beings in the environments in which we actually find ourselves. This is what we need to capture the intuitive notion of reliability that we require for epistemology. If I claim that my thermometer is reliable, it is no refutation to point out that it would not give an accurate reading on the sun. Similarly, if I claim to be able to determine accurately by vision whether I am standing in front of a beech tree, it would be no refutation of that claim to point out that I could not do this if I were receiving direct stimulation of the visual cortex in a physiological laboratory or if I were in a very thick fog. When I make a judgment of reliability—whether for an instrument, a documentary source, a psychological mechanism, or whatever—I have in mind, at least implicitly, a range of situations with respect to which the claim is being made. What happens outside that range is simply irrelevant.

With respect to this issue concerning the appropriate range of cases, there are parallel points to be made for the adequacy of grounds. Indeed, some of them were made earlier, near the end of the last chapter. This is the second way in which the reliability of ways of forming beliefs and the adequacy of grounds of belief turn out to raise essentially the same problems. In the next section we will see that the connection is even closer than that.

iii. Belief-Forming Mechanisms as Psychologically Realized Functions

Now I can return to my central task: challenging the assumption that there are no objective facts that determine a unique type to which a particular token belief-forming process belongs. I agree, of course, that a given process token belongs to innumerably many types. Like any other particular, a process token has indefinitely many properties to each of which is associated a type defined by that property. Nevertheless, some types, in this generous logical sense, are ontologically rooted, fundamental, and important in ways many others are not. Even if it is true that you belong to indefinitely many classes, such as *objects weighing more than ten pounds, objects that exist in the twenty-first century, objects reading this book,* and so on, it is still the case that membership in the class of human beings is fundamental for *what you are* in a way that many others are not, just because it is the *natural kind* to which you belong. I shall suggest that something analogous is true of belief-forming processes—that there are considerations that mark out for each process token a type that is something like its "natural kind", and hence that in thinking of belief-forming process types we are not awash in a sea of indeterminacy, as Feldman and others suppose.

Recall that in the previous section I gave reasons for focusing on the psychological states or processes that constitute the proximate cause of the belief in question when we treat belief-forming processes. But this limitation does not significantly reduce the embarrassment of riches where types are concerned. A purely psychological process will also be of indefinitely many types, including such undesirable candidates as *happening on a Wednesday* and *generating a true belief*. Moreover, it will belong to types of all levels of generality. If it is a visual belief-forming process, it will be of the type *forming a belief on the basis of such-and-such a kind of visual presentation, forming a belief about a tree, forming a belief about something in the vicinity, forming a belief on the basis of vision, forming a belief on the basis of perception*, and so on. We are still drowning in an unmanageable plurality.

But decisive help is near. The germ of it is to be found in Goldman 1979, from which I have been quoting, though, as we shall see, Goldman fails to take advantage of it to solve the generality problem.

> We need to say more about the notion of a belief-forming 'process'. Let us mean by a 'process' a *functional operation* or procedure, i.e., something that generates a *mapping* from certain states—'inputs'—into other states—'outputs'. The outputs in the present case are states of believing this or that proposition at a given moment. (1979, 11)

Thus every belief formation involves the activation of a psychologically realized *function*. That activation yields a belief with a propositional content that is a certain function of the proximate input. This function will determine both what features of the input have a bearing on the belief output and what bearing they have, that is, how the content of the belief is determined by those features.[8] In order to bring talk of reliability of belief formation closer to such paradigm examples of reliability as thermometers, let's say that a psychologically realized belief-formation function constitutes a

---

[8] 'Function' is used here in the mathematical sense, the sense in which addition is a function. Given any two or more numbers, the addition function will yield a unique output as their sum. A function in this sense is, of course, something abstract. That is why I had to specify that a belief-forming process involves the *activation* of a *psychologically realized* function, not just the function as a denizen of logical space.

psychological *mechanism*. If you don't like this terminology, either because it sounds too "mechanistic" or because it threatens to populate the mind-brain with unmanageably many separate black boxes, we can use other terms. We can think of the function as embodied in a *habit* of forming a belief with a certain propositional content that is a certain function of certain features of the input, or as a *disposition* to do that. Or if you prefer act-psychology, you can think of the subject's having the power to "take account" of certain features of inputs and, on the basis of that *taking-account*, to form a belief with a content that is a certain function of those features. The common thread running through all this is that it is part of the constitution of the psyche to be so disposed that upon being presented with a certain kind of input, a belief is generated with a content that is a certain function of certain features of that input. In the ensuing I will freely oscillate between speaking of habits and of mechanisms.

Although I have been giving this functional account of *belief-forming* processes, here too, as earlier with basing beliefs on grounds, a parallel account can be given of *belief-strengthening* processes and *belief-preserving* processes. There the output of the realized function is a belief strengthening or a belief preservation. But the structure of the account is the same.

Returning to belief formation, let's descend from these high levels of generality and look at some examples. Consider the formation of a visual perceptual belief that a maple tree is in front of one. The input will be a visual presentation of a certain sort, one that involves the perceived object's *looking* a certain way.[9] The mechanism that is activated will take account of certain phenomenal features of the presentation. Certain shape features, certain color features, the spatial distribution of various colored regions and contrasts with the surrounding field will be "picked up" by the mechanism whereas others will be ignored. Thus many details of the presentation could have been different without changing the content of the belief generated. The tree could have looked larger or smaller, the bark could have looked rougher or smoother, and so on. It all depends on what function is operative. If the function were one that delivered a belief about size or finely discriminated bark texture, some features that

---

[9] The details of the account will vary with one's favored theory of perception. Since I don't want to get into that here, I am striving for maximum neutrality. Nevertheless, my talk of "presentations" reflects my attachment to a theory of appearing, according to which perceptual experience consists most basically of objects, usually external physical objects, *appearing* to one in certain ways. Sense-datum theorists, adverbial theorists, and conceptual-propositional theorists of perceptual experience will not like my way of putting it. I believe, however, that the points I am making concerning the features of belief formation that are relevant to assessments of reliability are neutral with respect to different accounts of perceptual experience. I would invite those who take exception to my formulations to restate them in their favorite terms.

are irrelevant to whether one believes merely that it is a maple tree would have been relevant.

In this example I assumed that only the visual presentation functioned as an input. It is widely held that in every case of perceptual belief formation other beliefs of the subject play a role in shaping the doxastic output. Whether or not that is so, it is clear that in many cases the input is partly doxastic. Consider an "individual recognition" case rather than a "kind recognition" case like the last one. Upon seeing a house, I form the belief that it is your house. How can this be a reliable recognition, given that there are many houses in the world that look just like yours from a passing glance? Well, let's say that yours is the only one on this block of this street in this town that looks like yours. In that case it can well be that my identification of the house as yours is influenced by my knowledge (belief) that I am on this block of this street in this town, as well as by features of the visual presentation.

These examples may give the impression that the function involved in any perceptual belief formation is extremely specific, relating very detailed features of experiential input (together with propositionally specific belief input where that is present) to a unique belief content. In view of the heavy weather made by Feldman and others about the problem of navigating between a too specific and a too general process-type, it will be pertinent for us to consider for a moment where psychologically realized belief-forming functions stand on that dimension. In a word, they can be of various degrees of generality. Sticking with experiential input for the moment, we see that the function could be so specific as to take only precisely defined experiential features as input and issue only beliefs with a particular propositional content. But there are other possibilities. Consider attributions of color to perceived objects. Here we have what is plausibly regarded as a single function that maps the position of certain aspects of a visual input on several dimensions of color onto a belief that the object seen is of some more or less precise color. Here we can be confident that the function is unitary because of the systematic character of the mapping. But I take this to be the exception rather than the rule for perceptual belief formation. For most perceptual belief contents we don't have the possibility of systematic mapping that we have for color. But that does not imply that the function is always, or even usually, maximally specific. Think back on the maple tree example and consider apparent leaf shape as one of the relevant features of the input. Maple leaves are not all exactly the same shape, even if the belief output involves a particular type of maple, for example, sugar maple, rather than the more generic content of some maple or other. Hence the usual function realized by people who have some acquaintance with maples will accept any of a large number of different precise leaf shapes as contributing to the output of a belief that the object is a maple tree. This kind of generality is the rule rather than the exception.

Now consider a couple of inferential belief formations. On the approach I am suggesting, the functions involved in deductive inference will be principles of inference. Think of the hypothetical syllogism. I reflect that if I refuse your request for a raise you will quit your job, and if you quit your job I will be unable to find a replacement in time for carrying through a big contract that is impending. I, naturally, infer that if I refuse your request for a raise, I will be unable to find a replacement in time for that contract to be finalized. The function that yields a belief that is related in that way to the input beliefs is a psychological realization of the principle of inference called 'hypothetical syllogism'. Of course, we shouldn't suppose that only valid principles of deductive inference are psychologically realized. Some people, unfortunately, are so constituted as to regularly form beliefs related to the input beliefs in the pattern known as "asserting the consequent". Such a function would yield the belief that *it rained last night* from the input beliefs that *if it rained last night the grass would be wet* and *the grass is wet*.

Nondeductive inference presents a more complicated picture. If I arrive at a generalization from knowledge of various instances, I typically take into account not only the instances but also facts about the subject matter that indicate what kind of sample I need in order to reliably move to the generalization. As I pointed out earlier, some ranges of fact are more homogeneous than others and require less size and variety in the sample for a sound generalization. We must keep reminding ourselves that we are dealing here with what functions are psychologically realized, not just ones that are reliable. But I think we may safely assume that in many cases considerations of the sort just mentioned figure in the input to an induction by simple enumeration. Again, consider inference to the best explanation such as an inference to an explanation of a pool of water on the floor of my basement. The relevant inputs to such an inference will include not only beliefs about the current state of affairs in my basement but also a list of possible causes of the water's being there and considerations that bear on the likelihood of each of these possible causes having been operative.

iv. The Problem of Generality Solved

The time has come to apply all this to the generality problem. The application is very simple; it has probably already leaped to the eye of the reader. *The function determines the relevant type.* I form the visual belief that a car is parked in front of my house. What type of belief-forming process is such that its reliability is crucial for the epistemic status of that belief, so far as the epistemic status is determined by the reliability of the way that belief was formed? The type that is defined by the operative function, namely, *belief formations that proceed in accordance with the function that is involved here.* In other words, the particular process, by virtue of being a *functional* mapping of input features onto output content, has a *built-in* generality that is provided by the function. The function is something inherently general, and it defines the type the reliability of which, according to reliabilism, is crucial for the epistemic status of the belief in question.

Let me say a bit more about why the type defined by the operative function is the one to consider if we are interested, for epistemological purposes, in how reliably this particular belief was formed on this occasion. The type determined by the function has this special status just because it reflects or embodies the actual dynamics of the process, what is responsible for *this* belief with *this* content being formed on *this* basis. Hence if we assume, as we must if we take reliable belief formation to be an epistemic desideratum, that the epistemic status of a belief is, perhaps inter alia, a function of its proximate causal history, then from an epistemic point of view it is this type the reliability of which we should be interested in determining.

With respect to the visual belief that a car is parked in front of my house, it would be an immense labor to spell out the function involved here in complete detail since that would require enumerating the features of the visual presentation that led to my identifying what I saw as a car parked in front of my house. (Specifying the output side of the function—the belief content—is no problem.) I can identify the experiential input accurately, though not analytically, by using the content of the belief output. I can say that the mechanism generated the belief that there is a car parked in front of my house on the basis of an input that consisted in (using an adverbial idiom) *my being appeared to car-parked-in-front-of-my-housely*, or (using a presentational idiom) consisted in *an object's looking like a car parked in front of my house*. But whether we identify the perceptual input in analytically illuminating terms or in output-dependent terms, the basic point is the same. The type of process the reliability of which is relevant to the epistemic assessment of the belief is the one defined by the function, which is in turn defined by a certain way of going from input features to output features. The question of reliability that is of significance for the epistemic status of this belief is the question how reliable *this* habit is, the one defined by *this* function. The question is what the proportions of true beliefs would be in the outputs of activations of *this* habit over a sufficiently large spread of appropriately varied cases in typical circumstances. In other terms, the question has to do with the reliability of forming a belief *like this* on the basis of a perceptual presentation *like this*, where the relevant respects of likeness are determined by the constitution of the function realized in *this* mechanism.

As we have already seen, this point can be made more sharply with inferential belief-forming mechanisms since there the function can be more easily specified, at least for deductive inferences. If I form the belief that *Jim will come to the party* on the input of the beliefs that *Jim will come to the party if he is well* and *Jim is well*, then the belief formed here will be reliably formed provided my principle of inference is conditionally reliable—such as to lead to truths from truths, and the input beliefs have been reliably formed. The first of those two conditions will be realized provided that the principle that constitutes the function realized in the operative mechanism is modus ponens. (As we shall see later, this is not guaranteed by the fact that the inference exhibits that pattern.) In that case the process invariably yields true beliefs from true belief inputs.

Nondeductive inference, as we have seen, presents a messier picture. Here in order to be significantly reliable a function must be sensitive not only to formal properties of the argument but also to a variety of more substantive considerations—the character of the sample if it is an inductive generalization, various bits of relevant background knowledge, the field of competing explanations if it is an explanatory inference, and so on. Still, the basic point is the same. What the epistemic status of the particular output belief depends on, in addition to the epistemic status of the input beliefs, is the conditional reliability of the operative mechanism, that is, the extent to which the function realized by that mechanism would yield true belief outputs from true belief inputs in a suitable spread of cases. Or, to put it in terms of processes, the crucial issue is the conditional reliability of the process of going from belief input to belief output in accordance with that function, along with the epistemic status of the input.

So when we think of the reliability of belief-forming processes in this way, we are no longer faced with an indefinitely large multiplicity of types among which we have to find some way of making a choice. With the illumination shed by this way of construing belief-forming processes, the "Problem of Generality" as formulated by Feldman, Plantinga, Pollock et al. dissipates like mist before the morning sun. To be sure, it is still true that a particular process token is an instance of an indefinite variety of process types, including countless silly ones like *processes that take place on a Wednesday* and *processes that take place in the shower.* But now that we think of a belief-forming process as the functioning of a mechanism that embodies a (general) input-output function, we can ignore all that. The function defines the epistemologically relevant type, and we can forget about the rest.

When I introduced the input-output functional construal of a belief-forming process, I did so by quoting a suggestion of this from Goldman 1979. Amazingly enough, he failed to take advantage of this idea to solve the generality problem. Here is what he says about that problem in the very essay in which the functional construal was put forward.

> A critical problem concerning our analysis is the degree of generality of the process-types in question. Input-output relations can be specified very broadly or very narrowly, and the degree of generality will partly determine the degree of reliability. . . .
> It is clear that our ordinary thought about process-types slices them broadly, but I cannot at present give a precise explication of our intuitive principles. One plausible suggestion, though, is that the relevant processes are *content-neutral*. It might be argued, for example, that the process of *inferring p whenever the Pope asserts p* could pose problems for our theory. (12)

There is no hint that the identification of the function involved in a particular belief acquisition itself serves to define the relevant type of process. The discussion in Goldman 1986 goes beyond the above remarks, but, aside from the use of the propensity conception of reliability to dissolve the Single Case Problem, the additional suggestion amounts to the following.

> But how is it determined in each specific case, which process type is critical? . . . Let me advance a conjecture about the selection of process types, without full confidence. The conjecture is: the critical type is the *narrowest* type that is *causally operative* in producing the belief in question. (50)

But if my remarks in this chapter are on target, there is only one "type", that is, only one realized function, that is *causally operative* in a given case, apart from overdetermination. The function and the process type it defines can, of course, be characterized (not uniquely identified) in various ways because it has various properties, intrinsic and relational, beyond the constitution of the function that specifies its epistemically relevant character. But when we are interested in knowing what kind of process to check for reliability in order to assess the belief epistemically, the realized function that was actually operative in the belief generation gives us a unique answer to that.

v. Identity of Adequacy of Ground and Reliability of Process

At this point I will interrupt the treatment of reliability and return to the problem of understanding the degree of adequacy of a ground of belief in terms of the conditional probability the belief enjoys on the condition that it was based on that ground. You will remember that I settled on a frequency concept of probability as the objective construal of probability to use for this purpose. I then pointed out two problems this raises for treating the conditional probability of a particular token belief in terms of the relative frequency of true beliefs in a class of beliefs. These were (1) the problem of frequency classes: how do we pick one out of the many classes to which a particular belief token belongs, and one out of the many classes to which a particular ground token belongs, as the ones in which the frequency of true beliefs tells us what conditional probability to ascribe to that belief token? And (2) when that is settled, how do we determine the range of actual and possible cases involving beliefs of that class and grounds of that class to examine for the relative frequency of true beliefs among belief tokens of that class formed on the basis of ground tokens of that class? In the previous chapter I left these questions hanging, with the assurance that the answers would be forthcoming from the discussion of parallel problems that arise for the reliability of ways of forming beliefs. The time has come to make good on that promise.

The first step is to note that we have, as it were, stumbled onto the way to determine how being based on a certain ground gives a belief a certain conditional probability, in our treatment of a belief-forming process as involving a realized psychological function that maps features of the proximate input to the belief-forming mechanism onto features of the propositional content of the belief output. For what is there called an "input" to the belief-forming mechanism is just what in the previous chapter was called the "ground" on which the belief is based. The commonsense notion of forming a belief by basing it on a certain ground is given a formulation in cognitive psychology as the generation of a belief by a belief-forming mechanism that realizes a function that yields a belief the content of which is a certain function of certain features of the input (the "ground"). Hence with respect to the "reference class problem", the solution can be directly read off the solution to the "problem of generality" for belief-forming process types. The problems are the same expressed in different terminology, and the solution is correspondingly the same. As we have just seen, a belief's being based on a certain ground consists in its being generated by a belief-forming mechanism that embodies a function that has a built-in generality. The operative function consists of the taking of certain features of the input and thereby yielding a belief output with a certain content. So, in terms of belief-forming processes, the relevant process type is the one tokens of which proceed in accordance with the function operative in that token process. And in the *adequacy of ground-frequency probability* lingo, the relevant ground and belief classes are the ones the members of which function if and when they do in accordance with the function involved in the production of that belief token. Here too it is the operative function that determines the relevant general classes. The problems and their solutions for belief-forming processes and for basing beliefs on grounds are not only parallel. They are identical; only the terms in which they are expressed are different.

Let's look at how this identity works out in the case of one of the earlier examples. Take my formation of the perceptual belief that the large object in front of me is a maple tree. In terms of process reliability, what happens is this. An input-output function is activated, the input to which is a visual appearance, VA, and the output a belief *that it (the currently visually perceived large object) is a maple tree* (M). The function is one that maps certain features of VA onto a belief with propositional content M. The belief was reliably formed *iff* in a large range of (actual and possible) cases of the operation of that function in situations of the sort we typically encounter the belief outputs would be mostly true. Here is the description of the same belief formation in terms of adequacy of the ground on which the belief is based. The ground is again VA and the belief based on VA has the propositional content M. The ground is adequate *iff* in a large range of (actual and possible) cases of beliefs with content M being based on grounds with experiential content VA, these being in situations of the sort we typically encounter, the beliefs would be mostly true. VA and M are playing the same roles in the two descriptions. The only significant difference is that the process version does more to make explicit the structure of the psychological operation by specifying the realized function involved. In the basing version this is, so to say, concealed in the less analyzed notion of basing. But once we realize that for a belief to be based on a ground is just for that belief to be the output of a belief-forming mechanism that consists in a realized function of the sort specified in the process version, it can be seen that the difference is only in the degree of detail spelled out. More to the present point, the conferral of positive epistemic status on the belief by the way in which it is acquired depends on relative frequencies in the same way—the relative frequency of true beliefs in a sufficiently large and suitably constituted run of actual and possible cases of the operation of the function that was central in the particular case under scrutiny. The frequency notion of probability comes in more explicitly in the basing version, but it is implicitly involved in the process version as well. For to bring out what makes the particular process of belief formation a reliable one we have to bring out what would be the frequency of true belief outputs in a suitable range of cases of the operation of the function. And that carries with it the (unarticulated) implication that the belief outputs are rendered, by the process, probably true in a frequency sense of probability.

While tying up loose ends I will make explicit one further parallel that is embodied in the above discussion. Because of the intimate relation between a belief's being formed by a reliable process and its being based on an adequate ground, we can make a direct transfer to the latter of the treatment given at the end of section ii to the former of the problem of the appropriate range of cases. With respect to the question of the range of ground-belief pairs to be examined for relative frequency of true beliefs, we can make the same specification we gave there for the range of belief formations to be examined for a decision as to reliability. Here too the best we can do is to restrict relevant cases to ground-belief relationships of the sorts that we typically encounter. Again, this has just the right balance of significant content, and roughness and open texture, for the purpose.

I am far from the first to suggest that a frequency interpretation of probability is the one to use for epistemic probability. My most distinguished recent predecessor is Henry Kyberg.[10] It may help to emphasize important features of my version to make explicit some of my differences from Kyberg. I will not attempt to make a comprehensive list of these, which would require my going into the details of Kyberg's complicated views, as my aims in this book do not call for such an excursus. Briefly, then, Kyberg deals with propositions as bearers of probability while I have been putting beliefs in that role. This is not of the first importance since, as I have mentioned earlier, one can map propositional conditional probability onto belief-ground conditional probability. A more important difference is that Kyberg takes epistemic probability to be derivative from *knowledge* of frequencies whereas I take it to be constituted by the objective holding of frequencies, whether known by anyone or not. This difference leaves me to be comfortable with open-ended frequencies ranging over possible as well as actual cases since I am not constrained to restrict the range of relevant frequencies to those that are known by humans or any other cognitive subjects. And, finally, Kyberg's focus on known frequencies is paired with making probability assignments relative to one or another "rational corpus of knowledge" whereas the objective frequencies I envisage are free of any such relativity.

Since I have been quoting Plantinga at some length on probability, I should add a word about the relation of my account of epistemic probability to his. He distinguishes two components—an "objective" and a "normative". It is the objective component that he takes to be logical, and it is clear from the above discussion that I dissent from that, taking it to be of a frequency sort. But I also differ in not building in any normative component, characterized by Plantinga as its being "sensible or rational" to accept the

[10] See Kyberg 1974 and Bogdan, ed., 1982.

proposition in question. This difference is not a profound one. I agree that if a proposition is objectively probable on S's total evidence, it is rational for S to accept it. It is just that I see no compelling reason for making that part of what it means to say that it is objectively probable on S's total evidence. But I see no harm in doing it that way. I just find it cleaner and less complicated to keep Plantinga's objective and normative components separate and to think of the conditional probability status itself as a purely "objective" or "factual" matter.

I must make at least one possible qualification to the claim that the reliability of the process that results in belief B and the adequacy of the ground on which B is based are intertranslatable. The equivalence depends on (1) taking each belief-forming process to have an input-output functional structure and (2) supposing that each input to a realized belief-forming function can be just as well identified as what the belief is based on, its ground. Both of these can be questioned as true of all belief-forming processes. (I don't see any possibility of a sensible denial that both are true of most.) I don't see how there can be any doubt about (1) holding generally. Something must be responsible for the fact that the belief in question is formed at one time rather than another, and responsible for the belief formed having one propositional content rather than another. Otherwise we have a case of a belief arising "out of nowhere", and though I will recognize this to be conceivable, it seems unreasonable to suppose that it happens often enough to take into consideration in a general theory. But (2) might be contested for some cases. This will depend on several thorny issues—whether S must be conscious of what the belief is based on (no such condition is necessary for an input to a belief-forming process), how the basing relation is ordinarily spelled out, what it takes to have a *ground* of a belief, and so on. I have briefly given reasons for thinking that these questions are answered in such a way as to make the identification of inputs and grounds to hold universally. But I can hardly claim to have definitively settled the matter. Hence for present purposes I will simply say that the intertranslatability of the reliability of belief-forming processes and the adequacy of grounds of belief holds when and only when the above two assumptions are satisfied. The further discussion of the relation of epistemic desiderata 2 and 3 should be construed as limited to the cases in which these assumptions hold.

As for the view mentioned at the end of the last chapter, the view that process reliability and indicator reliability are quite different phenomena, it is clear that the above discussion thoroughly explodes that view. We have seen that a belief-forming *process is* the activation of a function that maps certain features of an input (ground, putative indicator of truth or probability thereof) onto the content of a belief output. And the epistemically relevant type to which it belongs is determined by the function in question. The reliability of such a process is given by the proportion of true belief outputs there would be in a large enough number of suitably varied activations of that function. But that also gives us the reliability of the "indicator" of the truth of belief that serves as the input to the realized function. A reliable indicator is one a sufficient proportion of its sufficiently numerous and varied functionings as an indicator (input) turn out to have true beliefs as output. And so reliability of process and reliability of indicator turn out to coincide, differing only in the emphasis on different parts of the belief formation. We speak of the reliability of the process when thinking of the entire proceeding, and of the reliability of the indicator when we are focusing on the input to the realized function and its relation to the output belief.

It is time to recall that the whole discussion in this chapter for cases where the ground or input is doxastic has been restricted to the ground-belief (input-output) relationship, neglecting the other contributor to adequacy (reliability), namely, the epistemic status of the ground (input). It is time to make that additional factor explicit. I don't have much to add on this. I am not prepared to produce a formula for computing the total epistemic probability of the belief (degree of reliability of its formation) from the epistemic status of the input and the conditional probability of the output on the input (conditional reliability of the process). I don't even see how to give a precise value to the epistemic status of the input on the basis of everything that contributes to that. So far as I can see, rough statements are the most we can manage. But at least I can say this. Where the ground (input) is doxastic, the conditional probability of the target belief on the ground (the conditional reliability of the process) can be related to the epistemic probability of the belief (the unconditional reliability of the process) in two ways. The simplest but less satisfactory way is to say that the conditional probability (conditional reliability) can be taken as unconditional on the assumption that the ground (input) is true. As pointed out earlier, that is the way in which conditional probability is usually thought of, and it could be a way to think of conditional reliability. This is less than satisfactory because the doxastic ground (input) isn't always true even where the unconditional reliability of the process is high, and it would be desirable, if not epistemically obligatory, to have a uniform way of treating all cases of high unconditional reliability. The second way is simply to add the caveat that the overall, unconditional epistemic probability of the target belief (the unconditional reliability of the process that yields the belief) is also partly dependent on the epistemic status of the ground (the input), where there is such an epistemic status. Without instructions on how to take that into account, this will not seem to be of much help. But it at least tells us this. The higher the epistemic status of the ground (input), the less the conditional probability (conditional reliability) is lessened by that input factor. If the epistemic probability of the input is 1, the conditional probability (conditional reliability) is not lessened at all. As the input probability diminishes from that limit, more is subtracted from the conditional probability (conditional reliability). This will make possible some rough statements of the overall resultant epistemic status of the target belief.

That completes the case for the substantial identity of epistemic desiderata 2 and 3, for the coincidence of process reliability and indicator reliability, and for the functional identity of the degree of adequacy of the ground on which a belief is based and the degree of reliability of the way in which the belief is generated.

vi. Objections and Complications

I will now consider some objections to my construal of the reliability of belief-forming processes and its application to the Generality Problem. (I assume that the points I will be making about this can be translated into *adequacy of grounds* terms, subject to the two assumptions laid out a few paragraphs back.) First, it may be objected (and has been objected in Swinburne 2001, Additional Note A, and in Feldman and Conee 1998) that there are still a large number of possible alternative process-types from which my functional conception of belief-forming processes does not make a unique choice. Are there not many different ways of carving up the psyche into distinct mechanisms or habits of belief formation? Depending on which of these we pick, won't we end up with one or another assignment of a particular process to a process-type, types that differ as to degree of reliability? Go back to my formation of the visual belief that there is a maple tree in front of me. Can't I think of the habit involved as one of (a) coming to believe that there is a maple tree in front of me on the basis of a visual presentation with such-and-such features, or (b) coming to believe that there is a maple tree in front of me on the basis of sensory experience, or (c) coming to believe that there is a tree in front of me on the basis of visual experience, or . . . ? That is, it looks as if I may think of the habit activated as possessing any one of widely varying degrees of generality (what Swinburne calls 'width'). Presumably, the reliability of these habits differs. Presumably, the reliability of the habit of forming maple-tree-in-front-of-me beliefs on the basis of visual presentations with just these features is much higher than the reliability of the more general habit of forming tree-in-front-of-me beliefs on the basis of some sensory experience or other. And does this not mean that we have still failed to pick out a unique relevant type?

NO. At least we are not still confronted with that problem if the assumptions I have been making are warranted. To properly respond to the above objection I need to distinguish the input and output sides. For the latter there are no alternatives as to how it is specified. We only have a particular case of belief formation at all if we have a belief with a particular propositional content. That gives us our starting point. It sets our problem of finding the realized function that is responsible for its acquisition. There is no question of there being various levels of generality at which to specify the output. If the belief the formation of which we are considering is a belief that there is a maple tree in front of me, that ties down the output side, and there is no scope for choosing between different ways of identifying it. If someone should suggest that the habit (the function) involved in its formation is one the output of which is a belief that there is a tree in front of me, or that there is a plant in front of me, that changes the subject. That is not the belief the formation of which I was investigating. If we assume that I believe everything entailed by something I believe (or to make it slightly more realistic, that I believe everything *obviously* entailed by something I believe), then if I believe that there is a maple tree in front of me, I *also* believe that there is a tree in front of me. But the latter designation is not a complete specification of the propositional content of the belief we are considering and hence does not suffice to individuate it. Therefore, a function that yields a belief that there is a tree in front of S on the input in question is *not* the function that is operative on this occasion. And so we need not worry about a plurality of alternatives for the level of generality at which to specify the output side of the operative function.

The input side and the function involved are a bit trickier because they, especially the function, are not so open to view. Just what features of the input are picked up by the mechanism and just how the function "uses" them to determine features of the output (i.e., just what the function is) is not so obvious. At this point the current objection forces me to become explicit about a basic assumption of my approach to the Generality Problem, namely, *psychological realism*. I assume that there is always a unique correct answer to the question "What mechanism, embodying what function, was operative in the generation of this belief?" I assume that just one way of generalizing from this particular input–belief output relationship reflects the actual psychological dynamics of the process. When I look out the window and form the belief that there is a maple tree there, there are, in the abstract, many functions that would yield a belief with that content from a visual presentation of that sort. The transition might be based on the leaf shape, the overall shape of the tree, the color of the leaves, the character of the bark, and so on, or some combination of such features. But I assume that only one of these possibilities is realized in this case. The mechanism that was operative embodied one of these ways of taking certain features of the concrete input rather than others as the ones that yield a belief with that content. Again, when my beliefs that *John will come to the party if he is well* and that *John is well* yield the belief that *John will come to the party*, there are many abstract possibilities as to the principle of inference involved. The mere fact that the inference exhibits a modus ponens form does not guarantee that this is the principle that was psychologically operative. I could have been utilizing a function that yields that belief on the basis of any beliefs about John, or on the basis of any set of beliefs one of which is a conditional, or . . . Nevertheless, according to my psychological realism, exactly one of those possibilities is realized in this case. And whichever one is realized, it is the reliability of that function, along with the epistemic status of the belief inputs, that is crucial for the epistemic status of the output.

Let me pause to note that in Feldman and Conee 1998 they make a big thing out of the point that a given input-output pair can be involved in many different functions and hence that specifying the input and output does not suffice to identify a function. They take that as a criticism of my position, even though in the article they are criticizing (Alston 1995) I recognize the point, as I did in the last paragraph, and there as here I tie it to the point that what goes into the individuation of the function is not the "raw" input in all its individual concreteness but rather what aspects of it are "picked up" by the mechanism and used, in accordance with the function, to determine the content of the output belief. This is illustrated by the two cases in the last paragraph, as it was in Alston 1995, but since it didn't catch the attention of Feldman and Conee, it deserves the underlining provided by this paragraph.

To return to the main thread of the discussion, like any form of realism, this one can be opposed. One can doubt or deny that the psyche really is determinate in this way, and here as elsewhere epistemological motives for antirealism are prominent. It may be claimed that we lack the access to the details of cognitive processes that would be required to determine in each case just what function is operative. One of Plantinga's objections to reliabilism is along these lines.

> Indeed, if, as Goldman suggests, the relevant type must be specified in psychological or physiological terms, we won't be able to specify any such types at all; our knowledge is much too limited for that. (Plantinga 1993a, 199)

This is not the place for a full-dress defense of psychological realism, but I will make a few points. First, the viability of reliable belief formation as an epistemic desideratum hangs on the viability of psychological realism. If there is no objective fact of the matter as to what input-output function is utilized in a given belief formation, then the notion of reliable belief formation is helpless before the Problem of Generality.

Second, we should not unduly inflate the epistemological requirements for psychological realism. It is reasonable to suppose that there are many objective facts we will never know about, and even facts we are incapable of knowing about. Details of the past of humanity, the earth, the solar system, and the universe present many examples of this. Hence less than ideal epistemic access to Xs is not fatal to realism about Xs.

Third, our cognitive access to belief-forming mechanisms is not as scanty as Plantinga makes it out to be. Although we can't peer into a psyche with some instrument and observe the little input-output functions doing their thing, we are in a similar situation with respect to many other matters about which we know something; and the approaches we use in those cases are available here too. When it is a question of what function was operative in my own case, I often have a "participant knowledge" of this. Though my knowledge of my own input-output mappings is far from ideally complete and although I am not immune to error, I typically can, by reflecting on what is going on, gain some significant degree of insight into what it was that led me to form a certain belief. In the perceptual cases, even if I can't spell out in detail the "atomic" perceptual cues that enabled me to recognize what I was looking at, still I have some insight into the look of the object that tipped me off; and I can recognize relevantly similar looks when they occur. In inferential cases I can often, if I am analytically inclined, formulate the principle(s) of inference on which I was relying; or at least I can recognize relevantly similar inferences when they occur. As for third-person cases, if I want to know what function was operative in Sam's inference about John's coming to the party, I can put him to the test in other cases with and without a modus ponens structure, and with or without the other features mentioned above. In that way I can try to find consistent patterns in the way he draws conclusions; and though success is not guaranteed, I might reach some fairly solid results. The perceptual cases are more difficult, but there too I can vary input-output relationships in such a way as to give myself a chance to find consistent, fairly stable patterns of relating perceptual presentation features to belief content. These techniques yield less than maximally conclusive results, for more than one reason. For one thing, a person might be utilizing a given function on one occasion, even though she doesn't do so regularly, often, or consistently.

For another thing, no matter how many competing hypotheses we have eliminated as to what function is operative on a given occasion, there are always more looming on the horizon. Nevertheless, by using techniques such as these, we are considerably better off than blankly ignorant as to what function is operative in a given case of belief formation.

Another point about my psychological realism. I don't want to overstress the determinacy and precision of belief-forming functions or, for that matter, belief contents. Indeterminacies to which all psychological states and operations are heir are to be found here as well. Some or all of my belief-forming habits may be such that there is some leeway as to exactly where certain perceptual features must be on relevant dimensions of size, color, pitch, and so on in order to generate a certain belief content. Even if the input sensitivity is perfectly precise, there may be some looseness in the way in which input features determine belief content. Indistinguishable inputs might on different occasions yield beliefs with somewhat different degrees of confidence. And so on. The psychological realism I espouse is committed only to a degree of determinacy of belief-forming mechanisms that is sufficient to make it worthwhile invoking them in thinking about the reliability of belief formation, as well as many other matters.

Here are two other complexities that would have to be recognized in an adequate theory of belief-forming processes. First, more than one habit might be involved in generating a particular belief. My belief that it is my wife's car that I see parked in our driveway might be generated both by a perceptual mechanism that takes account of features of my current visual experience and by an inferential mechanism that takes as input the belief that she told me when I left in the morning that she would be at home all day.[11] I don't think this kind of overdetermination poses any special difficulty for cognitive psychology, but it does require the epistemologist to make a decision as to which mechanism(s) is such that its reliability is crucial for a positive epistemic status of the belief. In this case I would suppose that, given that each process would have been sufficient by itself to produce the belief, it would seem reasonable to hold that the belief receives PES if either of the processes is sufficiently reliable.

The second complication is this. I have been talking as if every belief is generated by a single momentary input-output mapping. But many beliefs are arrived at only after a more or less extended period of deliberation,

---

[11] Note that this overdetermination by two different mechanisms working from two different inputs differs from the case mentioned earlier in which both visual presentation and background beliefs are required to generate the belief in question. In the present case, though not in the earlier one, each contributor could have been sufficient by itself to generate the belief.

search for evidence, weighing considerations pro and con, and so on. How are we to fit that sort of thing into the picture I have been painting? Here I believe that it is primarily the psychologist who has additional work to do. In developing the psychology of belief formation the cognitive psychologist has to decide how to represent the structure of these extended deliberative processes. For one thing, more than one input–belief output mapping could be involved. For another, the searches for relevant evidence and weighing of pro and con considerations are processes of a different character from belief acquisition. Perhaps we should say that the belief-forming process occurs only at the end of the deliberation (unless there are preliminary beliefs formed during the process), and that when it occurs it is of the simple, momentary sort of which I have been speaking. Or perhaps some other construal would be preferable. I am happy to leave this issue to the cognitive psychologist. So far as I can see, epistemology could work with whatever account seems best from the standpoint of psychological theory.

vii. Some More Serious Complications

A. The entire treatment in this chapter of belief-forming processes and their relation to basing beliefs on grounds has been on the assumption that such a process is limited to the operation of a functional input-output mechanism. But now I must face the fact that these are not the only kinds of processes that could reasonably be called "belief-forming processes". There are at least two ways in which belief-forming processes might differ from my chosen model. First, beliefs might result from processes that lack any input-output structure that is at all comparable to the phenomenon of a belief's being based on a ground. Indeed, it is at least conceivable that beliefs might eventuate from a process that involves nothing that would be properly described as psychological at all. In section v I dismissed this as a serious possibility for human beings, but even if there are such cases they are extremely rare and hence can be neglected in a general epistemology of belief.

B. A more serious consideration is that even where the final stage is of the functional input-output type, one could individuate the process more broadly by including earlier stages that lead up to that final stage and legitimately call it a belief-forming process. For example, if the proximate input is a perceptual experience, the process could be construed as including what is responsible for the formation of that experience. If the proximate input is a belief, the process could be construed as including what is responsible for that belief's being acquired or being activated at that time, and/or whatever is involved in coming to base another belief on that. This being the case, it might seem that we are faced with an indeterminacy as to just what process to take to give rise to a certain belief, an indeterminacy that can be resolved only by an arbitrary decision. Let's consider what to say about this.

First, can we restrict ourselves to the final stage in determining the extent to which the terminal belief has been formed in a reliable way? If so, we could say that it is the final stage that is crucial for epistemic purposes and that earlier stages can be ignored for an epistemologically relevant demarcation of the belief-forming process. And it must be admitted that if the process so construed passes the test of being such that it would yield a heavy preponderance of true beliefs in a suitable spread of cases, that would suffice for deeming it a reliable way of forming beliefs. We could still recognize that earlier stages have a bearing on the reliability, as they obviously do. If the visual appearance were not formed so as to reflect adequately the perceived object, that would adversely affect the chances of the resultant belief's being true. And if an input belief were not so formed as to be adequately grounded and so enjoy a PES, the output belief would not be rendered conditionally probable on being based on that input. But in both these cases the bearing of the earlier stage on the probable truth of the output belief comes through its bearing on the final input, the suitability of that to render probable a belief based on it. And so it still looks as if the final stage is all we need consider for epistemological purposes. It is worthy of note in this connection that the formulation I have been using for the reliability of a final process with doxastic input requires an adequately grounded input if the belief is to be unconditionally rendered probable. No such condition was built into the requirement for the reliability of a process with perceptually experiential input, but a parallel distinction could be drawn there between conditional and unconditional reliability, where the latter requires that the experiential input accurately reflects the perceived object. Why isn't this generally done? It may be partly because experiences that don't accurately reflect their object are much less common than inadequately grounded beliefs. Experiential inputs are largely produced by hard-wired mechanisms whereas belief formation is more subject to a variety of influences that can and often do go wrong. It may also be partly because unrepresentativeness of experiences is less easy to spot than inadequate grounding of belief.

But it remains true that some earlier stages are more epistemically desirable than others. The fact that they influence the probability of truth for the final belief output guarantees that, even if that influence does go through their influence on the final input. Moreover, they are worthy of attention for other reasons. They may be the explanation for a particular instance of a generally reliable type of belief formation yielding a false belief. That could happen because as a result of earlier stages in the process the final input lacked an epistemically desirable feature—being adequately grounded for a doxastic input and adequately reflecting the perceived object for a perceptual experience input.

C. There are further complications. Another class of influences on the epistemic status of the output belief consists of relevant evidence unknown to the subject. There is a considerable literature devoted to this topic. One of the staple examples concerns barns, an example introduced by Ginet and exploited by Goldman and many others. A father, while driving his young son through the country and identifying objects they pass, points to what he takes to be a barn and says "That's a barn". From the relatively brief glimpse he gets of it, the object looks just like a barn to him. As it happens, the area is full of fake barn facades that had been used for filming a movie. But what the father identified as a barn was a real barn, one of the very few in that vicinity. What should we say about the epistemic status of the father's belief that it was a barn? The standard treatment is to say that the belief was justified but did not count as knowledge. But I have ruled out that reaction for purposes of this book on both counts. In any event, it is clear that S's situation as described is less epistemically desirable than it would have been had there been fewer fake barn facades in the vicinity or had S's perception of the object been sufficient to enable him to discriminate it from a mere barn facade. And so here too there is something other than the final stage of the belief formation that has a bearing on the epistemic status of the belief. And here the influence on the final belief is not through its influence on the final input.

Examples of this sort are by no means restricted to perceptual belief formation. There are many examples in the literature of relevant evidence beyond S's ken that has an adverse effect on the epistemic status of a belief the input to which was purely doxastic. Let's say the detective, S, has strong reasons for believing that the butler committed the murder and he proceeds to charge him, unaware that the cook had just confessed. Again, there is something other than the final input-function–belief-output process that has a bearing on the epistemic status of the output. Here the unknown evidence is such as to show the final belief to be false. If S had been able to take account of it, there would have been a different final stage with a somewhat different input, a different function, and a different output belief.

So what should we say about these kinds of cases? For one thing, unlike the factors in B, they provide no reason for extending the belief-forming process. They are not further parts of a process leading to the belief, nor are they taken account of in the belief-forming process in question. The only influence they have on the general reliability of the process is, like the factors in B, that they are responsible for some false or otherwise epistemically disreputable outputs that count against the general reliability score. Hence they are worthy of notice as possible explanations of particular instances exhibiting a negative outcome.

One thing worth noting about these kinds of factors is that if they are unusual, as in the barn case and cases where unbeknownst to the subject a suspect has just confessed to a murder, they will automatically be excluded as factors influencing the reliability of a process-type by the restriction of cases to those "of the sort we typically encounter". But if they are of frequent occurrence in actual cases, as holds for something as unspecific as *some unknown relevant evidence*, then any influence they have on the computation of the general reliability of the process in question is already taken into account in the general formula.

D. Going back to the barns for a moment, note that the case illustrates two kinds of factors other than the final process that have a bearing on the epistemic status of the output. The relevance of evidence S does not possess we have already discussed. But we also made reference to S's inability to discriminate a real barn from a fake barn facade on the basis of the momentary fleeting glimpse he had of it. This introduces another factor that influences the epistemic status of belief outputs, namely, the discriminative and other cognitive capacities of the subject. That was not easy to notice in this case because that lack of discriminative capacity is so widely shared and not at all distinctive of this subject. But we can easily describe cases in which differences between subjects in this respect have a bearing on the epistemic status of a belief output. This can be illustrated for both doxastic and experiential inputs. For the former, consider the fact that subjects differ widely in their ability to discriminate valid from invalid deductive inferences and in their care to avoid too hastily jumping to conclusions of nondeductive inferences. For experiential inputs, consider the wide variation in abilities to perceptually discriminate different species of trees or of dogs or different makes of automobiles. The same intrinsic kind of visual input would lead one subject to identify a dog as an English setter and another to identify it as Scotch terrier. No doubt these two subjects would be employing different functions in going from the input to the belief. And so this kind of factor has a different role to play in the discussion from the other two I have been introducing. The main issue it brings up concerns a choice hitherto unmentioned in the discussion of the reliability of belief-forming processes, namely, over what range of subjects a belief-forming process-type should be construed as ranging. Up to now I have been tacitly assuming that it would range over something like all normal fairly mature human subjects. But that is not the only possible choice. It could range over all subjects with a certain level of one or another cognitive capacity. Or at one extreme it could be limited to one particular individual, or one at a certain period of time.

Again, our choice between alternatives must needs be on the basis of what is needed for epistemology. Just as with the first two choices, what is needed is something more general rather than something more particular or something of lesser scope. Since in epistemology we are seeking generalizations that apply to all reasonably normal and mature human subjects, it is that level of generality that we should aim for in our generalizations about, for example, the conditions of one or another epistemic desideratum.

E. Thus far in this section I have been focusing on reliability of processes. The considerations I have brought out could be reproduced with only minor modifications for the question how to construe the adequacy of grounds. All the factors recognized above as influencing the reliability of a belief-forming process also figure as influences on the epistemic status of a belief based on a certain ground. But there is one crucial difference. What launched the above examination was a question as to what boundaries to put on a given belief-forming process. Should we continue to construe it in terms of the final stage alone, or should it be extended backward in time? But there is no parallel problem for the adequacy of the ground of a belief. Here the very way the desideratum is specified leaves no room for a boundary-setting problem. Nothing prior to or external to the basing of a belief on a ground can be part of that on which the belief is based, however much it influences the epistemic status of the belief. Nevertheless, all the rest of the earlier discussion of the strengths and weaknesses of various factors can be applied to the adequacy-of-grounds desideratum.

It is time to sum up the results of the discussion in this section. The main conclusion is that we have found no compelling reason for construing belief-forming processes for the purposes of epistemology in any way other than the final-stage construal I have been developing and applying in this chapter. It is compatible with this to recognize the bearing of earlier stages on the conditional probability of the belief output. But that bearing always obtains via the bearing of the factor on the input to the final stage. As for relevant evidence beyond the subject's ken, we found that if it is of an unusual type, it is ruled out of consideration in the computation of the degree of reliability of the process by the restriction to "situations of the sort we typically encounter". While if it is commonly encountered, it will automatically be taken into account by that computation. As for the range of subjects over which these desiderata range, we concluded that the interests of epistemology are best served by concentrating on a fairly broad class of normal, fairly mature cognitive subjects.

All this is in addition to whatever support for our concentration on these desiderata as we have been construing them is forthcoming from the fact that they have been very prominent in the epistemology of belief from a justificationist perspective. That is fortunate because I am well advised to aim at some deeper reason for proceeding as I do than the fact that this is the way it is generally done. I fancy that the considerations of this section provide a somewhat deeper set of reasons for the prominence of these desiderata, as so construed, in the epistemology of the last fifty years or so.

viii. Proper Functioning of Cognitive Faculties

Now we can go into some detail concerning desideratum 4, the idea that a belief is formed by the proper functioning of one's cognitive faculties. This notion has become influential through Plantinga's important account of what he calls 'warrant'. Plantinga, like myself, wants nothing to do with the term 'justified' in epistemology. His term of choice for a central positive epistemic status of belief is *warrant*, defined as a quantity enough of which serves to convert true belief into knowledge. Here is a formulation of the conditions for warrant from the end of chapter 2 of Plantinga 1993b.

> ... a belief has warrant for me only if (1) it has been produced in me by cognitive faculties that are working properly (functioning as they ought to, subject to no cognitive dysfunction) in a cognitive environment that is appropriate for my kinds of cognitive faculties, (2) the segment of the design plan governing the production of that belief is aimed at the production of true beliefs, and (3) there is a high statistical probability that a belief produced under those conditions will be true. Under those conditions, furthermore, the degree of warrant is an increasing function of degree of belief. (46–47)

Note that since this principle is restricted to the *production* of a belief, it must be supplemented with parallel considerations concerning the strengthening and preservation of a belief, just as we have done with desiderata 2 and 3. Consider it done. And as with other material from the literature I have been discussing, it must be remembered that my interest in this is significantly different from the author's. Plantinga's interest in giving an account of warrant is to spell out what it takes to turn a true belief into knowledge. Since I am leaving knowledge aside here, my concern is different. I am interested in whether Plantingian warrant is an epistemic desideratum, as I have laid out the requirements for that, and if so, how it is related to other epistemic desiderata.

First, it is clear that Plantinga's conditions for warrant qualify it as directly truth-conducive in the sense of their satisfaction providing strong support for taking the belief in question to be true. This is guaranteed by his condition (3). In fact, that condition by itself is equivalent to reliability of belief formation as I have explicated that, provided we interpret "statistical" probability of truth not as a proportion of truths in some closed set of actual cases but rather as a frequency in an indefinitely large set of actual and possible cases, as in my explication of reliability.

But if (3) is enough by itself to guarantee truth conducivity, the question remains of whether the other clauses make any contribution to truth conducivity or whether (3) is bearing that whole load alone. This issue is complicated by the fact that as (3) is formulated, it is not independent of the other clauses; it specifies that beliefs "produced under these conditions", that is, satisfying (1) and (2), will be probably true. Hence there is no possibility of (3)'s going it alone. But we can still ask whether (1) and/or (2) are truth-conducive on their own, or whether warrant enjoys that status only on the condition that (3) is added. I won't engage in a quixotic attempt to raise this question for (1) and (2) separately, since they are so formulated as to work together hand in glove. Taking them together, it seems clear that their satisfaction at least comes close to entailing a high probability (of a frequency sort) of truth for a belief, B, on condition of that satisfaction. For if B is produced by faculties that operate according to a design plan that is aimed at truth (2), and if they are functioning properly (in accordance with that design plan) in an environment suited to their functioning (1), then it seems inescapable that any belief so produced would be highly likely to be true. How would a faculty with that kind of function be "functioning properly" in the kind of environment in which that is its proper function if it were not doing what it is its function to do, at least by and large? Only by and large, because external obstacles or interferences can prevent any human faculty or mechanism from producing the result it was designed to produce even if it is functioning as properly as you like. A radio receiver might fail to bring in a broadcast not because of a malfunctioning of its interior apparatus but because of an external electrical field that interferes with reception. But the combination of (1) and (2) would seem to ensure that any belief for which they hold enjoys a high likelihood of truth.

So it looks as if there was no need for Plantinga to add condition (3) to his account of warrant in order for it to be epistemically valuable. But our interest in this chapter is in the converse question. Are (1) and (2) needed in addition to (3), that is, the belief's being formed reliably, to ensure truth conducivity? As we have seen, we can't put the question in just that way. But suppose we disengage (3) from its dependence on (1) and (2) and formulate it as follows.

> 3A) The belief was formed in such a way that there is a high statistical (frequency) probability that it is true.

(3A) is equivalent to our construal of a belief's being formed reliably. We can then ask whether (1) and (2) add anything to the truth conducivity of (3A).

Since (3A) in this version straightforwardly implies that a warranted belief enjoys a high conditional probability of truth, the only way that (1) and/or (2) could add anything to this would be by ratcheting high probability of truth up to a necessity of truth, and they certainly don't do that. Thus, though (1) and (2) tend toward a preponderance of true beliefs in the output of faculties that meet these conditions, they don't really add anything to the truth conducivity of (3A). Hence they are best thought of as an explanation of the high probability of truth for a warranted belief that is merely stipulated by (3A) without explanation. The explanation is that the belief is one produced by the proper functioning of a faculty that meets the conditions embodied in (1) and (2).

Plantinga has an argument for the necessity of the proper-functioning clause for warrant. But that is based on taking warrant, by definition, to be what converts true belief into knowledge. He deploys a raft of imaginative counterexamples against the claim of reliability to perform this role. Here is an example.

> ... suppose (contrary to what most of us believe) the *National Enquirer* is in fact extremely reliable in its accounts of extraterrestrial events. One day it carries screaming headlines: STATUE OF ELVIS FOUND ON MARS!! Due to cognitive malfunction ... I am extremely gullible, in particular with respect to the *National Enquirer*, always trusting it implicitly on the topic of extraterrestrials. (And, due to the same malfunction, I don't believe anything that would override the belief in question.) Then my belief that a statue of Elvis was found on Mars is in fact based on a reliable indicator ... and I don't know or believe anything overriding this belief. But surely the belief has little by way of warrant. (Plantinga 1993a, 191)

The reason for saying that the belief lacks warrant is that I surely don't *know* that a statue of Elvis was found on Mars, and if the belief had warrant and if, as we are supposing, it is true, I would know it. Plantinga's suggestion as to why I don't know it is that the belief was not formed by the *proper functioning* of the cognitive faculties involved. I will not contest the claim that cognitive malfunction is involved here. But I do think that a case could be made for the claim that given the assumptions built into the case, I would know that a statue of Elvis had been found on Mars, and that the reason we find this so counterintuitive is that it is difficult to take seriously, even for purposes of an imaginary case, that the belief is true or that the *National Enquirer* is reliable about extraterrestrial matters. But here I am not concerned to argue with Plantinga about his alleged counterexample but only to point out that that is not my concern. My only claim is that whether or not reliable belief formation, as I have explained that, is sufficient to make true belief into knowledge, it is clearly a directly truth-conducive epistemic desideratum. If the requirement of proper function of cognitive faculties is needed for knowledge, it is certainly not needed, and not shown to be needed even if the alleged counterexamples are genuine, for epistemic desirability. Hence (3A) alone qualifies Plantingian warrant as a directly truth-conducive desideratum. And, if we leave aside knowledge and its conditions, the whole package of (1), (2), and (3A) is best construed as reliability of belief formation (3A) together with an explanation of that—(1) and (2).

It is also worthy of note that 4 differs from 3 in that the reliability component of the former, namely, (3A), is not construed, as I have construed 3, in terms of a functional input-output relationship. Hence it does not require for a belief to be warranted that it be based on a ground. And hence it lacks the virtual equivalence with 2 that is enjoyed by 3. Thus it is a form of reliable belief formation that can be embraced by one who denies or doubts, as we have seen Plantinga do, that every belief has a ground.

Plantingian warrant is also different from my functional account of belief-forming processes in working with much larger cognitive units. The cognitive faculties distinguished by Plantinga are such as perception (or perhaps separate perceptual modalities), memory, introspection, rational intuition, and reasoning of various sorts. Whereas the input-function-output units involved in the above account of belief-forming processes cut things up much more finely. This appears more sharply for the noninferential processes. Even if, as suggested above, some perceptual belief-forming mechanisms are less than maximally specific, still many of them are. And the point holds even more strictly for memory, introspection, and rational intuition. This is not to deny that proper functioning of cognitive faculties, with faculties individuated as Plantinga does, is a directly truth-conducive epistemic desideratum but only to mark one important respect in which this desideratum differs from reliability of belief-forming processes as I have explained that. In this respect warrant goes along with some versions of desideratum 5, which will be treated in the next three sections.

ix. Intellectual Virtues: Sosa and Goldman

The concept of reliable belief formation that is involved in my development of 3 is the concept of a particular way of going from one or more beliefs or experiences of a certain kind to a belief with a certain kind of content. As such, it is impersonal. It is not restricted to a certain individual subject. Indefinitely many subjects can avail themselves of the *same* way of forming beliefs, the same realized input-output function. (This impersonality is shared by 2 and 4.) However reliable various realized input-output belief-forming functions are, this tells us nothing about the reliability of a particular individual's belief formation. It tells us nothing about the relative frequency with which the beliefs formed by S, or that would be formed by S, are true. And this, the *reliability of a cognitive subject with respect to belief formation*, is something in which we are often interested. The interest may be in how good S is at hitting the mark with respect to a restricted class of beliefs—concerning ancient Greek history, the doings of friends and acquaintances, baseball statistics, the potentialities of graduate students, or whatever. At the limit we may be interested in S's reliability at belief formation concerning *anything* to which she turns her attention. In discussions of reliability these two notions—reliability of ways of belief formation, and reliability of a subject at forming true beliefs—are often conflated or at least not clearly and explicitly distinguished. But they are very different.

The topic of the reliability of cognitive subjects brings us to the last of the desiderata in Group II.

5. Belief B was formed by the exercise of an intellectual virtue.

I am not prepared to give in this book an extended treatment of what an intellectual virtue is and what it is for a belief to be formed by the *exercise* of an intellectual virtue, a treatment that is at all comparable in scope and depth to my treatment of adequacy of grounds and of the reliability of a way of forming beliefs. Partly this is because I have not thought long enough or deeply enough about intellectual virtues and their functioning in belief formation to have any well-considered views on the subject, much less original well-considered views. And partly it is because I cannot give extended treatment to all candidates for epistemic desiderata without inflating the book to an intolerable extent. Hence I restrict my treatment to candidates in which I am more interested and about which I have more of significance to say. What I shall do in this section, then, is of exemplary modesty. I aspire only to get a sense of the conditions under which the role of intellectual virtue in belief formation would be a truth-conducive role, and then refer the reader to literature in which the topic is developed in greater detail. Again, I have to say that although this discussion, like the literature with which I am interacting, is specifically about belief formation, we must keep in mind that if intellectual virtues play a key role there, they can be expected to play a similar role in belief strengthening and belief preservation.

What is nowadays called "virtue epistemology" is a sprawling, diverse, even chaotic territory. There is not even a rough commonality as to what counts as an intellectual virtue, much less how it functions in belief formation or how this bears on epistemic status. I will resist the temptation to pretend that the field is more unified than it is, and I will illustrate the diversity by focusing on a few interesting cases.

There are several major divisions between virtue epistemologists. One concerns how to think of intellectual virtues and where to look for them. Another has to do with the place of virtues in epistemology as a whole. A third has to do with the relation between intellectual and moral virtues. I will begin the discussion with the second of these differences. On the one hand, one could be interested in intellectual virtue as an addition to the more usual epistemological concerns with belief and knowledge. A study of intellectual virtue is a study of a kind of epistemic value of subjects of belief and knowledge, ways in which *persons* can be better or worse epistemically. This could become a department of epistemology without impinging markedly on the departments more familiar from the epistemological literature. But one might also seek to use intellectual virtue to give a novel treatment of the more familiar topics of knowledge and justified (rational, warranted, credible . . .) belief. This latter emphasis bulks large in the recent literature on the subject.[12] Explanations of knowledge and justified belief in terms of intellectual virtue have mushroomed and taken center stage. Confining myself to a short treatment, I will concentrate on this more popular type of virtue epistemology, though, as usual, replacing 'is justified' with 'has positive epistemic status'.

---

[12] This could be, and often is, combined with using the new approach to treat epistemic fields that have been mostly ignored in recent times, such as understanding.

I begin with Ernest Sosa. His initial introduction of intellectual virtue runs as follows.

> Let us define an intellectual virtue or faculty as a competence in virtue of which one would mostly attain the truth and avoid error in a certain field of propositions F, when in certain conditions C ... a faculty or virtue would normally be a fairly stable disposition on the part of a subject *relative to an environment*. Being in conditions C with respect to propositions X would range from just being conscious and entertaining X—as in the case of "I think" or "I am"—to seeing an object O in good light at a favorable angle and distance, and without obstruction, etc. (Sosa 1991, 138–139)

It is clear from Sosa's disjunction of 'virtue' and 'faculty' that, as he says, he is thinking of a virtue as a (fairly stable) competence or ability. And in the course of his discussion he takes intellectual "virtues" to be such things as perceptual capacities, reasoning capacities, memory capacities—pretty much the sorts of things Plantinga calls 'faculties'. Further spelling out the reference to "an environment" in the above quotation, he points out, for example, that "relative to our actual environment A, our automatic experience-belief mechanisms count as virtues that yield much truth and justification. Of course relative to the demonic environment D [controlled by the Cartesian evil demon] such mechanisms are not virtuous and yield neither truth nor justification". (1991, 144).

Neglecting the many subtle distinctions Sosa draws within the epistemic justification territory, we can get the general idea of the way in which he seeks to get epistemological mileage out of what he calls 'virtue' by saying that he takes justification (at least the most basic sort of justification that he calls 'aptness') of a belief B relative to an environment E to consist in B's resulting from what relative to E is an intellectual virtue as defined above.

Here are a couple of more explicit later formulations.

I. S has an intellectual virtue V(C,F) relative to environment E if and only if S has an inner nature I such that

if (i) S is in E and has I,
    (ii) P is a proposition in field F,
    (iii) S is in conditions C with respect to P, and
    (iv) S believes or disbelieves P,
then (v) S is very likely right with regard to P. (1991, 284)

II. S believes P out of intellectual virtue V(C,F) iff

    (a) S is in environment E such that S has intellectual virtue V(C,F) relative to E,

(b) P is a proposition in F,
(c) S is in C with respect to P, and
(d) S believes P. (1991, 287)

Then, again ignoring a lot of the complexities of the view, we see that the rough idea is that S is justified in believing that P, which is in field F *iff* S believes P out of intellectual virtue V (C,F).

So far it looks as if this view amounts to a kind of reliabilism about justification with very large units (faculties) for generalizing over particular belief formations. The main distinction would be that the reliable belief formations that count as generating justification are restricted to those that stem from relatively stable belief-forming *dispositions* or *capacities*. (Sosa does not sufficiently distinguish between these.) These dispositions or capacities are termed 'virtues' in apparent disregard of what are called intellectual virtues in most of the tradition. (We'll see what that looks like in the discussion of Zagzebski below.) I suppose that Sosa's rationale for using 'virtue' in this way is that from Plato and Aristotle on, virtues are regarded as relatively stable and deep-seated excellencies of character, and the reliable belief-forming dispositions Sosa calls 'virtues' are clearly intellectual excellencies.

If we move out of "justification" talk and into "epistemic desideratum" talk, there can be no doubt that the formation of a belief out of an intellectual virtue, as construed by Sosa, is an epistemically desirable feature of a belief since it renders the belief very likely to be true and so entails that, just as reliable belief formation and forming a belief on an adequate ground do. And the possession of an intellectual virtue, since it makes possible the formation of beliefs out of intellectual virtue thereby, is itself an epistemic desideratum of the subject. Apart from the distinctions between levels of justification, which I have passed over, I can't see that Sosa's way of securing this result enjoys any superiority over desiderata 2 and 3 other than ensuring that what makes for the epistemic desirability of the belief is something relatively stable in the subject. This is a common thread that runs through most of current "virtue epistemology". What becomes the heart of the matter, the root from which other epistemic desiderata spring, is an intellectual excellence in the cognitive subject. It is in terms of this that epistemic desiderata for beliefs (and also knowledge) are explicated. This shift to a focus on excellencies of the subject (or agent) is common to virtue epistemology and to the emphasis on virtue in much of contemporary ethics.

I want to stress that the foregoing brief exposition of Sosa's virtue epistemology is severely truncated and hence does not begin to give an adequate idea of the complexity, power, and subtlety of his position. To go further in that direction the reader is referred to Sosa 1991.

A version of virtue epistemology very similar to Sosa's (as Goldman acknowledges) is found in Goldman's "Epistemic Folkways and Scientific Epistemology", chapter 9 of Goldman 1992a. One can anticipate which of the pair in the title Goldman considers to provide (at least the promise of) pure epistemological gold and which gives us only raw unrefined ore. Intellectual virtues are assigned mostly to the ore, the epistemic folkways, which constitute "our ordinary epistemic assessments", whereas "scientific epistemology" deals with the reliability of processes of belief formation. Since my present concern is with virtue epistemology, I will concentrate here on Goldman's treatment of epistemic folkways.

> The basic approach is, roughly, to identify the concept of justified belief with the concept of belief obtained through the exercise of intellectual virtues (excellencies). Beliefs acquired (or retained) through a chain of "virtuous" psychological processes qualify as justified; those acquired partly by cognitive "vices" are derogated as unjustified.... The hypothesis I wish to advance is that the epistemic evaluator has a mentally stored set, or list, of cognitive virtues and vices. When asked to evaluate an actual or hypothetical case of belief, the evaluator considers the processes by which the belief was produced, and matches these against his list of virtues and vices. If the processes match virtues only, the belief is classified as justified. If the processes are matched partly with vices, the belief is categorized as unjustified....
>
> I shall assume that the virtues include belief formation based on sight, hearing, memory, reasoning in certain "approved" ways, and so forth. The vices include intellectual processes like forming beliefs by guesswork, wishful thinking, and ignoring contrary evidence. Why these items are placed in their respective categories remains to be explained.... I plan to explain them by reference to reliability. (157–158)

Note that the treatment is from the standpoint of the evaluator of beliefs rather than the subject of beliefs (though the subject, of course, might also figure as evaluator). Though Goldman does not make this explicit, he is presumably taking the process-types he calls 'virtues' and 'vices' to be relatively stable dispositions of the subject, as Sosa does. In any event, his virtue epistemology is distinguished from straight reliabilism in a somewhat different way from Sosa's. For Goldman the epistemic evaluation of beliefs has a two-level structure. The virtues and vices are selected on the basis of reliability or unreliability, but the epistemic evaluation of beliefs is carried out by consulting the lists of virtues and vices, not directly from considerations of reliability. As Goldman points out, this is analogous to rule utilitarianism, where considerations of utility are used to formulate general rules of conduct, with particular actions being assessed by reference to those rules rather than directly from considerations of utility.

There is much more to Goldman's account of epistemic folkways, but to round off this brief exposition I need to say something about the other half of the dichotomy, "normative scientific epistemology". Goldman insists that this should preserve continuity with the folkways, at least to the extent of keeping reliability as the court of last appeal. But it will seek improved accounts of virtuous and vicious processes by using the results of cognitive psychology to obtain more adequate accounts of the nature of our belief-forming processes and their individuation and interrelations. The bottom line for our present concerns is that Goldman's conception of an intellectual virtue, and the ones he emphasizes, are in the same ball park as Sosa's—roughly, ways of forming beliefs that are more or less reliable. Again, we have basically a form of reliabilism with a bit of frosting in the form of more or less stable dispositions on the part of cognitive subjects to form beliefs in certain ways. As with Sosa the main claim of the virtues to be epistemic desiderata stems from the reliability requirements in the background.

x. Intellectual Virtues: Zagzebski

My final exhibit in this rapid survey of virtue epistemologists is Zagzebski 1996. This book I regard as the richest, most original, and most powerful contemporary essay in virtue epistemology. As such, any brief treatment will be even more fragmentary and inadequate than my account of Sosa and Goldman. Again, my concern will be to determine whether Zagzebski has developed a feature of beliefs that is epistemically desirable from the epistemic standpoint defined in terms of the truth goal. As you will see, extracting such a feature from her virtue-based epistemology requires doing a certain amount of violence to her thinking. But once it is understood what my purpose is and that it does not include a faithful adherence to her own views, I believe that she will forgive me for making this use of her work.

Zagzebski's notion of intellectual virtue, and her consequent identification of particular virtues, differs sharply from that of Sosa and Goldman. Her lists, modeled on much of the traditional literature from Aristotle on, comprise what we might call fairly well entrenched dispositions to conduct one's intellectual conduct in one way rather than another. Rather than faculties of belief formation, like those of Sosa and Goldman, they are habitual ways of cognitive behavior each of which can typically be manifested in the exercise of more than one of the Sosa-Goldman faculties. They primarily have to do with relatively high-level cognitive activities involving deliberation, search for evidence, weighing of pro and con considerations, and the like. Here is a typical list.

> Examples include intellectual carefulness, perseverance, humility, vigor, flexibility, courage, and thoroughness, as well as open-mindedness, fair-mindedness, insightfulness, and the virtues opposed to wishful thinking, obtuseness, and conformity. One of the most important virtues, I believe, is intellectual integrity. (Zagzebski 1996, 155)

The general account of the nature of a virtue, applicable to both moral and intellectual virtue (between which Zagzebski sees no sharp difference), is, broadly speaking, Aristotelian in character, with some modern innovations.

> A **virtue**, then, can be defined as **a deep and enduring acquired excellence of a person, involving a characteristic motivation to produce a certain desired end and reliable success in bringing about that end.** What I mean by a motivation is a disposition to have a motive; a motive is an action-guiding emotion with a certain end, either internal or external. (137)

Several things are to be noted about this definition. First, unlike faculties, a virtue is acquired. Faculties may appear only at a certain stage of maturation, and they can be modified, but they have a strong innate basis. Second, a virtue is essentially a motivation to produce a certain end, and one has the virtue only if one is generally successful in bringing about that end. Since motivation is at the heart of the matter, Zagzebski holds that "each virtue is definable in terms of a particular motivation. For example, benevolence is the virtue according to which a person is characteristically motivated to bring about the well-being of others and is reliably successful in doing so" (165). As for intellectual virtues, she holds that "the intellectual virtues can be defined in terms of derivatives from the motivation for knowledge and reliable success in attaining the ends of these motivations" (166). Thus all intellectual virtues have the same ultimate aim, differing only in aiming at different means to that end.

It is beginning to sound as if this virtue epistemology, though very different in its details from the Sosa-Goldman type, will have a similar bearing on the truth conducivity of having and acting on intellectual virtues.

Though Zagzebski portrays acting out of intellectual virtue as aimed at *knowledge* rather than at *true belief*, since she also takes knowledge to involve true belief we still have the truth goal in a central place. But things are not so simple.

> ... the intellectual virtues ... are all forms of the motivation to have cognitive contact with reality, where this includes more than what is usually

expressed by saying that people desire truth. . . . [U]nderstanding is also a form of a cognitive contact with reality, one that has been considered a component of the knowing state in some periods of philosophical history. . . . [I]t is a state that includes the comprehension of abstract structures of reality apart from the propositional. . . . Although all intellectual virtues have a motivational component that aims at cognitive contact with reality, some of them may aim more at understanding, or perhaps at other epistemic states that enhance the quality of the knowing state, such as certainty, than at the possession of truth per se. (167)

So the ultimate aim of intellectual virtues ranges over more than true belief. But since it does include that, I will focus on that part for my purposes, and consider whether the possession of, and acting from, intellectual virtues as portrayed by Zagzebski is a desideratum from the epistemic point of view as I have characterized that, and moreover an epistemic desideratum of the primary sort that I have put under the rubric *truth-conducive* desiderata. I will now cite some of Zagzebski's epistemic definitions to give a partial idea of how this works out.

A **justified belief** is what a person who is motivated by intellectual virtue, and who has the understanding of his cognitive situation a virtuous person would have, might believe in like circumstances.

An **unjustified belief** is what a person who is motivated by intellectual virtue, and who has the understanding of his cognitive situation a virtuous person would have, would not believe in like circumstances. (241)

Do these last two definitions, along with the above account of the nature of an intellectual virtue, imply that actions that lead to a belief and are motivated by an intellectual virtue thereby lead to a belief that is likely to be true? To answer that question we need to be more explicit both about the aim of an intellectual virtue and about the force that 'justified' carries with it here.

It looks as if we could settle the question in the affirmative just by citing a statement that specifies the intended force of 'justified'.

A key difference between knowledge and justifiedness is that the latter is a quality that even at its best only makes it *likely* that a belief is true. Justifiedness is a property that a belief has in virtue of being a member of a *set* of beliefs of a certain kind. Similarly, we call a *person* justified in having a belief because she has a property that (among other things) *tends* to lead her to true beliefs. (268)

Does that settle the matter decisively with respect to truth conducivity? I'm afraid not. We still have to look at the distinction between the ultimate and the proximate defining motivation of an intellectual virtue. If the only aim that is essential to a given intellectual virtue were the acquisition of knowledge, then the clause in the definition of 'virtue' that requires reliable success would guarantee that one could not form a belief out of an intellectual virtue without the belief's being likely to be true. But given that the only reliable success that is required for its being the case that one forms a belief out of a given intellectual virtue is the success in achieving the end of the motivation that defines that intellectual virtue in distinction from other intellectual virtues, that changes the picture. Given the motivations that are distinctive of the different intellectual virtues on Zagzebski's account, it is wildly implausible to suppose that success in realizing their ends would make a belief likely to be true. Consider a couple of examples, *perseverance* and *open-mindedness*. To be successful in the former is, naturally, to persevere (up to a reasonable point) in seeking knowledge about something. But it is clear that one could persevere as long and as assiduously as you like without forming a belief that is likely to be true. Such is the fallibility of human nature. The same can be said of all the other paradigmatic intellectual virtues cited by Zagzebski. To take the other one just mentioned, one could be paradigmatically open-minded in collecting and appraising evidence and in taking seriously objections to one's views and still reach conclusions that are not likely to be true.

What seems to have happened here is that Zagzebski has failed to keep in mind the distinction between the ultimate and the proximate defining end of each intellectual virtue. Hence she is led to overinflate the epistemic consequence of forming a belief by acts motivated by an intellectual virtue. Moreover, what she would have needed for modest truth conducivity is not the ultimate end her account ascribes to all intellectual virtues—the acquisition of knowledge. Reliable success in achieving that end would give her too much for justified belief as contrasted with knowledge. It looks as if what she would need to get the results she claims in the passage last cited for justified belief is an ultimate aim at true belief. If her definitions of justified belief would require success in attaining that ultimate aim as well as the proximate end of an intellectual virtue, then a justified belief would thereby be likely to be true, and its being justified would be an epistemic desideratum by my lights. Her account could be modified in this direction. But that would disturb the unity of her theory, in which the ultimate motivation inherent in intellectual virtues is the same whether we are thinking of them as generative of justification or of knowledge.

The above discrepancy in Zagzebski's virtue epistemology is interestingly connected with her difference from Sosa and Goldman over where to locate intellectual virtues. As we have seen, the latter identify intellectual virtues as reliable ways of forming beliefs and so have no difficulty in taking the exercise of intellectual virtues, and at a second remove their possession, as truth-conducive epistemic desiderata. But Zagzebski's intellectual virtues are further removed from the actual processes of belief formation. They are dispositions to conduct oneself in ways that are conducive, if the situation cooperates sufficiently, to forming beliefs in reliable ways. Hence there is more room for slips between cup and lip, and hence there is a more tortuous route from success in the defining aim of a motivation in Zagzebski's account to a property of beliefs that is directly truth-conducive.

xi. Conclusion on Intellectual Virtue

My tentative conclusion from this survey of virtue epistemologies is as follows. (It is tentative both because of the small sample of epistemologists examined and because of the incomplete treatment of each one.) In order to get truth-conducive epistemic desiderata out of the possession or exercise of intellectual virtues, we have to build into such virtues a reliable way of forming beliefs. This is done in Sosa's and Goldman's accounts but at the price of using 'virtue' in a seemingly arbitrary way. It looks to all the world that what we have in both cases is a reliabilist account of the epistemic status of belief that differs from other versions of reliabilism only by the restriction to well-entrenched and relatively stable reliable ways of forming beliefs. And it looks as if all the truth conducivity comes from the reliabilist underlay and none of it from the intellectual-virtue frosting. Zagzebski uses 'virtue' in a much more traditional and intuitively congenial way, but she fails in her attempt to develop from that an epistemic status for beliefs that is truth-conducive. She might be able to remedy this defect, but it would require a great deal more attention to the relation between the proximate and a (suitable) ultimate end of the motivation she takes to be definitive of intellectual virtues. The upshot is that our examination has not found much promise in virtue epistemology for distinctively epistemic desiderata of belief.

I want to emphasize that nothing I have said has any tendency to show that an attention to intellectual virtues has no importance for epistemology. My interests in the above are limited, being confined to a search for truth-conducive epistemic statuses of beliefs. I have said nothing, for example, about Zagzebski's virtue-oriented account of knowledge. Nor have I looked into the possible values for epistemology of the concentration on epistemically valuable features of cognitive subjects that comes out of a study of epistemic virtues. But as far as my program in this book is concerned, I do not find much of distinctive value in virtue epistemology.

CHAPTER 7

ADDITIONAL EPISTEMIC DESIDERATA

i. Group III Desiderata

The previous two chapters, devoted to the directly TC desiderata, are the longest in the book. I take this to be warranted by the primary role of directly TC desiderata in epistemic evaluation, as that was explained in Chapter 3. I can now go on to what needs to be said about the undiscredited desiderata that are more indirectly related to the truth goal, those in Groups III and V. I can refer the reader back to Chapter 3 for the reasons for taking these desiderata to be at least indirectly related to the truth goal. After a brief reminder of the main points of that discussion, I will go on to clear up a few more issues concerning these desiderata.

First, here are the Group III and Group V listings from Chapter 3.

III. *Desiderata that are thought to be favorable to the realization of truth.*

6. S has some high-grade cognitive access to the evidence, etc. (and perhaps to its sufficiency).
7. S has higher-level knowledge, or well-grounded belief, that B has some positive epistemic status and/or as to what is responsible for that.
8. S is able to carry out a successful defense of the positive epistemic status of B.

V. *Goals of cognition that have intrinsic value as such over and above truth, but have that value only on the presupposition of truth.*

12. Explanation
13. Understanding
14. Coherence
15. Systematicity

The Group III items all consist in higher-level epistemological knowledge or well-grounded belief, the potentiality for this, or something that requires this. Their main claim to truth conducivity comes from the extent to which higher-level epistemological knowledge or what it makes possible is a help in ensuring, so far as we can, that the beliefs we form are true rather than false. The basic idea is that if we are able to monitor the epistemic status of candidates for belief, that puts us in a position to see to it, so far as we have control over such matters, that the beliefs we form are of high positive epistemic status and hence probably true on the condition that they are based on the ground on which they are based. It must be pointed out that this advantage obtains only for PES that implies probability of truth. If that status is of the sort emphasized by certain internalist epistemologists and discussed in Chapter 5, section iii, then these Group III desiderata are not even indirectly truth-conducive, and such value as they have must be sought elsewhere. In that case they will not be *epistemically* valuable, as I have explicated that kind of value.

The Group V desiderata are related to true belief not as a means thereto but as presupposing it. Although they are of intrinsic importance on their own, that importance depends on the belief in question being true or on the system of beliefs in question having a high proportion of true beliefs. A coherent system of mostly false beliefs, or an inaccurate explanation of a phenomenon, or a theory that unifies a lot of diverse phenomena but fails to get its subject matter right may have some value or other, perhaps aesthetic, but it is of no particular value for the cognitive enterprise.

Now for some further points. All the items in Group III are subject to variation in degree along different dimensions. The cognitive access can be more or less direct. At a maximum there is what Ginet (1975, 34) calls "direct recognizability", defined as follows: ". . . if a certain fact obtains, then it is directly recognizable to S at a given time if and only if, provided that S at that time has the concept of that sort of fact, S need at that time only to reflect clear-headedly on the question of whether or not that fact obtains in order to know that it does". At the other extreme there is the possibility of determining that the fact obtains by engaging in extensive and complex research over a considerable period of time. And there are various intermediate degrees of ready access. Strongly internalist epistemologists like Chisholm and Ginet make it a requirement for something counting toward the justification of a belief that the subject be able to ascertain it just on reflection. They have little or no interest in lesser degrees of access. But on my nonjustificationist approach all degrees of access to the epistemic status of beliefs are epistemic desiderata of varying degrees of magnitude. The more direct the access, the greater its epistemic value, but even the more indirect, unsure, and tortuous access is of more epistemic value than no access at all.

I should note that my rejection of justificationism looks particularly attractive when that epistemology takes the extreme internalist form of requiring Ginet's "direct recognizability" as a condition for anything contributing to the justification of a belief. For since, at most, current conscious states of the subject and simple self-evidence meet this requirement, the position is doomed to extreme paucity of what can bestow justification on beliefs. It is only by the most extreme measures that this internalist justificationism can represent contingent beliefs about things beyond the subject's current experience as justified. For some cases in point see Chisholm 1989 and BonJour and Sosa 2003, chapter 5.

Desideratum 7 ranges over a wide variety of cognitive relations to epistemic statuses of beliefs. Knowledge stands at the summit of the hierarchy, and below it are various grades of well-groundedness of belief. They can be arranged in different orders—strength of grounds, strength of conviction, resistance to contrary considerations, and so on. Since knowledge, we assume, presents a fixed maximum that does not admit of degrees, it is not surprising that it should have been the focus of most of the attention in discussion of 7, but strongly supported belief that falls short of knowledge should not be ignored. When one holds that higher-level cognition of the epistemic status of a belief is part of the analysis of the concept of having such an epistemic status, circularity threatens. For example, if one holds that part of the concept of being justified in believing that p is that one is justified in believing that one is justified in believing that p, one is in the unhappy position of using the concept of being justified in believing that X in the definition of being justified in believing that X.[1] But that is no problem for what I am doing here, partly because I am not dealing with the justification of belief and partly because I not offering definitions of epistemic concepts. Hence I am free to recognize higher-level epistemological knowledge or well-supported belief as an epistemic desideratum without worrying about circularity.

[1] This requirement also suffers from generating an infinite regress. See Alston 1989, chap. 9.

ii. Group V Desiderata

Turning to Group V, let's first consider 12, explanation. It's clear enough that understanding why things happen, why facts obtain, is one of the main things we seek in our cognitive endeavors. Even if we possess an enormous quantity of knowledge of, or well-supported belief in, particular facts, if there is no grasp of why the facts that obtain do so, we are missing something crucially important for the intellectual life. Acquiring explanations of various facts and phenomena is one of our chief intellectual aims. And the fact that we seek the *correct* account of why something is the case underlines the point that we have completely reached the goal of explanation only if we have discerned the *true* explanation of the explanandum in question; and in this way explanation has its cognitive desirability only when associated with truth, or at least the probability of truth. But it may be questioned whether explanation qualifies as a cognitive desideratum in the same way as truth. For, it might be said, explanations are simply one kind of subjects of truth, one sort of proposition that is either true or false. Some propositions attribute properties to objects, some record events or happenings, some specify mathematical quantities, some indicate logical relations, and so on. We don't list property attributions, event records, logical relations, and so on as epistemic desiderata. Why should explanation be put on a list of epistemic desiderata when these other types of propositions are not?

That's a good question. Its force comes from the fact that not all propositions that are subject to truth values are explanatory in character, just as not all of them have to do with logical relations, property possession, and so on. But where explanation differs from the others is the way it spreads over all subject matters. Whenever any claim is made about anything other than an explanation, one can seek an explanation of its being so rather than otherwise. We can ask, "Why does this object have this property?", "Why did this happen where and when it did?", "Why does this proposition entail that proposition?", "Why does this substance weigh more than that one?", and so on. So explanation is one sort of thing we can seek with respect to any subject matter whatever. Hence it has a sort of universality as a goal of cognition that is lacking for the other kinds of propositions with which the objection was comparing it.

Many books have been written on the subject of explanation—what it is to give an explanation of something, what the conditions are for an attempted explanation to be the correct explanation, what the major kinds of explanation are, how they are related to one another, and so on. I can't go into all that in this book. I will have to work with an unanalyzed concept of an explanation, recognizing that it hides a multiplicity of distinctions, and be content with bringing out the way in which explanation as a cognitive goal is related to truth, and hence that it is, and how it is, an epistemic desideratum.

Though I put understanding (13) as a separate item on the list, it is best treated in terms of the other items in Group V, since their achievement all counts as one or another form of understanding, as I will bring out in due course. There are other forms of understanding as well, but I must forego any attempt at a comprehensive treatment.

Now for coherence and systematicity. The latter may seem to be just another term for coherence. And indeed coherence is a term that is variously understood. Explanation is often subsumed under it as well. It is often thought that one respect in which one system is more coherent than another is that the former involves more explanations of items in the system. But since explanation has virtues of its own apart from considerations of anything naturally called 'coherence', it deserves separate treatment. As for systematicity, the idea I have in mind might better be expressed by 'unification', which is perhaps less likely to be confused with the total coherentist package although it is often taken to be a contributor to coherence. The best way to handle these messy problems is to think of this group of desiderata to consist primarily of coherence, with special attention to two features—explanation and unification—that are often thought of as contributors to coherence.

I have evaded long enough the task of giving some idea of how I am thinking of coherence as an epistemic desideratum. I don't have anything original to say on this. I find the account in BonJour 1985 to be as good for my purposes as any. BonJour begins with a sketch of the intuitive idea.

> Intuitively, coherence is a matter of how well a body of beliefs "hangs together"; how well its component beliefs fit together, agree or dovetail with each other, so as to produce an organized, rightly structured system of beliefs, rather than either a helter-skelter collection or a set of conflicting subsystems. It is reasonably clear that this "hanging together" depends on the various sorts of inferential, evidential, and explanatory relations which obtain among the various members of a system of beliefs, and especially on the more holistic and systematic of these. (93)

He then goes on to enunciate various principles mostly governing comparative coherence of systems.

(1) A system of beliefs is coherent only if it is logically consistent.
(2) A system of beliefs is coherent in proportion to its degree of probabilistic consistency.

(3) The coherence of a system of beliefs is increased by the presence of inferential connections between its components and increased in proportion to the number and strength of such connections.
(4) The coherence of a system of beliefs is diminished to the extent to which it is divided into subsystems of beliefs which are relatively unconnected to each other by inferential connections.
(5) The coherence of a system of beliefs is decreased in proportion to the presence of unexplained anomalies in the believed content of the system. (95-99)

Explanation enters into the account of the intuitive idea, in (5), and also by the fact that it is covered by talk of "inferential connections" in (3) and (4). Unification is featured in (4) and also in (3).

The discussion of coherence in recent epistemology is mostly centered on the view that coherence figures in a necessary and sufficient condition for the justification of beliefs.[2] The usual idea is that a belief is justified *iff* it fits sufficiently coherently into a system of coherent beliefs. The fit of the individual belief into the system is "sufficiently coherent" if it makes a sufficient contribution to the coherence of the entire system. Thus, though the total system is the primary source of positive epistemic status, this "trickles down" to individual beliefs by virtue of their membership in the system. There are serious and, I would say, fatal objections to this coherentist view of epistemic justification. First, it seems clear that there is a potential infinity of equally strongly coherent systems of beliefs that are mutually incompatible. And we can't have both sides of infinitely many contradictory pairs to be equally justified. Coherentists try to handle this by restricting the scope of the view to actual systems of beliefs, though this will work, of course, only if there are no incompatible actually held belief systems that are strongly and equally coherent. Perhaps that condition is satisfied, but it leaves the position dependent on contingent issues as to what cognitive subjects actually believe. Second, since justification, on coherentism, depends solely on the internal relationships between beliefs in a system, it seems to leave no room for perceptual input into the system. BonJour seeks to get around this difficulty by recognizing what he calls "cognitively spontaneous beliefs", beliefs that are not inferred from other beliefs. These will cover beliefs that are thought by many noncoherentist epistemologists to owe their epistemic status to sensory experience rather than to the way they fit into a system of beliefs. But BonJour claims to be able to accommodate fresh perceptual input into the system by distinguishing how the beliefs originate

---

[2] See BonJour 1985 and Lehrer 1990.

from what provides their justification, the latter being their membership in the system rather than their origin from sensory experience or whatever.

Perhaps the most serious objection to a coherentist theory of justification comes from the question why we should suppose that fitting into a sufficiently coherent system is either necessary or sufficient for being probably true. Doubts about the necessity come from the apparent fact that, for example, in normal sense perception I get probably true beliefs about my environment even if they, or some of them, do not fit coherently into the total system of my beliefs at all. After all, we can get information from perception that strongly goes against much of what we antecedently believed about a certain subject matter. Doubts arise about the sufficiency because of a lack of sufficient reasons for supposing that coherence of a system is a strong indicator of the truth of its constituents. In BonJour 1985 he struggles valiantly to still such doubts but, as I argue in Alston 1993a, chapter 4, unsuccessfully. A sufficiently internalist epistemologist may not take the lack of truth conducivity to be a black mark against a theory of justification, but BonJour is not one of that number. And in any event, from my view of desirability from the epistemic point of view, a feature of belief can be directly an epistemic desideratum only if it is truth-conducive.

If there are no sufficient reasons for taking fitting sufficiently coherently into a sufficiently coherent system of beliefs to be an adequate indication of truth for individual beliefs, then what makes the coherence of a system of beliefs a goal of the cognitive enterprise and hence intrinsically valuable from the epistemic point of view? We have already seen that if it is a goal of the cognitive enterprise, it has that status only on the assumption that the beliefs in the system enjoy at least a substantial probability of truth; and so that lets it in the back door, so to say, as an epistemic desideratum. But why should we suppose that it is itself a goal of cognitive endeavor? What cognitive aims are satisfied by coherence? Of course, we could just say that the cognitive aim that is satisfied by coherence is the aim at coherence, taking it as intuitively obvious that we get more satisfaction out of systems that are more rather than less coherent. But it would be desirable to dig more deeply into the structure of cognitive motivation than that.

We have already seen that coherence is a complex affair depending for its realization and its degree on a number of distinguishable factors, two of which appear on the list of Group V desiderata. So perhaps the best way to attempt a deeper digging is to treat the component factors separately and ask, with respect to each, why we should suppose it to be a goal of cognition. I have already done that for explanation. And what about unification? I think the situation there is similar to that for explanation. Here too the acquisition of probably true beliefs is part, but only part, of the story.

The distinctive beliefs here are those the contents of which are (a) the overarching principles that unify a disparate group of phenomena, laws, regularities, and so on and (b) the beliefs about how the latter are related to the former. For example, the development of scientific chemistry, involving the periodic table, the list of elements, the principles of chemical combination of elements into compounds and chemical interactions between compounds, and so on, makes it possible to recognize patterns of a relatively few types in a vast congeries of processes that on the surface appear to have nothing in common. Consider the discovery that such apparently diverse processes as the rusting of iron, the souring of milk, and the burning of wood are all cases of oxidation. So the unification achieved by chemistry is in part the acquisition of a lot of true and probably true beliefs. But there is more to it than that. The systematic character of the whole theory is something more than the sum of its parts. Seeing it all together as the pieces of a grand design and understanding each part in terms of how it fits into the total scheme and how it is related to other parts is something beyond acquiring some additional probably true beliefs. This is one of the respects in which "understanding" is often something that goes beyond a set of true beliefs, though it does also rest on true beliefs. Explanation is also a kind of understanding, as is the understanding of texts, the understanding of people, and so on. These are all cognitive goals and cognitive values that are something other than the truth of propositionally shaped beliefs though presupposing probably true instances of beliefs. So, like the case of explanation, the achievement of systematicity involves the acquisition of probably true beliefs of distinctive kinds and also involves intrinsically valuable forms of understanding that, though built on and presupposing various probably true beliefs, add to the intrinsic cognitive value contributed by those beliefs.

CHAPTER 8

WHERE PARTICULAR DESIDERATA ARE OF SPECIAL IMPORTANCE

i. Introduction

We have now surveyed a number of the most important ED, features of beliefs and complexes thereof that are desirable and valuable from the epistemic point of view, construed in terms of true belief as the central goal of cognition along with certain ancillary goals. I do not claim to have dealt with all ED that have to do with belief, but I believe the most important ones have been covered. The most obvious exception to this claim is knowledge. If being a case of knowledge is a feature of beliefs, that is certainly a crucially important epistemic desideratum that has been neglected. But that was by design. As I warned the reader at the outset, this book is devoted to an ED approach to the epistemology of belief as contrasted with knowledge, leaving the latter for separate treatment.

We have dealt with the *elucidation* of each desideratum, going into issues that arise when we seek as deep an understanding of them as possible and responding to problems and difficulties concerning their viability. We have explored their *interrelations*, which of them are fundamental and which are derivative. Thus we have completed our treatment of three of the topics concerning ED announced in Chapter 3. Only the fourth, *importance*, remains. Of course, much of the foregoing is relevant to that issue. The elucidation of each of the desiderata and the portrayal of their interrelations, especially the way in which they are related to the goal of true belief, have significant implications for their importance to the cognitive enterprise. But those implications are of a blanket sort. They are implications for the importance of any epistemic desideratum, the only qualification to this coming in the distinction of more and less fundamental desiderata from the epistemic point of view. But what remains to be done under the heading of importance is to explore the ways in which one desideratum will be of greater importance and concern than others in certain kinds of contexts.

ii. Reliability

I begin with reliability of belief formation. In Chapter 6, section ix, I emphasized the distinction between reliable belief formation in the sense of desideratum 3 and the reliability of a subject, either generally or with respect to some restricted set of beliefs. The former concerns the proportion of true to false beliefs that would result from the activation of a particular belief-forming mechanism in a large and suitably varied spread of cases in situations of the sort we typically encounter. The reliability of a belief-forming mechanism is not subject relative, for its degree of reliability is a matter of proportion of true beliefs in a total spread of outputs for any subjects in whom the relevant function is or would be activated. Hence the degree of reliability of a particular way of forming beliefs in the sense of 3 tells us nothing about the reliability of a particular subject as a source of true beliefs, either generally or with respect to a particular subject matter. But we can consider how reliable a particular individual subject is at forming beliefs, in general, for a certain subject matter, or by the use of some particular faculty. Let's call this *subject reliability* R1 to distinguish it from the reliability of a particular belief-forming mechanism across subjects, which I will call R2.

One context in which R1 is of special interest and importance is that in which we are evaluating candidates for a position that calls for making judgments on matters of practical importance. Since most jobs involve making judgments only on certain matters, we will be interested in how reliable a candidate is in getting it right about the results of clinical tests of drugs, about the strength of the evidence against a murder suspect, about the quality of the outcome of a certain food recipe, or about the load capacity of a bridge. But there are some cases, for example, the position of head of state, where a much more general reliability of judgment is very important. In any event, where we are evaluating an individual job candidate, the reliability we are concerned with is R1 rather than R2. Another context in which R1 is of central importance is that in which we need to ascertain some matter of fact and need to choose among several possible informants.

Here we will be concerned to pick an informant that we have reason to believe is reliable on that kind of issue.

Contrast these contexts with the following. (1) I want to find out on my own the correct answer to a certain question. Here, so long as I arrive at an answer on the basis of very strong evidence (2 on the list), it is of no practical concern to me whether I am *generally* reliable in my judgments about everything on which I make judgments or with respect to issues like the present one. Here the interest in getting the truth on this particular issue overshadows any concern for my having some more general truth-yielding propensity. (2) I am interested in determining whether a belief of yours is based on a sufficient reason, perhaps a belief about the mood of a close friend. Here again the desideratum that is most relevant is, obviously, 2, rather than any more general disposition of yours, whether to form true beliefs generally or beliefs like this only on sufficient reasons.

Remember that in Chapter 6 we pointed out that *reliability of belief-forming processes* and *believing on the basis of an adequate ground* are intertranslatable provided we can make two assumptions: (1) Every belief-forming process can be construed as the activation of an input–belief output function, and (2) every input to such a function can be described as a ground on which the belief is based. In that discussion I gave some reasons for these assumptions. Proceeding on that basis we can just as well put the point of the preceding paragraph by saying that in such contexts as these it is the reliability of a particular belief-forming process (mechanism, function) that is the most salient epistemic desideratum.

iii. Group III Desiderata

Now consider the higher-level desiderata in Group III. Consider the first two—having knowledge or well-founded belief[1] concerning the epistemic status of lower-level beliefs or having the capacity to acquire such. Where are these desiderata particularly salient? For one thing, whenever we are concerned to evaluate the epistemic status of other people's beliefs, for in order to do that we need to be able to determine what those statuses are. This holds for our first context, which involved ranking job applicants. There, it will be recalled, we needed to assess how reliable a candidate was in making true, or well-supported, judgments about various things. And to do that we would have to be able to determine whether in the test cases the

---

[1] In the future I will omit the 'or well-founded belief' disjunct. It will be tacitly understood where appropriate.

candidate knew the right answer or could make a well-grounded judgment. The same holds for picking a reliable informant. To determine how reliable a given informant is we have to be able to determine the truth value or epistemic status of her alleged information. And our last case—determining whether a belief of yours is based on a sufficient reason—obviously requires that I can tell what your belief is based on and whether it does count as a sufficient basis for the belief.

These are all cases of knowledge about the epistemic status of someone else's beliefs. But what internalists frequently take as necessary for justification of a belief is such higher-level knowledge of the epistemic status of one's own beliefs. To be sure, from my justification-free perspective, that is no reason to ignore the epistemic desirability of higher-level knowledge of the epistemic status of another's beliefs. And it obviously is epistemically desirable wherever it is relevant, as in the above examples. Nevertheless, higher-level knowledge of the epistemic status of one's own belief is also epistemically desirable for reasons we gave in Chapter 3, primarily the point that it provides a guide that will help one encourage the formation of probably true beliefs and discourage the formation of probably false beliefs. This insight provides a clue to contexts in which first-person epistemic knowledge is particularly important. Generally speaking, they are contexts in which rather than simply forming beliefs, like ordinary perceptual, introspective, and memory beliefs, in an automatic, "mechanical" fashion without the need for any critical reflection or internal monitoring, one engages in a significant amount of reflection, deliberation, exploration of alternatives, search for pro and con reasons, and the like before fastening onto a position on a certain issue. In short, these are cases of relatively sophisticated searches for correct answers to questions, where it is not immediately apparent what the correct answer is and where considerable searching and comparative evaluation is called for. Various candidates for the correct answer are scrutinized and evaluated for their epistemic credentials. All this obviously requires that the subject have the capacity to discern what epistemic status a particular candidate would have if it were accepted. And it requires one to be able to identify the epistemic status of an acceptance of the finally chosen position in order to be satisfied that a reasonable choice has been made. These contexts range from high-level investigations in science, history, philosophy, theology, technology, and the like, through detective work, medical diagnoses, and airplane crash investigations, to the most humble inquiries into where one has left one's glasses and why the clock is not working properly. Wherever there is a need for inquiry that involves comparative evaluation of alternative answers to questions, it is crucial to be able to determine the epistemic status of the alternatives.

Now for a brief glance at the third item in Group III, *being able to make an effective defense of the epistemic status of one's belief.* Here the kind of context in which this desideratum is of prime importance can be read directly off the above formulation. It is the kind of context in which it is important for one to defend the epistemic status of one's belief. These are primarily situations in which one's belief is challenged, opposed, or doubted, situations in which the expression of one's belief is met by "Why do you think that?" or "Why should anyone suppose something like that?" or "What possible reason could there be for thinking that?", and the like. Anything that calls for a defense of the epistemic status of one's belief makes for a context in which this desideratum is salient.

iv. Deontological Desiderata

In Chapter 4 I disqualified alleged deontological desiderata on the grounds that they failed the test of making a significant contribution to the realization of the truth goal of cognitive activity. Despite that, it is not clear that they lack value altogether, even if it is not value from the epistemic point of view as I had defined that. And so it is worthwhile to consider contexts in which they are particularly interesting or important. Let's recall the list we were working with.

9. B is held *permissibly* (one is not subject to blame for doing so).
10. B is formed and held *responsibly*.
11. The causal ancestry of B does not contain violations of intellectual obligations.

I will concentrate here on 9 and 11. They differ in that 9, by virtue of applying terms like permitted (required, forbidden) to beliefs, makes the false presupposition that believing is sufficiently under effective voluntary control to make the application of those terms appropriate. While 11 applies that deontological triad of terms not to believings themselves but to actions like searching for evidence and carefully evaluating alternatives that are uncontroversially under effective voluntary control. Hence I will focus on 11 and leave to one side the disqualified 9. Relative to what contexts is it important to consider whether 11 holds with respect to a certain belief?

To go into this matter thoroughly we would have to spend quite a lot of time determining what intellectual obligations people have, under what conditions they have them, and so on. But limitations of space prevent that, and, fortunately, it is not really necessary for identifying the main sort of context in which it is important to determine whether 11 holds with respect to a certain belief. For whatever one's intellectual obligations are, if one has violated them and this has made a significant contribution to one's acquiring a certain belief, then one can be blamed for this, just as one can be blamed for other states and conditions which are not themselves under effective voluntary control but which are often due to what one did and didn't do that is under voluntary control—conditions like weight or cholesterol level. Consider a student who is "guilty" of a howler, for example, supposing that Jane Austen wrote *Middlemarch*. I am considering not whether the student should be marked down on a test for this but whether he should be held to be culpable, properly upbraided for making such an elementary mistake. This will depend on what could have been expected of him. If it was within his capacities, with sufficient study time, to get straight on who wrote what, and if there were no overriding obligations that prevented him from using the time in this way, he could properly be blamed for academic dereliction. But if, for whatever reason, he was incapable of mastering the material, it would not be in order to hold him responsible for his mistake. Note that these concerns are not distinctively epistemic. If this case is typical of those in which the desideratum in question is of considerable importance, we must conclude that its relevance is other than epistemic.

v. General Philosophical Assessment of Beliefs

Thus far I have been focusing on *practical* interests for which one or another epistemic desideratum is of special importance. I am sure that philosophical readers will be anxiously, and perhaps irritatedly, waiting for me to turn my attention to the role of various desiderata in philosophical reflections on the epistemic status of beliefs. Before turning to that, I want to make the point that the epistemic assessment of beliefs in the thoughts and social interactions of daily life is of relevance to those philosophical reflections. Considerations that are of importance for epistemic evaluation in daily life have a *prima facie* claim to attention in systematic epistemology. Correlatively, if a certain consideration is of no interest in a variety of contexts of daily life, as we have seen higher-level epistemic knowledge not to be, that is something that should be duly noted in attempts to develop a systematic epistemology of belief. In that spirit here are a couple of morals I would like to draw for epistemology from the above survey.

First, one may well be struck by the way in which different desiderata are salient in different contexts. Where there is a keen interest in the reliability of the subject, the reliability of particular belief-forming mechanisms retreats into the background. Where having adequate reasons for a belief is crucial, the general reliability of the subject is not so important. It remains to be seen what the impact of this is on the more impersonal context of philosophical epistemic reflection, but that reflection ignores this point at its peril. Second, the most striking implication of this diversity is the fact that in everyday life there seems to be no single desideratum or set of desiderata that are epistemically crucial in all contexts. This is a further reason for doubting that there is any one epistemic status, such as "justification", that is uniquely of central importance epistemically across all contexts of epistemic assessment.

When I consider how to go about a distinctively philosophical epistemic evaluation of beliefs, I find that the abandonment of *justification* as a unique central dimension of epistemic evaluation makes an enormous difference. At first we seem to be adrift without a anchor, at a loss for what to seek and for what criteria of better and worse epistemic statuses to use. I have distinguished a variety of epistemic desiderata, each of which has a title to that status and each of which is of prime importance in certain contexts. To be sure, apart from the special interests of particular practical contexts, some of these desiderata, the directly truth-conducive ones in Group II, have turned out to be more fundamental from the epistemic point of view than others, and one might think that these are the ones that should be concentrated on in a disinterested philosophical assessment of beliefs. But what makes higher-level knowledge of epistemic statuses of lower-level beliefs or the degree of coherence of systems of beliefs less worthy of "philosophical" consideration than reliability of belief formation or adequacy of reasons for belief? To be sure, the former, as we have seen, are less directly related to the truth aim, but so long as they *are* related they call for some attention in a comprehensive epistemological theory.

I think we have to bite the bullet and admit that the loss of justification as the key epistemic virtue of beliefs does leave us with an irreducible plurality of epistemic desiderata and forces us to undertake the baffling task of integrating them somehow into a comprehensive epistemology of belief. Of course, I have not junked propositional knowledge along with epistemic justification, and that might provide the anchor for the need of which we feel. But in this book I am attempting to go it alone with belief, forsaking for the moment any help we might get from considering how the various ED for belief relate to knowledge.

And yet the situation is not as bleak as the last two paragraphs would suggest. In fact, the discussion in Chapter 3 as to how the various epistemic desiderata are interrelated gives us what we need for an organization of a systematic epistemology of belief from the present point of view.

The desiderata in Group II, those that are directly truth-conducive, are the ones that are of the greatest interest and importance for the epistemology of belief, due to the overriding importance of true belief as a goal of our cognitive endeavors. For example, Alston 1993a, which is concerned with examining all the most prominent attempts to provide a noncircular argument for the thesis that sense perception is a source of beliefs about the external environment that possess positive epistemic status, is entitled *The Reliability of Sense Perception*. The title reflects the centrality of the reliability of ways of forming beliefs for their epistemic status. Just because of the overriding interest of having our beliefs be true rather than false, philosophical interest in the epistemic status of beliefs of a certain category has largely focused on the two most basic truth-conducive desiderata—how adequate are the grounds of the belief (and hence how probable is it that the beliefs so grounded are true) and the nearly equivalent question of how reliable are the ways in which such beliefs are generally formed. The primacy of these desiderata is also reflected in the fact that skeptical attacks on beliefs concerning the past, the future, other minds, high-level scientific theories, and God are most often directed to the question of how adequate are their grounds and how reliable are the processes by which they are formed.

To be sure, this primacy of the directly truth-conducive must be balanced by a recognition that secondary, derivative epistemic desiderata deserve consideration in a philosophical examination of the epistemological credentials of beliefs. Indeed, these derivative desiderata are so intimately entangled with the more basic desiderata that they are not infrequently confused. Consider why this should be so. Consider the high-level epistemic knowledge desiderata in Group III. If we attempt to determine whether, say, perceptual or inductively formed beliefs generally have adequate grounds or are generally formed in a reliable way, we find Group II and Group III desiderata both involved in the discussion, playing different roles. The question we are trying to answer is, for example, whether normal perceptual beliefs have adequate grounds and what they are. That is, we are trying to determine whether normal perceptual beliefs have a certain directly truth-conducive desideratum from Group II. But in order for this investigation to succeed, the investigator's beliefs must themselves have a derivative Group III desideratum of being a knowledge of, or access to knowledge of, the epistemic status of lower-level beliefs. Since one can't determine whether certain beliefs possess a Group II desideratum without some of one's own beliefs realizing a Group III desideratum, it is easy to conflate the two, and many epistemologists have fallen into this trap. For documentation of this charge see

Alston 1980. Nevertheless, when it comes to satisfying the most basic aims of cognition, it is the desiderata that entail a probability of truth for beliefs that occupy the primary place.

vi. Assessment of Perceptual Beliefs: Preliminaries

As I pointed out in the beginning, this book deals with meta-epistemology, not with substantive epistemology. We are charting a course for an epistemology of belief in terms of a variety of epistemic desiderata rather than in terms of justification, not embarking on that course, at least to any considerable extent. Nevertheless, it will not be amiss to give more of an idea than I have thus far of how the epistemological treatment of a certain class of beliefs would look on this approach. I will do so with respect to perceptual beliefs. And before I launch that, some more general preliminary distinctions and principles must be laid down to guide us.

First, there is the distinction between two categories of grounds of belief—those that consist of other beliefs, *doxastic* grounds, and those that consist of something else, primarily experience (*experiential* grounds). Notice that this distinction sidesteps altogether the tricky issue whether some beliefs have positive epistemic status without being based on any grounds at all. Apart from the controversial issues discussed in Chapter 5 in response to a view of Plantinga's that not all beliefs have grounds, there is the view held by some epistemologists that there are beliefs that enjoy a positive epistemic status just by being the beliefs they are, just by being the kind of beliefs they are or having the content they do. In Alston 1976 I defend the idea that beliefs to the effect that one is in a current conscious state are what I called "self-warranted", needing no ground other than themselves to enjoy positive epistemic status. And other philosophers have other candidates for beliefs that are ungrounded and yet justified, warranted, or whatever term of PES is favored. A full-dress substantive epistemology will have to deal with the question whether there are such beliefs, and if so where they are to be located and how to handle them. But for this trial run we can leave all that to one side and restrict ourselves to beliefs that do have grounds to which they owe what PES they possess. Since beliefs with doxastic grounds have traditionally been called *indirectly* or *mediately* grounded whereas those experientially grounded have been called *directly* or *immediately* grounded, I shall feel free to use those terms. This terminology comes, of course, from the foundationalist idea that any belief that gets its positive epistemic status from other beliefs stands at the end of a chain of belief that is grounded at the beginning by one or more experiences. Otherwise the chain of belief-support would stretch back infinitely, or else circle around on itself and suffer from circularity. Thus it is only experientially grounded beliefs that are, so to say, *directly, immediately* connected with the "world" whereas doxastically grounded beliefs are only *indirectly, mediately* connected to the world through the chain of belief-supports stretching back to one or more experiential grounds. A comprehensive substantive epistemology of belief would need to consider whether this foundationalist picture is adequate or whether it needs to be replaced by something else, or perhaps modified in some way. But, again, we can leave those issues about the overall shape of a total system of beliefs to one side in this trial run. They will be lightly treated in Chapter 11.

Another matter that needs to be addressed concerns the distinction between epistemic beliefs that have to do with the epistemic status of lower-level beliefs and those lower-level beliefs themselves. To be sure, level distinctions can be made on various bases, but we will be concerned with the distinction between beliefs that are not about the epistemic status of other beliefs (call them *lower-level*), and beliefs that are (call them *higher-level*). The reason this distinction is of particular interest here is that when we come to the question whether a given belief, or class of beliefs, enjoys a certain truth-conducive PES, the question arises as to whether a higher-level belief about this can be experientially grounded or must, if grounded at all, be doxastically grounded. It does not seem on the face of it that the epistemic status of a belief is something we can have adequate grounds for accepting without having *reasons* for it in the form of knowledge, or well-grounded belief, that the necessary conditions for that epistemic status are satisfied in this case. Given what it takes for a ground to be adequate (a large proportion of true beliefs that would be forthcoming from a properly constituted run of beliefs based on that ground) or for a way of forming beliefs to be reliable (ditto), it seems incredible that one could know that such conditions are satisfied just by one's direct experience. The satisfaction of those conditions is not the sort of thing one can experience. If that is so, then when we seek to answer questions about the epistemic status of beliefs, if our answers are to achieve PES they must be doxastically grounded. And this is so whether the epistemic status of the lower-level belief that is the object of the inquiry is a function of doxastic or experiential grounding. Again, it is crucial not to confuse the epistemic status of a non-epistemic belief and the epistemic status of the belief about the epistemic status of that first belief, or to confuse the sorts of grounding for the beliefs on the two levels. See Alston 1976 and 1980 for a detailed elaboration of this point.

vii. The Nature of Perception

We need to consider how the class of perceptual beliefs is to be delimited. As the term suggests, a perceptual belief is one about a perceived object that is formed on the basis of perception. It is better to put it this way than to say simply that it is a belief about what one perceives. One can have many beliefs about a perceived object that are not based on the perception. Thus I might see and recognize a book on my desk, remembering that I had agreed to review it. The belief that there is a book on my desk with such-and-such a title is based on my seeing it, but the belief that I had agreed to review it is not; it is based on memory.

But using this definition without further qualification gets us into serious problems. To appreciate this we must make a detour. There are a number of different views on the nature of perception. And since the epistemology of perceptual belief has to do with the relation between the belief and perception, the account we give of that relation will have to differ for different views of perception. I will consider as much of that variety as is important for our present interests.

First, there is the view that the perception of objects is necessarily conceptually structured.[2] There can be no perception of an object that does not involve conceptualizing the object as so-and-so. Call this the *conceptualist* view. And some of those who take this line go further and hold that there can be no perception of an object that does not involve one or more beliefs about the object (or at least tendencies to form such beliefs).[3] Call this the *doxastic* view. Now if these views amounted to no more than the recognition that normal adult perception of the external environment involves seeing things as so-and-so, under the concepts of so-and-so, and involves believing various things about them (or tending to do so), it would be quite uncontroversial. When, standing on the sidewalk, I look about me and see other pedestrians and cars parked along the curb and cars going by along the street, I conceptualize what I am seeing as pedestrians and cars, believe of some cars that they are parked while others are moving, and so on. But it is not uncontroversial that these conceptualizations and beliefs are essential to perception, that there could be no perception of these objects without them. On the contrary, there is the opposed view that what is minimally essential to and distinctive of perception is a nonconceptual or preconceptual *presentation* of an object to consciousness, its appearing to one as so-and-so—its looking a certain way, sounding a certain way, and so

---

[2] See Heil 1983; Pendlebury 1987; Runzo 1977, 1982; Searle 1983.
[3] See Armstrong 1961 and Pitcher 1971.

on, where looking so-and-so does not amount to one's seeing it *as* so-and-so, where the latter involves the application of a general concept to the object. Call this the *presentational* view. In the typical case this perceptual presentation will then give rise to conceptualization of and belief about the object, this latter being so smoothly blended phenomenologically with the presentation that it requires determined analysis to distinguish them.

The opposition that has the most obvious bearing on the epistemology of perceptual beliefs is that between the presentational and the doxastic view. On the latter it would seem that perception comes on the scene too late to be a ground of perceptual belief, at least if, as we have been assuming, the ground of a belief must be distinct from the belief itself. If we are to find a ground of a perceptual belief that is part of a perception, it seems that we must look elsewhere. There would appear to be no alternative on this doxastic view of perception to finding the ground of a belief about a perceived object outside the perceptual situation in the ways in which the belief fits in with other beliefs of the subject. Such a view naturally fits into a coherentist epistemology, though it need not go all the way in that direction. Whereas the presentational view has no trouble in taking perception as a ground of the perceptual belief to which it gives rise. The view that holds that perception of an object essentially involves conceptualizing the object, but that stops short of holding belief to be essential, occupies an intermediate position here. It does not take a perceptual belief about O to be part of the perception of O, but it also does not hold the belief to be as distinct from the perception as the presentational view does.

But speaking of perceptual beliefs as those "based on perception" is too crude a formulation to deal with all aspects of the subject matter. To get a more refined framework for dealing with our epistemological concerns, we must distinguish between perceptual experience (PE), the conscious experience involved in perception, and anything else that is necessarily involved in the perception of an object. We may think of PE as the experiential aspect of a perception. Using that term, we can now define 'perceptual belief' (PB) as follows.

B is a perceptual belief = df. B is about a perceived object O, and B is either (a) (at least partially) based on a PE of O or (b) is part of a perception of O.

The "at least partially" qualification for (a) reflects the fact that a particular belief about a perceived object, say that a certain perceived house is Sally's house, might be partially based on the way it looks and partially on my knowledge that I am in the block of the street on which she lives. In this discussion I will be focusing on the PE part of the basis for the belief, but this is not meant to imply that background beliefs and knowledge cannot also figure in the total basis.

In the definition the (a) disjunct takes care of the presentational view of a perceptual basis, and the (b) disjunct handles the doxastic view. Conceptualism is left uncomfortably straddling the fence, and I will leave it there for purposes of this quick sketch.

To get back to the epistemology, if we are to investigate the epistemology of perceptual beliefs, we must make some choice between the views of perception I have been distinguishing. In Alston 1998 and 1999 I argued against conceptualist and doxastic accounts of perception and plumped for the presentational account. I will follow that in this discussion, thinking of a perceptual belief about perceived object O as based on a PE of O, that is, on a presentation of O. But this is not the end of the matter. Among those who take perceptual beliefs to be based on PE, there are several significantly different views of that. The presentational view, which I and others have called the *theory of appearing*, is the one I was contrasting with conceptualism and the doxastic view in the above. But the *sense-datum* view and the *adverbial* view also take PE to be a distinguishable part of the perception of an external object. (Each of these views is held in several different forms, but I won't be able to go into that here; a generic presentation will have to suffice.) These views of PE differ as follows.

The most basic divide is between presentationalism and the other two. Presentationalism is a form of direct realism. On that view when I perceive an object (usually an external object), the perceived object itself presents itself to me as so-and-so, appears to me as so-and-so. It looks red, grainy, rough, or like an apple tree. The perceptual experience is *constituted* by the object appearing as so-and-so. Where, as usually, the object is something in the external environment, the experience is not purely intra-mental. It is irreducibly relational, with one relatum being the subject or, if you prefer, the subject's consciousness and the other relatum being the external object. The other two views take PE to be purely intra-mental. The sense-datum view agrees with presentationalism in taking PE to have a subject-object structure. It is an awareness, a consciousness *of* something. But even where the experience is involved in the perception of an external object, the object that figures as such in PE is not external to the mind. It is a mental, or mind-dependent, object; it is not a physical object. Roughly speaking, it is the subject of the qualities the perceived object appears to have. These internal objects of which the subject is directly aware and which function as intermediaries between the subject and the external perceived object are called *sense data*.

Adverbialism also takes PE to be purely intra-mental but to lack any subject-object structure. It is not an awareness *of* anything. It is a *way* of being conscious, on a par in that respect with feeling excited, relieved, or depressed but different from them in that it is involved in the perception of external objects as the experiential aspect of that.

So when, as we ordinarily say, an object, O, looks red to S, the presentationalist will take that as the bottom-line formulation of S's experiential state. It is simply a matter of O's looking red to S, and that is a not-further-analyzable state of affairs. But the other two views give further analyses. The sense-datum view is that S is aware of a red sense datum that, somehow, represents an external (apparently) red object and thereby makes possible a perception of that object. The adverbial view is that by being conscious in a certain way ("redly"), S is thereby enabled to perceive an (apparently) red object.

It is clear that the sense-datum and adverbial views have a lot of work to do to fill out their positions. In particular they have the job of specifying how it is that being directly aware of a sense datum or being conscious in a certain way enables S to perceive an external object O. This problem arises for them, and not for presentationalism, just because of the split between PE, securely ensconced in the mind, and the allegedly perceived object in the external environment. They must be brought into a suitable connection. The most common way of doing this is in terms of causality.[4] By virtue of causing the awareness of the sense datum or being conscious in a certain way, O is thereby perceived by S. But this immediately runs into the point that many other items, both internal and external, are also involved in the causal chain leading to the PE. And so there is the problem of explaining how it is that one of the causal contributors figures as the perceived object while the others do not. In Alston 1990 I argue that this problem is insoluble, and that none of these views that treat the perceived object as externally related to the experiential aspect of perception can be successful. As just pointed out, presentationalism is spared this problem, but its opponents take this as a vice rather than a virtue, alleging that it has simply buried the difficulties with which its competitors are faced by helping itself to an unanalyzed notion of the presentation of an object to a subject. Another objection to presentationalism is that it cannot handle hallucinations, in which an experience phenomenologically indistinguishable from veridical perception occurs without an external object. Whereas the other views have no trouble with this. Here the fact that PE is represented as purely intra-mental and only externally related to any external object is an advantage. Hallucination is just the PE without any external object to which it is related in veridical perception.

---

[4] Some accounts are more complex. For a multifactor view, see Goldman 1977.

In Alston 1999 I present and defend presentationalism, called there the "theory of appearing", and, inter alia, make some suggestions as to how it can handle hallucinations. But I have no space to further discuss these issues here. Suffice it to say that I will consider how the epistemology of perceptual belief looks on all the positions I have mentioned and say something about the strengths and weaknesses of each.

viii. The Truth Conducivity of Grounds of Perceptual Beliefs

Now I can turn to the discussion of the question whether perceptual beliefs enjoy directly truth-conducive desiderata, and if so how. Since this is designed not as a substantive discussion of the issues but rather as a consideration of what is involved in carrying on such a discussion, I will be much concerned with *how* to go about answering the questions, what devices to employ, what data to seek, what issues to explore, what considerations are relevant, and so on. Let me remind you once again that I will feel free to oscillate between the adequacy-of-grounds version and the reliability-of-ways-of-forming-beliefs version of the most basic directly truth-conducive epistemic desideratum.

It may seem that I could have skipped what was presented in the last section, namely, the variety of views as to the correct account of perceptual experience. For, it might be said, wouldn't the investigation of the adequacy of the grounds for perceptual beliefs or the reliability of ways of forming them be investigated in the same way regardless of how PE is correctly characterized? At least that is true for any of the views that permit the ground for some perceptual beliefs to be PE of a preconceptual character. However we decide among presentationalism, sense-datum theory, and adverbialism, the investigation of whether or under what conditions a PB is adequately grounded or was formed in a reliable way would be the same. We would seek to determine, for a particular perceptual belief content, whether in a large and suitably constituted run of cases of a belief with that content being based on PE in the way we usually do, or of the parallel belief-forming process, there would be a large proportion of true beliefs. And that investigation would proceed in just the same way, regardless of which theory of PE we adopt. So long as we can identify PE grounds without having decided on what the correct theoretical characterization of PE is, it looks as if the determination of the adequacy of a certain PE ground for a certain PB content would proceed in the same way.

It is undeniable that this frequency-count approach to the determination of adequacy of ground or reliability of belief formation does not require a decision between alternative views of the nature of PE, so long as we can identify the same PE type in different cases. But there are special difficulties where the ground is a preconceptual experiential state. Even if we can reliably distinguish different PE contents in the first-person case, the investigation cannot restrict itself to cases involving the investigator. That would hardly count as a "properly constituted" sample. And identifying the variables in third-person cases poses all the notorious problems of reliably ascribing experiences to other subjects. I don't mean to suggest that we are totally incapable of doing this, but any claim to have done so in an objectively satisfactory way would be highly controversial. For this and for other reasons it would be desirable to be able to approach the investigation in some other way, not necessarily instead of this frequency-count approach but at least in conjunction with it.

This is where the relevance of the differences between the competing accounts of PE comes in. If it were the case that we can understand better how being grounded in a PE would endow a PB with positive epistemic status on one view as to the nature of PE than on others, and if there are other reasons for favoring that view, this would give an additional boost to whatever results we got from the purely empirical data for concluding that being grounded in a PE in the way we usually do would endow a PB with positive epistemic status. Let's see what we can find along these lines.

This is not the place for me to argue for presentationalism, though if I were to go substantive, I would readily do so. (For a sketch of the argument, see Alston 1999.) But I will indicate an advantage of this view of PE over its two main competitors in making clear how a PE grounding could strongly support taking a perceptual belief to be probably true. The basic point about presentationalism is this. It takes a PE to consist in an object O's appearing to the subject S as so-and-so, O's looking heavy, grainy, disheveled, like a maple tree, or like a Victorian house. If we take as a minimal PB about O a belief that O *looks* grainy or like a maple tree, then O's looking grainy is a maximally truth-conducive ground for the belief that O *looks* grainy. It not only renders that belief probably true; it makes it certainly true. There is no possibility of that belief with that ground being false since the content of the belief simply reproduces the content of the appearance. There is an identity of content here. Of course, that doesn't render it certain that O *is* grainy or a maple tree. Things aren't always what they look to be, even if the subject and the conditions of perception are completely normal. Nevertheless, the fact that O looks P is certainly a consideration in favor of the claim that O is P. That looking is sufficient to endow the belief that O is P with a significant degree of probability on condition of being based on that looking. So a PE as construed by presentationalism clearly and incontrovertibly renders a very minimal belief about its object true and makes a significant contribution to the probability of truth for stronger beliefs about O.

Now what about the competing views of PE? They differ from presentationalism in that the PE itself is purely intra-mental; its content is distinct from the perceived object. Thus they present us with a gulf to be bridged. To understand how S's awareness of a sense datum with certain qualities, or S's being conscious in a certain way, provides an adequate, or even a significantly positive, ground for some belief about O, we have to see how the purely internal PE as characterized in one of these ways is related to O so as to provide a ground for believing anything about it. On these views there is no intrinsic feature of the PE itself as a ground that enables us to see how it makes any contribution to the probable truth of any belief about O. I take this to be obvious on the face of it for the sense-datum view. How could the fact that I am aware of a sense datum with one set of qualities rather than another tell me anything about some object in the external environment? Adverbialism, on the other hand, might seem to be in a better position. Why shouldn't being appeared to grainily or being appeared to mapletreely at least render it probable, or even true, that O looks grainy or looks like a maple tree, in the same way that a presentational PE would? But this supposed advantage is an artifact of the way in which these modes of being conscious are specified. They are specified in terms of supposed properties of the perceived object, thereby obscuring the fact that they could perfectly well exist without the perceived object bearing the corresponding properties and, indeed, without there being any perceived object there at all. If we are in dead earnest that these are simply ways of being conscious, then they present us with just as much of a gulf between that and the epistemic status of any belief about the perceived object as the sense-datum view does.

To be sure, the advocates of these views are not at a loss for presenting a case for the relevance of PE on their construals to the epistemic status of perceptual beliefs. The main story is causal. Since there are regularities in the way in which the properties of perceived objects affect the properties of PEs of subjects to which the former make a causal contribution, it is via these regularities that the sense-datum or adverbial PE can contribute to the probable truth of ascriptions of those properties to the perceived object. And don't yield to the temptation to say that this shows that on these construals of PE, what grounds PBs is not the PE itself but an inference from facts about the PE to facts about the object, and hence that we don't have a purely preconceptual experiential ground at work. For that would be to confuse what grounds the PB with what it takes to realize *that* the PB is thereby adequately grounded. It would be a level confusion of the sort mentioned earlier. But what we can say is that the understanding of how the PE can be an adequate ground of a PB is much more complex, and involves a greater battery of assumptions that require independent support and are more or less controversial, than what we encounter in understanding the epistemic contribution of a PE ground to the grounded perceptual belief on the presentationalist account of PE.

The foregoing is a sparse discussion of what we run into when we consider the project of showing that, and how, a PE can be an adequate ground for some kinds of perceptual beliefs. Obviously, a comprehensive epistemology of perceptual beliefs would involve bringing a variety of propositionally shaped reasons into the picture along with the PE involved, as well as discussing the epistemic contributions of PE in more detail. And that is more than I am prepared to undertake in this book. But at least this section provides a sample of some of the things involved in trying to determine if, and if so how, perceptual beliefs can enjoy a directly truth-conducive epistemic desideratum.

In this discussion we have been freely making use of what we take ourselves to know about matters relevant to carrying out the project, about the truth value of outcomes of belief-forming processes, about causal relations between perceived objects and PE, about how sequences of cases of belief formation have to be constituted to enable us to draw inferences about the proportion of true beliefs in a long run, and so on. And philosophers, especially but not solely under the banner of *skepticism*, have raised serious questions about whether we are entitled to assume we know, or have well-supported beliefs about, these things when we are engaged in epistemological inquiry concerning the epistemic status of lower-level beliefs. If we take these questions seriously, we are forced into ultimate questions about the epistemology of epistemology, about the epistemic status of epistemic attributions and epistemic principles. In the foregoing, indeed throughout the entire Part I of this book, I have been proceeding as we ordinarily do in any investigation or inquiry, taking ourselves to have available any things we reasonably take ourselves to know or have well-supported beliefs about, using ordinary standards for this. But the ultimate questioners just mentioned challenge our right to assume this. Part II will take up this challenge and seek to arrive at the best way to respond to it.

PART II

ULTIMATE QUESTIONS: THE EPISTEMOLOGY OF EPISTEMOLOGY

CHAPTER 9

CRITICAL QUESTIONS ABOUT EPISTEMOLOGICAL METHODOLOGY

i. The Demand for a Final Settlement

As intimated at the end of the preceding chapter, there will be those who are not satisfied with the "naturalistic" approach to epistemic evaluation that involves making use of whatever we take ourselves to know, or to believe on an adequate basis, when we epistemically evaluate a belief or a class of beliefs. For, they will say, we are just taking for granted the positive epistemic status of our beliefs in what we take to be the case when we rely on them in the examination of our target belief(s). And why this partiality? Why should we simply take it for granted that some beliefs have positive epistemic status while we critically examine the credentials of others? How can this procedure be justified?

We might well respond that we can't do everything at once. I can't simultaneously determine whether you have adequate reason for supposing that Gerda is planning to file for divorce, and also determine the epistemic status of all the beliefs I rely on in carrying out that investigation. And obviously I can't get at the epistemic status of your belief about Gerda's plans from behind a veil of ignorance. I have to make use of certain suppositions if I am to have any basis for whatever judgment I make as to whether you have adequate grounds for your claim. And if questions are raised about those suppositions, I can, if I consider the questions to be serious, look into the epistemic credentials of the beliefs I was relying on in the initial investigation, proceeding, of course, in the same spirit. So why are you dissatisfied?

It is not hard to see what leads the objector to be dissatisfied. Each of these investigations of epistemic status leaves another investigation hanging that involves exactly the same kinds of issues. It seems that we are not getting anywhere. In order to answer doubts about what was assumed in the original evaluation, we are driven to make further assumptions that give rise to the same questions; and so on ad infinitum. Nothing ever gets finally, definitively settled.

My initial response to these remarks is to ask my interlocutor whether she is equally unsatisfied with this kind of situation when it concerns non-epistemic inquiry. Suppose the investigation is as to whether a bridge has been weakened too much to support heavy trucks. Here too I make use of various beliefs I take to have adequate support—about the state of the various structural parts of the bridge, its age, past problems with it if any, and so on. And I do so without trying to determine what the epistemic status of those beliefs are. Doing so would take so much time and effort that I would never get to the resolution of the problem I started with. And even if I were able to carry out that higher-level investigation, I would perforce be relying on other beliefs to do so, the credentials of which were not critically examined. It seems clear that this "always something hanging over" feature applies to any inquiry into anything, whether we begin with an epistemic problem or not. Are we going to be dissatisfied on these grounds with the results of any attempts to answer any question whatever? This would lead to a total skepticism about any claim to knowledge or well-grounded belief about anything.

To this my interlocutor would, no doubt, reply that there is a crucial difference between starting with an epistemic question and starting with a non-epistemic question. In the latter case, as with the question about the bridge, we don't get into an infinite regress until we reach an epistemic question at the second stage. If someone doubted the accuracy of what I am supposing in concluding that the bridge is strong enough for heavy trucks, if the doubt is about the truth of what I am supposing rather than its epistemic status, then that can be investigated in just the same way as the initial question about the bridge, by going on whatever we suppose ourselves to know or reliably believe about what is relevant to the issue. And either at the initial stage or at some subsequent stage we might well, and presumably will, come to some assumption about which no doubts arise. But when the initial question is about the epistemic status of some belief, then to settle that, or any further epistemic question in the regress, we have to take for granted something of exactly the same sort, something that should require critical examination if the initial claim to epistemic status does. It is the endless repetition of just the same sort of claim to epistemic status at each stage of the regress that makes the procedure unsatisfactory because it is not "getting anywhere".

But why should that make a difference to the satisfactoriness or the reverse of the process? In both cases we begin with a question to which we are trying to find an adequately supported answer. And in order to support such an answer, we provide certain reasons for supposing it to be true. In principle, we could raise a question about the accuracy, or epistemic status, of those reasons, that is, the beliefs that those reasons are correct. And if that question is raised, we are forced into a parallel situation at a second remove. Why should we suppose that the content of the questions and the reasons given for an answer at one or another stage makes a difference to the acceptability of the proceeding? If we can give an acceptable resolution of the question about the safety of the bridge without continuing a regress of reasons (or claims about the epistemic status of beliefs) ad infinitum, why can't we claim the same status for the inquiry that begins with a question about the epistemic status of a belief?

I think that we have probed deeply enough to uncover the basic assumption that is at the root of my opponent's position. It has to do with what the goal of epistemology should be. It should aim at establishing epistemic conclusions in a final, definitive way with no unsupported assumptions left over. This is often put in terms of giving "an answer to skepticism". The skeptic challenges us to show that we have some knowledge or some beliefs that are adequately grounded or reliably formed, or have some other truth-conducive status. And until we can do this without leaving any assumptions, particularly epistemic assumptions, not sufficiently established, we have not met the skeptic's challenge. Thus the assumption driving the dissatisfaction is an assumption about what it takes to establish a claim to knowledge or well-grounded belief. It is the aspiration for a final, definitive establishment that makes use of no assumptions (beliefs, claimed knowledge) that are themselves not established that leads to the dissatisfaction we have been trying to understand and assess.

The skeptical challenge that this aspiration is aimed at meeting will be discussed in the next chapter, where I will distinguish a number of different forms of skepticism and consider what should be said about each. For now, I want to examine the basic assumption just identified and consider what it would take to meet its demands, and if this turns out to be impossible, consider how this should affect our view of the human epistemic situation.

ii. The Inevitability of a Regress

The first thing to note about the demand for a final definitive establishment of an epistemic claim, with no reliance on any unestablished claims, epistemic or otherwise, is that it seems to be in principle unsatisfiable. The considerations of the previous section indicate that no matter how long we pursue the attempt to validate ever higher assumptions about the epistemic status of beliefs, there will always be other such assumptions that have not yet been established. For assuming, as I have, that no belief about an epistemic status of belief can be immediately supported by experience, to adequately support a claim about the epistemic status of a belief, we must rely on other beliefs to do so. In relying on them to give adequate support to the former belief, we are assuming that they themselves enjoy a suitable positive epistemic status. And to establish the credentials of that assumption we are forced into an exactly parallel situation at the next higher level. Thus there is no way in which we can end this process by reaching a stage at which no epistemic assumptions are left unestablished. And if this is what the skeptic requires before admitting that anyone has any adequately grounded beliefs, we must tell him that he is crying for the moon. (More on the skeptic in the next chapter.)

Let's go into this in a bit more detail. Though it seems impossible that any adequate nondoxastic, experiential support could be given for a belief to the effect that a certain other belief has a truth-conducive epistemic status, suppose that this were possible. Suppose that for any of the regresses we have been envisaging there would be a stage a finite number of steps up at which we could just "see" by rational intuition that the assumptions being made at that stage enjoy a sufficient PES. Would that constitute the satisfaction of the demand we are considering?

NO. But to see that it would not, we have to move up a level. Since on this scenario our warranted confidence in the epistemic status of the assumption is not based on other beliefs the epistemic status of which would continue the regress, there is not the same propulsion toward a continuation of the regress that we have where all the epistemic claims have to be doxastically supported if they are to give an adequate support for the belief at the previous stage. Where that is the case, in order to support the epistemic claim the subject has to assume that the beliefs he uses to provide that support themselves have sufficient PES, and that continues the regress in just the same way. But on the present (unrealistic) assumption of immediate support for an epistemic claim, the support comes not by way of another belief whose epistemic status raises the same kind of question on a higher level but by way of a rational intuition or some other kind of nondoxastic experience. And so we don't get exactly the same sort of question at that level. But we still get a question that prevents everything from having been settled with no loose strings dangling. For although S, in supposing that she has adequate support for her belief C that the lower-level belief B has sufficient PES, is not thereby assuming that some further belief has enough PES to enable it to adequately support her belief that C, she is assuming that the nondoxastic support she relies on (explicitly or implicitly) has sufficient epistemic efficacy, as we might put it. It is not as if no such assumption about the epistemic efficacy of the supposed immediate support is involved when one takes C to have sufficient PES. Without making, at least in practice, the assumption that the nondoxastic basis is a sufficient basis for C, she would not have supposed that she was entitled to accept C, that is, to believe that B has sufficient PES. Hence the regress continues on a higher level. Now the question is as to what basis she has for D, the belief that the nondoxastic basis for C is adequate to do the job. And so we have another fork in the road. Either the support for D is doxastic or nondoxastic. If the former, we have the same situation we had for the stages we discussed earlier. If nondoxastic, we have the situation envisaged in this last scenario. Either way the regress continues, and the problem about the epistemic status of a belief that gave rise to the whole process has still not been finally and definitively resolved, with no loose ends dangling.

In the discussion thus far we have been implicitly assuming that as we go though the stages of the process, no beliefs, epistemic or otherwise, that have previously been supported make a reappearance. That is what forces an infinite regress; at each stage we depend on one or more beliefs that have not yet been established. But if one or more previously established beliefs pop up at a later stage, we have a different story. Now the trouble is with circularity rather than with the inability to halt a regress. To take a simple illustration, the support for A involves assuming that B, support for which involves assuming that C, support for which involves assuming that A. This means that the last support for A depends on assuming, inter alia, A. But of what value is that? Any proposition is such that it is true if and only if it is true. Though this doesn't leave loose ends dangling in the same way as the unending regress, it does not leave us in any better epistemic position.

At this point the coherentist could enter the discussion by objecting to the whole assumption of a linear process of epistemic support, opting instead for resting everything on the overall coherence of a system in which mutual support of beliefs is not only tolerated but welcomed. I have already given reasons for rejecting such a thoroughgoing coherentist epistemology, and we will return to it later. But for now I want to point out that the above argument for the unsatisfiability of the skeptic's demand for final, definitive settlement of all issues with no loose ends dangling presupposes a linear model of epistemic support, one rejected by coherentism.

iii. Attempts to Avoid the Regress: Doxastic Practices

Thus far we have not succeeded in removing the initial impression that the requirement that the epistemic status of beliefs be established without leaving any questions about epistemic status dangling is in principle unsatisfiable. At this point we could give up the aspiration to satisfy this requirement and relapse into a (perhaps dissatisfied) acceptance of the "naturalistic" approach to epistemology as the only one that is possible for our human condition. This is a near relation of one of the positions called "contextualism" in epistemology. This is the view that any inquiry (into epistemic status or anything else) takes place in a context that is defined by certain things that are taken for granted and about which any search for grounds or any critical examination is out of order, in that context. The things taken for granted can be subjected to critical scrutiny subsequently but only in another context the framework of which is constituted by other assumptions that, for the nonce, are given this privileged status of being immune from critical examination. This position renounces the aim at determining the status of all knowledge (well-founded belief) claims "all at once", without making use of any unexamined knowledge claims in doing so. John Dewey, an eminent contextualist, once said in perhaps the only pithy statement he ever made, "In the last analysis there is no last analysis". Something like contextualism is what we have seen, thus far, to be the inescapable human cognitive condition.

But before settling for this, let's explore alternatives. It has been suggested more than once that the kind of regress we have been envisaging can be stopped if we reach a stage at which what is on the table is something that it makes no sense to doubt or deny. This status has been claimed for a variety of items—truths of deductive logic, beliefs about one's current conscious state, commonsense beliefs that in fact no one doubts, principles of induction, and others. The most prominent twentieth-century advocate of such a position is Ludwig Wittgenstein, but there are many others.[1] To go into all the ins and outs of such a position would fill too much space to be undertaken in this book. I will content myself with making one point. Practically any attempt to defend such a position rests heavily on a verificationist constraint on what makes sense. The idea is that since we can't specify

---

[1] See especially Wittgenstein 1969.

any way in which we could empirically test, for example, the supposition that the world came into existence five minutes ago with all the apparent memories, records, buildings, and so on that we take to indicate a much earlier origin, neither that supposition nor its denial is intelligible to us. And hence it is misguided to look for considerations that tell for or against it. In response to this I say that it is obvious that the supposition is intelligible, obvious that we understand what it would be for the world to have come into existence five minutes ago. And it is so obvious that it is preferable to something as dubious and controversial as the verifiability criterion of meaningfulness. So I will not treat this position as a live alternative.

There are also more indirect attacks on the practice of raising skeptical doubts about things of which we are normally confident. These attacks typically trace such doubts to the uncritical acceptance of dubious and/or false ways of thinking about belief, knowledge, evidence, truth, epistemic support, and the like.[2] Again, I could go into the pros and cons of such positions at the cost of winding up with a multivolume treatise. But I will dodge that by making the point that doubt about p is not a necessary condition for the meaningfulness or importance of raising questions as to what adequate support, if any, there is for a belief that p. We can quite properly be interested in what epistemic status that belief has, and what gives it that status, without ever having any doubts as to its truth.

But there is a kind of alternative to the contextualist, naturalistic approach that I will take more seriously. This is the attempt to establish very general conclusions about the epistemic status of large classes of beliefs and then apply those conclusions to particular members of a given class. This is a top-down method as opposed to the bottom-up method exemplified by starting with a question about the epistemic status of a given belief and then going on to analogous questions about beliefs that are utilized to answer that initial question, thus giving rise to the regress that has been bothering us. This top-down approach is designed to provide a way to stop such regresses but, so to say, in a wholesale rather than a retail manner. Instead of looking for a particular stage in the regress where no questions of epistemic status can be raised, we seek to answer that question for an indefinitely large class of beliefs in advance of any critical examination of particular beliefs. That puts us in a position, when the need for a particular examination arises, to apply the general conclusion to the particular case.

Thus there are attempts to establish the general reliability (general well-groundedness) of normal perceptual beliefs, memory beliefs, introspective beliefs, beliefs based on rational intuition, enumerative induction, inference

---

[2] See, e.g., M. Williams 1991.

to the best explanation, and so on. In previous publications I have discussed this matter in terms of what I called *doxastic practices* (hereinafter *DPs*).[3] A DP is a general way of forming beliefs of certain types. We could think of it as a family of belief-forming practices or, to tie it into the discussion in Chapter 6, a family of belief-forming *mechanisms*, psychologically realized input–belief output functions. In Chapter 6 I argued that the psychological dynamics of belief formation determines the individuation of such a mechanism. The realized function determines when we have that mechanism rather than some other. But a DP is a family of such mechanisms grouped together because of similarities between them, and there is no unique way of grouping belief-forming mechanisms into DPs. There are various ways in which different mechanisms can be similar, and depending on which of these we fasten on, we get different groupings. The most intuitively salient similarities have to do with inputs, outputs, functions, and another feature that I will mention shortly.

Input similarities will figure prominently for experiential inputs. Visual experiences involve distinctive kinds of phenomenal content, differing in this way from auditory, tactile, gustatory, and olfactory content. Analogously, memory inputs and self-evidence inputs each seem to have a common phenomenal character. This gets us started with distinctive DPs for perceptual beliefs in various modalities, memory beliefs, and beliefs in self-evident truths. Commonalities in the output beliefs also play a role. Perceptual beliefs are distinctive in being beliefs about perceived objects. Of course, not all beliefs about perceived objects are perceptual beliefs; for example, there can be memory beliefs about (previously) perceived objects. And, as I pointed out in section vii of the last chapter, I can hypothesize something about a currently perceived object, thus forming a belief about a currently perceived object that doesn't count as a perceptual belief. But if we put together the output belief's being about a perceived object and the input being (at least in part) an experience characteristic of one of the sensory modalities, we have perceptual DPs pretty well pinned down.

Inferential DPs are another matter. Here input and output are both beliefs that can be of any sort, embodying any propositional content whatever. We might demarcate inferential DPs just by their having purely doxastic inputs. But it is also the case that any inferential belief formation is of a type that is individuated by the function, by the principle of inference involved. As I have already pointed out, these functions can be much more simply and precisely stated for both valid and invalid deductive inferences than for various sorts of nondeductive inferences, but the point holds

[3] See Alston 1991a, chap. 4.

across the board, though we are often hard pressed to specify precise functions for nondeductive inferences. Individuation by the realized function does not work for experiential DPs, at least not for the large units in terms of which this discussion is being carried on. In Chapter 6 I pointed out that the functions realized by belief-forming mechanisms for perceptual beliefs are generally quite specific and differ radically among themselves. This contrasts sharply with inferential functions, each of which can remain constant with widely varying inputs and outputs.

Next I should say something about why I choose to work with wide-ranging DPs of the order of visual beliefs generally and memory beliefs generally, rather than identify each particular DP with a particular realized function, even for those with experiential input. The reason will appear when we come to epistemic questions about the reliability of DPs. The crucial point is that DPs tend to fall into large groupings of mechanisms of the sort we have been mentioning because there are important commonalities in such groups with respect to the factors that bear on the reliability or unreliability of the specified mechanisms. That will be fleshed out below.

The next point is that DPs can be of various degrees of generality, and there is no reason to think that one position along such a dimension is the only possible one. We can think very generally of a perceptual DP or less generally of a visual DP, an auditory DP, and so on. The former is best construed as a disjunction of the latter. And there are choices as to how fine to cut each of these in terms of input type. Since perceptual beliefs can be formed just on an experiential input or by a combination of that with background beliefs, we could divide each general perceptual DP and each less general visual, tactile, and so on DP into two DPs depending on whether background beliefs are included in the inputs. With respect to inferential DPs, we can for certain purposes think in terms of as large a grouping as deductive inferences generally. For other purposes a more specific class of valid deductive inferences, or something still more specific like *modus ponens inferences*, is needed. But again there is no one right way of slicing the pie. Different relevant epistemic points can be made about DPs at different degrees of generality. For example, the point that a deductive inference is conditionally reliable *iff* it is impossible for the premises to be true and the conclusion false is a point that holds for deductive inference generally. Whereas for each specific type of deductive inference, what we have to consider is the specific realized function involved.

Remember the point made in Chapter 6 that for doxastic inputs, but not for purely experiential inputs, we have to distinguish between conditional and unconditional reliability of the belief-forming process or mechanism. That applies to DPs as well. An inferential DP is conditionally reliable if it reliably transfers truth or PES from premises to conclusion. It is unconditionally reliable if that condition holds and the input beliefs are true and/or have sufficient PES. No such distinction applies to a DP with purely experiential input since the notions of truth and epistemic status do not apply to its inputs. This distinction must be kept in mind in the following discussion.

Another point is that for at least most DPs the most that could be reasonably claimed for them on the unconditional side is *by-and-large* unconditional reliability. No sensible epistemologist would think that all perceptual beliefs, all memory beliefs, or all beliefs based on rational intuition are true or even probably true, and the same holds for beliefs based on inference. Perfect reliability is usually not a live possibility. Even if all beliefs based on introspection of current conscious states are reliably formed, and even true, that is the exception rather than the rule. Of course, beliefs arrived at by valid deductive inference are thereby guaranteed to be conditionally perfectly reliably formed; but for unconditional reliability we need premises that are true, or have sufficient PES, and we can't expect that condition to be satisfied in every case. So the most we can expect by way of unconditional reliability for at least almost any DP is that it is by-and-large reliable. And this means that all its outputs are only *prima facie* probably true on condition of being an output of that DP, that just by being an output of that DP there is a prior *presumption* that it is probably true. And this means in turn that it can be taken to be probably true unless there are sufficient reasons to the contrary. It is to be taken as innocent until proved guilty. Please note that this reservation is quite different from the one that is involved in the notion of unconditional reliability. Here it is not that the reliability has to do solely with the way it transfers epistemic status from input to output, though that may be involved as well. It is rather that the *unconditional* reliability that is involved is only *prima facie*, subject to being canceled out by contrary considerations.

One reason for mentioning the prima facie status at this stage of the discussion is that it brings onto the scene another factor that is involved in the individuation of DPs. I use the term 'overrider' for anything within the subject's knowledge or well-grounded belief that cancels out the prima facie presumption of probable truth a belief has by virtue of being the output of a certain DP. Associated with each DP is what we can call an "overrider system", a set of criteria for what would function as an overrider if it were present in the subject's knowledge or well-grounded belief. Different DPs have characteristically different overrider systems. For example, beliefs formed by perceptual DPs can have their presumption of probable truth overridden by abnormalities in the functioning of the subject's relevant perceptual faculties. Whereas beliefs formed by an explanatory inference can have their prima facie probable truth overridden by neglect of other possible explanations. And, for all cases, anything that would show the belief to be false or probably false overrides the presumption of probable truth.

I believe that this is enough of an introduction to the notion of a DP to serve as a framework for the discussion of attempts to show the reliability of certain very general and basic DPs, like the ones I have been using as illustrations. There is much more to be said about DPs, but for that I refer the reader to the material cited in the last footnote.

iv. Epistemic Circularity

I can now turn to a consideration of attempts to establish the by-and-large reliability of DPs. For the sake of concreteness I will discuss this issue with respect to a particular class of beliefs—normal perceptual beliefs. The force of 'normal' here is to restrict it to perceptual beliefs that are formed in the way we usually do. That does not mark a completely precise boundary, but it does exclude some things, for example, beliefs formed under hypnosis, under the influence of hallucinatory drugs, or guessing as to what something is when one can't see it well enough to identify it. I have carried out an extensive critical examination of arguments for the general reliability of normal perceptual beliefs in Alston 1993a and in only slightly less detail in Chapter 3 of Alston 1991a. Please remember that the discussion in the last chapter of the bearing of various accounts of perceptual experience on the question whether such experience constitutes a truth-conducively adequate ground for perceptual beliefs based on it was conducted from a "naturalistic" standpoint in which we feel free to assume relevant things we take ourselves to know or well-groundedly believe; whereas in the present discussion we are exploring the possibility of establishing the general reliability of our usual ways of forming perceptual beliefs without taking anything for granted about which a reasonable doubt could be raised.

There is more than one reason for denying the cogency of such arguments for that reliability. Some of them have to do with dubious patterns of argument or unresolved problems about the premises. But even if all these are cleared up, there remains a difficulty that is widely applicable to such arguments, what we may call *epistemic circularity*.

I can best introduce the concept of epistemic circularity by looking at a maximally simple argument for *the general well-groundedness (reliability of mode of formation) of normal perceptual beliefs (PBs)* (call this conclusion 'RP') in which that defect is particularly obvious. This is a track-record argument. Take a suitably constructed sample of perceptual belief formations and check the belief outputs for truth value. Then take the proportion of true beliefs in that sample as an estimate of the reliability of that mode of belief formation. Let's assume that the sample is sufficiently large and properly varied to satisfy standard sampling criteria and say that the result we get from the argument is RP, that normal perceptual belief formation is highly reliable.

So far well and good. But how do we determine the truth value of the beliefs in our sample, for example, B1? Since B1 is a perceptual belief, the natural way is simply to take another look, listen, or whatever to determine whether B1 is correct. B1 is 'That's a Volvo'. To determine whether B1 is true I (or someone else who is able to recognize a Volvo on sight) take a look to determine whether what the subject of B1 was referring to really was a Volvo. But then, in taking that premise of the argument ('S formed B1 and B1 is true') to be true, we are taking normal perceptual belief formation to be a reliable mode of belief formation. That is, we are presupposing the conclusion of the argument in taking that premise, and other like premises, to be true. And that is a kind of circularity. It is not the most direct kind of logical circularity. We are not using RP as one of our premises. Nevertheless, we are assuming RP in using normal perceptual belief formation as a way of generating premises for the argument. If one were to challenge our premises and continue the challenge long enough, we would eventually be driven to appeal to RP in defending our right to those premises. And if I were to ask myself why I should accept the premises, I would, if I pushed the reflection far enough, have to assert RP explicitly. Since this kind of circularity involves a commitment to, a reliance on, the conclusion in order that our premises be well grounded, it is properly called *epistemic* circularity.

As I pointed out earlier, direct track-record arguments are not the only way, even if the most basic way, to establish reliability of belief formation. Shortly, I will mention another attempt to do this with respect to sense perception, and a great many more are to be found Alston 1993a. At this point I am using the track-record argument only to give an initial idea of epistemic circularity.

The reason why epistemic circularity is important in this context is that arguments that are infected with it would seem to have no force. If we have to assume RP in order to be entitled to premises for an argument for it, how can the argument provide support for RP? If our assumption of RP is warranted before we give the argument, how does the argument add to the PES of RP? Wouldn't we just be marching in the same place without advancing? But things are not that simple. Surprisingly enough, as I argue in Alston 1986a, epistemic circularity does not prevent us from using an argument to establish its conclusion. At least this is the case if, as I have claimed earlier, having an adequately grounded belief that p is adequately grounded, or an adequately grounded belief that implies that p is adequately grounded, is *not* necessary for one's belief that p *being* adequately grounded. So long as my belief that p *is* adequately grounded, I am entitled to use it as a premise in an argument even if I don't also have an adequately grounded higher-level belief that the belief that p is adequately grounded. Hence even if I do have that higher-level belief based on an adequate ground, that is not necessary for my being entitled to take p to be true and to use it as a premise in an argument. Perhaps I would not be inclined to use p as a premise in an argument unless I took it to be adequately grounded, but the force of the argument doesn't depend on that; nor does it depend on that higher-level belief's being adequately grounded. The force of the argument, its being sufficient to establish its conclusion, depends only on the arguer basing the premises on an adequate ground and on the form of the argument. Thus epistemic circularity, unlike the simple form of logical circularity in which the conclusion appears as a premise, does not of itself prevent the argument from being used to establish its conclusion.

To put the point another way, what is necessary for the PES of the premises is only the truth of RP, not that S has adequate grounds for taking it to be true. So long as RP *is* true, then S will have at least prima face adequate grounds for those premises (and epistemic circularity itself cannot bring it about that this prima facie presumption is overridden), and that permits the argument to be cogent even if S does not have adequate grounds for the prior assumption of RP, and even if S does not realize that he is making that assumption. And so, despite appearances, the argument could be cogent even though it is epistemically circular.

But even so an epistemically circular argument for RP does not satisfy the usual aspirations of those seeking to determine whether normal perceptual beliefs are generally reliably formed. What I just pointed out is that *so long as RP is true*, an argument for it that is epistemically circular by virtue of assuming RP in practice can still be used to show that RP is true. Or, more exactly, the epistemic circularity will not disqualify it. So long as the argument is otherwise satisfactory, it can still do the job. But we get this result only if RP is, in fact, true; otherwise the perceptual beliefs that figure among the premises will not be reliably formed. *If and only if* RP is true, it can be shown to be true by an otherwise satisfactory argument that assumes RP in putting forward premises as it does. But that is not going to help anyone who is unsure about the matter and wants to find out *whether* RP is true. Assuring this person that *if* RP is true, then an epistemically circular argument can show it to be true will not settle his question. It was precisely that condition about which the person was unsure.

Here is another way of bringing this out. The point I have just been making about showing RP to be true can be made about any belief-forming practice, no matter how disreputable. We can just as well say of beliefs based on crystal-ball gazing that if and only if that is a reliable way of forming beliefs, it can be shown to be reliable by a track-record argument that is epistemically circular by virtue of our using the same way to check the beliefs formed on that basis for their truth. At least this is true for any way of forming beliefs that will give results that are consistent with each other. That will ensure that a track-record argument shows the process to be 100 percent reliable. And even if the process only almost always gives mutually consistent results, we can still show by the simple track-record argument that it is a highly reliable way of forming beliefs. This is not what we are after. When we ask whether various ways of forming beliefs are reliable, we are interested in discriminating those that are reliable from those that are not. Hence the mere fact that if a process is reliable it can be shown to be reliable by using that process to check its own results fails to make that discrimination, fails to discriminate between those processes that are in fact reliable from those that are not. Epistemically circular arguments will not make that discrimination.

v. Avoiding Epistemic Circularity

I have been examining track-record arguments for the reliability of PBs in general and have concluded that because of epistemic circularity they cannot give us what we are looking for. But suppose the target of the argument was narrower than PBs in general. Let's look at some narrower classes of beliefs, still staying within PBs. We will see that this makes an important difference to the vulnerability to epistemic circularity.
Where the target of the track-record argument is PBs generally, ranging over all sensory modalities, it seems particularly obvious that we cannot check perceptual beliefs for truth without relying on perceptual beliefs to do so. The reliance does not have to be of the maximally simple sort that involves using direct perception to determine whether it is the case that p in order to check the truth value of a belief that p. It could involve perceiving other things that one has sufficient reason for supposing to be a strong indication that p. Thus, if the belief to be checked is that a British Airways plane flew over the Syracuse, New York, area around noon on February 5, 2002, I could check it by examining the records of relevant flight controllers. But then I would still have to rely on the accuracy of my perception of those records. And if some check on the reliability of those flight

controllers is needed, I could consult their supervisors or check their files for any indication of defective performance or the reverse. But then I have to rely on my perception of those things. If we try to imagine checking on the accuracy of a perceptual report without making any use of sense perception to do so, we are totally at a loss. It is clearly the office of sense perception to acquaint us with particular facts about the world that are inaccessible to us in any other way, particular facts that are contingent and cannot be ascertained just by considering how things necessarily go in general. Even so minimal a check as determining whether a perceptual belief goes along with what people normally perceive under those circumstances (a) would not be a decisive indication that just that was accurately perceived by that believer at that time and (b) would involve reliance on perceptual evidence to support the claim that this is the sort of thing that people normally perceive.

But if the target of the investigation were much narrower, we would not necessarily run into epistemic circularity in attempting to show it to be reliable. The narrowest target would be a particular belief formed by S at a particular time. But we need not get that narrow to make the present point. Consider the class of perceptual beliefs with a given propositional content, for example, that *the perceived object is a peach pie*. We could do a frequency count of true beliefs for such a class without including any perceptual beliefs from this class among the premises. We could rely on other perceptions to check for truth value in each case, for example, how the object tastes, its color pattern, how it smells, what the label on the package says, and so on. And the class could extend further without running into epistemic circularity. How about all perceptual beliefs about pies? Could we check each such belief for truth value without relying on any perceptual beliefs about pies? We could if we had sufficient evidence (not involving perceptions of pies) of lawlike connections between other perceivable states of affairs and states of affairs involving pies. And this is not obviously impossible. At some point, though, a line would be crossed beyond which we would no longer be immune to epistemic circularity. And, presumably, this would come well before the widening gets as far as all perceptual beliefs. Think of the class of visual perceptual beliefs. Could we check all such beliefs without relying on any visual perceptual beliefs? It seems dubious. It's dubious that lawlike dependencies across sensory modalities are that extensive. And perhaps the line would be crossed much before that. What about the class of perceptual beliefs about books? Could we check every such belief for truth value without relying on any perceptual beliefs about books? There is, of course, the omnipresent possibility of reliance on testimony. I could check the accuracy of my perceptual belief that you own a copy of *Emma* by asking you whether you do and listening to your answer. But if in order to do a thorough check on the original perceptual belief I would have to have sufficient reasons for considering you a reliable source of information about books, or about your books, it looks as if I would have to rely on some perceptual beliefs about books in order to ascertain that you are to be trusted in what you assert about books or about your own books.

In any event, wherever the line is drawn the basic point is that there are classes of perceptual beliefs in the determination of the reliability of which we run into epistemic circularity and cases where we do not. Hence at this point it looks as if we could avoid epistemic circularity altogether by keeping our targets narrow enough.

But that is not so easy. For one thing, as epistemologists we are interested in very general questions about the conditions under which we have adequate grounds of belief or reliable belief formation, and these questions will not go away just because we have difficulties in answering them. And there is a much more theoretical reason that does not depend on contingent facts about our interests. This has to do with what would happen if we pushed our inquiry far enough. To illustrate this, let's not start so far down the specificity scale as a particular belief with a particular content but take something more general than that. Start with visual perceptual beliefs and suppose, contrary to what I was suggesting earlier, that the accuracy of any accurate visual PB can be established by using touch and audition alone. But then, unless we are parochially concerned with vision, we will be equally interested in the general reliability of audition and touch. Suppose again that this can be established by relying on PBs formed by two other sensory modalities—smell and taste. How about the reliability of those? Take taste. If its reliability is established by relying on taste, we are once more embroiled in epistemic circularity. If it is established by relying exclusively on PBs formed by other sensory modalities, it will have to be by one or more of the others that appeared earlier in the regress. For the repertoire of human sensory modalities is limited. Say the reliability of taste is established by reliance on vision and audition. We are still involved in epistemic circularity, but the circle is larger. Vision is validated by audition and touch, which are validated by smell and taste, which (assuming the story with smell is the same as with taste) are validated by vision and audition. Thus the situation is this. We assume that the general reliability of any class of PB formations can be validated only if we rely on the general reliability of some class of PB formations. Given that assumption, even if the reliability of any class narrower than the whole can be validated by reliance on other classes of PB formation, if we push the inquiry far enough, we will run into a larger circle in which the chain of reliance involved in establishing reliability will eventually circle back to the class from which we started. And so we are forced to the conclusion that narrowing the class of PBs the reliability of whose formation we are concerned with does not enable us to escape epistemic circularity in arguments designed to establish this but only postpones the evil day.

vi. The Pervasiveness of Epistemic Circularity

If it were only a simple track-record argument for the reliability of our normal ways of forming PBs that is infected with epistemic circularity, and if we could find other satisfactory arguments for the same conclusion, the above results would not be of much significance. But epistemic circularity turns up with surprising frequency among arguments for this sort of conclusion. In Alston 1993a I survey a large number of such arguments and conclude that any argument for RP that is not otherwise disqualified suffers from epistemic circularity. I can't claim to have examined every argument that has been put forward, much less all possible arguments. But I believe that the sample is large enough and representative enough to give strong support for the conclusion. I refer the reader to Alston 1993a for most of the details, restricting myself here to one argument, where epistemic circularity surfaces where least expected. This argument is set out in somewhat greater detail in Alston 1993a, Chapter 3, section v.

The argument depends on Wittgenstein's claim of the impossibility of a necessarily private language. What Wittgenstein denies is not the possibility of a de facto private language, one that in fact is understood and used by only one person, but rather the possibility of a language that only one person *could* understand.

> But could we also imagine a language in which a person could write down or give vocal expression to his inner experiences—his feelings, moods, and the rest—for his private use?—Well, can't we do so in our ordinary language?—But that is not what I mean. The individual words of this language are to refer to what can only be known to the person speaking: to his immediate private sensations. So another person cannot understand the language. (Wittgenstein 1953 #243)

The argument from this to RP that I will present here is due to some unpublished remarks of Peter van Inwagen. He is not to be held responsible for the exact form I give it. Nor do I mean to imply that he is committed to any argument of this general sort, or that he is not.

Let's use the term 'public language' to cover a language that is used in common by members of a social group, a language the terms of which mean what they do by virtue of public rules for their use. The Wittgensteinian position on the impossibility of a private language could be put as follows:

(1) If (alleged) term 'P' cannot figure in a public language, it has no meaning.

But:

(2) If RP is false, there can be no public language.

The reason for (2) is that a public language gets established by way of social interactions in which the participants find out by perception what other participants are saying and doing. Think of first language learning. This is possible only by getting reliable perceptual information about the linguistic and other behavior of one's fellows. How else would one come to realize what various words mean and how to make and understand acts of communication?

But then, if we skip some obvious steps, by hypothetical syllogism from (1) and (2):

(3) If RP is false, then no term can have a meaning.

But in raising the issue of the reliability of our normal formation of PBs, we suppose ourselves to be using language meaningfully. And if we are not using language meaningfully, we have failed to raise that issue or any other. Hence:

(4) If no term can have a meaning, we cannot raise the issue as to the truth of RP.

Therefore, by transposition from (4):

(5) If it is possible to raise the issue as to the truth of RP, then terms can have meaning.

By transposition from (3):

(6) If terms can have meaning, then RP is true.

And from (5) and (6) by hypothetical syllogism:

CRITICAL QUESTIONS ABOUT EPISTEMOLOGICAL METHODOLOGY 209

(7) If it is possible to raise the issue as to the truth of RP, then RP is true.

Thus there is no real possibility that RP is false. If it were, then there could not be so much as a question as to its truth. If there is such a question, it can have only an affirmative answer.
  It does not seem that this argument depends in any way on the evidence of the senses until we ask how we know that (2) is true. The support for it appealed to the way in which people acquire their first language. But how do we know that this is the way it is done? That is not the only conceivable way. Conceivably, human beings might be born with innate knowledge of a language. We know that in fact people acquire their first language by observing the behavior of other members of their social group, and we know this by relying on our sense perceptions of what goes on in first language acquisition and reasoning from those perceptual data. And so it takes only a little digging to discover that this apparently purely a priori argument does after all depend on empirical evidence acquired through perception. And in crediting this empirical evidence we assume, in practice, that forming perceptual beliefs in the way we normally do is a generally reliable mode of belief formation.
  Suppose that I am mistaken about these and the other arguments for the general reliability of the formation of normal PBs. Suppose, for example, that one of the many a priori arguments succeeds in showing this without relying on any PBs to do so. What then? Well, there is still the question of how we know that the beliefs that figure as premises in this a priori argument are reliably formed. And that is a question of just the same sort as the one we have been struggling with vis-à-vis PBs. Let's say that the a priori argument in question draws on rational intuition and deductive reasoning for its force. To generalize, we have the question whether beliefs based on rational intuition and beliefs that certain forms of deductive argument are valid are reliably formed. Consider an argument to this effect. If some of its premises are just such beliefs, we are back in epistemic circularity of the simplest kind. If it relies on beliefs from other sources—memory, perception, inference to the best explanation, or whatever—then there is a question as to whether they are reliably formed. And the same alternatives pop up there for any argument for a positive answer to this question. Are some of the premises of the argument drawn from the same set of beliefs the generally reliable formation of which the argument is designed to establish? If so, epistemic circularity rears its head again. If not, the same question arises for the general class of beliefs to which those premises belong. It is clear where this is going. If we continue to validate classes of beliefs by reliance on other classes of beliefs, either we get into an infinite regress or we find

ourselves arguing in a circle. Since the number of broad sources of human beliefs is severely limited, we can ignore the former horn of the dilemma and concentrate on the latter horn. If we continue to pursue the question whether beliefs from a certain source are reliably formed, then we will at some point come back to the source or sources from which we started. Say, to simplify, that in arguing for the reliable formation of PBs we rely on beliefs formed by rational intuition. And to argue for the reliable formation of those we appeal to beliefs based on memory and introspection. And to argue for the reliable formation of those we appeal to perception and inductive inference. And to argue for the reliable formation of beliefs based on inductive inference we appeal to perception and rational intuition. So to simplify still further, for any class of beliefs we were interested in, C_1, its formation is validated by appeal to beliefs of a class, C_2, the formation of which is validated by appeal to beliefs of a class, C_3, that are validated by appeal to beliefs of class C_1. Having come back to the starting point, the circle recycles endlessly. And so it turns out that our way of forming beliefs at any stage of the process is indirectly supported, at least in part, by beliefs of just the same sort. This tells us that beliefs of a certain type, say PBs, are reliably formed if and only if they are reliably formed. An indisputable conclusion, but one bought at the price of vacuity. Again, this is something that holds for any process of belief formation whatever, and hence it tells us nothing about which classes of beliefs are formed reliably. So even if beliefs of every broad class can be shown to be reliably formed by arguments that take premises only from other broad classes, we are still mired in epistemic circularity when we look at the big picture that takes in the entire range of human sources of belief.

CHAPTER 10

SKEPTICISM

i. Types of Skepticism

If I have been right in the preceding chapter, whenever we try to show that a certain way of forming beliefs is a reliable way, we become entangled, one way or another, in epistemic circularity. And if I have been right, epistemically circular arguments for reliability are of no value in discriminating reliable from unreliable belief-forming processes. These conclusions could easily lead to skepticism about the reliability of all belief-forming processes or the adequacy of any grounds for belief. In the end I will argue that it need not. But first, we must become clearer about the many varieties of skepticism. Epistemic circularity seems to support some forms of skepticism and not others. Eventually, I will argue that we need not relapse into even the forms that it seems to support. But I will be in a position to do that only after a thorough consideration of the kinds of skepticism, and what should be said about each. I will begin by distinguishing kinds of skepticism.

First, there is specifically *epistemological* skepticism. In the broadest sense a skeptical position involves a denial of or doubt about something, usually if not invariably about something that is generally or widely accepted, or at least widely accepted by the audience to which the skeptical remarks are addressed. Thus I can be a skeptic about religious doctrines, about the stock market, about weather predictions, about the chances of the Tennessee Titans winning the NFL championship, about Saddam Hussein's denial that Iraq had chemical or biological weapons, about George W. Bush's having a promising program to improve the economy, and so on. These all involve doubts or denials concerning alleged nonepistemic facts. But distinctively epistemic skepticism is directed to alleged epistemic facts, to allegations that someone has knowledge or well-grounded beliefs about certain matters, or to the possibility of knowledge or well-grounded beliefs about certain matters or in general. It is easy to confuse these because in supporting a position opposed to a skepticism of the first sort, for example, about the Christian doctrine of the Incarnation, one would typically be adducing reasons for supposing the doctrine to be true, and if one were successful in this, one would at the same time be representing oneself as having a well-grounded belief in the doctrine. But there is still a difference in the explicit focus of the controversy. To show that Jesus Christ was God incarnate is one thing, and to show that one has a well-grounded belief that Jesus Christ was God incarnate is something different, even though succeeding in the former would also put one in a position to show the latter. One way to see the difference is to note that the converse does not hold. One could show that one has a well-grounded belief in the Incarnation by showing that one's grounds render it probably true but, depending on our concept of showing, fall short of showing that it is true. Moreover, to show that the doctrine is true has no bearing on whether someone else, much less people in general, have a well-grounded belief in it. So the distinction is important.

Within the area of skepticism about epistemic claims, there are the following important differences.

I. *What epistemic status the skeptic is skeptical about.* The main difference here is between *knowledge* and *adequate grounds for belief* (or *beliefs formed in a reliable way*). The other differences listed below apply to each of these choices.

II. *Particular-general.* The epistemic claim about which one is skeptical can concern a particular belief or it can be a more general claim about all beliefs of a certain type—beliefs about the past, about the conscious states of other people, about morality—or, as a limiting case, it can be about all beliefs whatsoever. I can be skeptical about your claim to know that Jim is planning to resign, or I can be skeptical about the possibility of anyone knowing what some human being is going to do in the future, or, at the extreme, skeptical about the possibility of anyone's having an adequate reason for any belief whatever.

This difference between epistemic claims, and skepticism about them, that concern restricted subject matters and those of unqualified generality is important enough to deserve a special rubric. Let's distinguish between *local* and *global* skepticism, where the latter is not restricted to any particular subject matters whatever.

III. *Positive-negative* differences. These have to do with whether the skeptic is putting forward a substantive claim of his own or only taking a negative attitude toward epistemic claims of others. In both cases these can be either particular or general, and if general either global or local.

   A. *Substantive skepticism.* This involves making a substantive claim of a skeptical sort. Thus one may assert that no one really knows anything at all (global), or anything about the unobservable submicroscopic structure of physical objects or about anything beyond one's own conscious experience (local). The substantive skeptic assumes quite a burden in undertaking to argue for such sweeping statements, as we shall see. Hence he may be forced back into a more modest stance.

   B. *Challenge skepticism.* This kind of skeptic simply issues a challenge to all comers to *show* that they know something or have adequate reasons for some beliefs. And if the challenge is more than an empty gesture, he will undertake to show that whoever takes up the challenge is unable to meet it. Thus his main work consists in attempting to refute attempts to establish an antiskeptical position. Here too we can have both particular and general forms, and among the latter both global and local varieties. This brand of skepticism is, so to say, a shadow of substantive skepticism. Where the substantive skeptic undertakes to establish that not-p, the challenge skeptic undertakes only to show the failure of all attempts to show that p. Since philosophers are notoriously better at refuting opponents than they are at establishing their own positions, challenge skepticism may well look more promising than its substantive cousin.

IV. There can be different *degrees of severity in the criteria* assumed by the skeptic for the epistemic statuses about which she is skeptical. Consider the different degrees of rigor in the standards for knowledge. A good recent example of a global substantive skeptic about knowledge is Peter Unger. In his 1975 he defends the position that no one knows anything, and in order to defend this highly skeptical position, he assumes that for a cognitive state to count as knowledge it must be certain, in a strong sense of the term that implies not just truth but the *impossibility* of mistake. Skeptics of this ilk from ancient Greece down to the present are often told that they are setting the standards for knowledge much too high. And so the argument then becomes one of what is the best or correct or most defensible way of thinking of knowledge. Such arguments can often turn into question-begging when the antiskeptic takes as a decisive refutation of the skeptical opponent that if knowledge requires certainty, then most of what we ordinarily consider to be knowledge would fail to win that title. To which the skeptic responds that this is precisely his position.

Leaving such arguments aside, the basic point is that there is a direct correlation between the strictness of the criteria for the epistemic status in question, on the one hand, and the ease of establishing substantive skepticism and the difficulty of overthrowing it, on the other. Moving over to skepticism about the adequate grounding of beliefs, if it is held that this requires reasons that are themselves adequately grounded and also logically entail the target belief, then it is not difficult to show that we have relatively few adequately grounded beliefs.

V. Now I want to distinguish different ways of supporting a substantive skeptical position. Each of these will have both global and local versions, and if the latter, various kinds of localization.

　A. *The inability to rule out alternative possibilities.* Here the argument is that (focusing on knowledge) there are possibilities such that if they are realized, then one doesn't know anything, or anything of a certain sort. Restricting ourselves for now to the global version, we can call this *Cartesian Skepticism*, after its most famous exposition. This is not say, of course, that Descartes was a "Cartesian skeptic" or any other kind of skeptic. It is rather that this is the kind of skepticism that he was worried about and sought to refute. The alternative possibility (or alleged possibility) that gave him this concern was that the world is ruled by an omnipotent evil genius who has arranged things in such a way that when it seems most clear to us that something is true it is false. Contemporary versions prefer the idea that each of us is a brain in a vat programmed in such a way that we have just the kinds of experiences and resultant beliefs that we do have. Or, alternatively, that our cognitive states are fiendishly manipulated through remote control by hyperintelligent extraterrestrial beings who have arranged things in the way envisaged by Descartes for his evil genius.

　　This form of argument for global skepticism about knowledge sets the standards for knowledge very high. To require for knowledge that p that one have ruled out every (alleged) possibility that if realized would make the proposition that p false, or even that one is capable of doing so, is to put a heavy burden indeed on the aspirant to knowledge, one that it may be impossible to satisfy. At least, neither Descartes nor any of his followers in this enterprise have succeeded, or, to make a more modest claim, it is not clear that they have done so. And we confidently take ourselves to know many things with respect to which this demand has not been met.

B. *The inability to find adequate grounds for beliefs of a certain kind, in beliefs that are themselves adequately grounded.* This support for skepticism comes only in local versions since it presupposes that there are some beliefs that are adequately grounded (or, in a knowledge version, that there are some things that we do know). One common skeptical position of this sort takes beliefs about one's own current conscious states to be the only empirical beliefs that enjoy a PES apart from support by other beliefs with PES. And then the claim is that nothing else, or at least no beliefs of certain types, can receive adequate support, either directly or indirectly, from a foundation that is restricted in the way just specified. Since Hume in his most skeptical moods is a historically famous advocate of this kind of skepticism, I will call it *Humean Skepticism*, though allowing this term to range over any skepticism of this form even though the fillings are specified differently.

C. I have sketched these two ways of arguing for skepticism not to discuss them further but as a contrast to the way that involves epistemic circularity. The general type of which this is a species seeks its support in *the impossibility of adequate support for the epistemic assumptions that are presupposed in our claims to knowledge or adequately grounded belief.* Since the skepticism attributed to the ancient Greek skeptic, Pyrrho, was given this kind of support, among others, I will term it *Pyrrhonian Skepticism*. If one were to support a skepticism about a certain class of beliefs such as perceptual beliefs by seeking to show that any attempt to support the claim that perceptual beliefs formed as we ordinarily do are formed reliably, or are adequately grounded, runs into epistemic circularity, this would be a form of Pyrrhonian skepticism. And a parallel global variety could use the argument of Chapter 9, sections iv–vi, in an attempt to establish that if we push the attempt to demonstrate the validity of criteria of well-foundedness far enough, we will run into epistemic circularity no matter what belief or class of beliefs it is from which we begin.

Where does Pyrrhonian skepticism that is supported by an argument from epistemic circularity stand on the dimension of severity of criteria presupposed for well-grounded belief? Can it be met by a successful attempt to weaken the criteria? Well, it would be highly controversial to demand of knowledge or well-grounded belief that the subject have actually carried out a demonstration of the validity of general principles presupposed that is not subject to epistemic circularity. But it is more difficult to carry through the claim that not even the possibility of such a demonstration is required for genuine knowledge or genuinely adequately grounded belief. Consider the fact brought out in the preceding chapter that any way of forming beliefs, no matter how disreputable, can be shown to be reliable if we countenance epistemically circular demonstrations, and the implication from this that epistemically circular arguments fail to discriminate reliable ways of forming beliefs from blatantly unreliable ones. Given this, we cannot rest content with epistemically circular arguments. And so if the reliability of the way of forming a certain belief (alternatively, the epistemic principle assumed in accepting it) can be supported only by an epistemically circular argument, we must relapse into skepticism or else challenge the assumption that a satisfactory argument must be possible for presupposed epistemic principles or criteria if the beliefs presupposing them are to be adequately grounded. I will seek to avoid skepticism by taking the latter route.

But first I want to point out that the problem currently before us—how to live with the pervasiveness of epistemic circularity—does not have to be posed in terms of how to escape the clutches of skepticism. This is unquestionably a dramatic way of putting the problem. The figure of the skeptic has enlivened many an introductory philosophy course and kept the students from relapsing into slumber. But it is not necessary for a calm, fully mature consideration of the problem. We could, without being at all inclined to take skepticism seriously, and without being genuinely fearful of falling prey to it, undertake to consider the epistemic status of epistemically evaluative principles. Are they, all or some of them, directly based on experience, or do they have to be supported by sufficient reasons in order to have a high PES? Is it required that they have a high PES in order that lower-level beliefs that fall under them have a high PES? If they must be sufficiently supported in some way to be rationally acceptable, what alternatives are there for this support? Must it be the kind of support that renders them highly probable, or will some other way of showing them to be rationally acceptable do the job? These are questions about the epistemology of epistemology that can be pursued without constantly looking over one's shoulder to see if the skeptic is gaining on us.

But having said this, I shall continue to discuss the problem in the more dramatically attractive way of considering what response we should make to the substantive or challenge skeptic who is armed with the thesis that epistemic circularity is omnipresent in attempts to establish the validity of basic epistemic principles and criteria.

ii. Disarming the Pyrrhonian Skeptic

A first step in dealing with the global substantive Pyrrhonian skeptic is to note that his position renders him dialectically immobile. Since he holds that the pervasiveness of epistemic circularity makes it impossible for us to have an adequately grounded confidence in the reliability of any general way of forming beliefs, and since he furthermore holds that this implies that no beliefs can be adequately grounded, he has cut himself off from the possibility of supposing any beliefs at all to be adequately grounded. This leaves him without entitlement to a reliance on any premises for any argument in support of any conclusion whatever, including his own position. He can, of course, hold that position, but since he is unable to give any reason for us to take it seriously, we need not suppose that taking it seriously is a reasonable option for us.

To be sure, by the same token we are not able to present a refutation of his position that he would be in a position to appreciate or recognize as such. For the same disability that prevents him from marshaling an argument for his position prevents us from producing a refutation of his argument that is not question-begging when directed to him. For any such refutation would employ premises we are assuming in practice to be adequately grounded, and he is committed by his position to denying that those premises or any other premises can be. As far as an argument between us is concerned, we remain in suspension, facing each other in a dialectical void, neither of us able to move a step. But, of course, my attempts to decide what attitude to take toward the epistemic circularity difficulty is not restricted to arguments with my skeptical opponent. I can proceed on the basis of what I take to be well-grounded beliefs whether he is prepared to recognize them as such or not. Eventually, I will have to come to terms with the epistemic circularity difficulty, as applied to those premises, as well as to anything else I suppose to have a PES. But I can't begin to do so by starting out with what the global substantive skeptic allows me, namely, nothing. To come to terms with it I have to proceed on the basis of what I take myself to believe on adequate grounds, and then circle back to whatever rationale I can give for those takings, along with their near relations.

Let's consider what this dialectical situation implies for the question of how we should regard epistemic circularity. Remember that the problem is posed by the fact that any attempt to show the reliability of a particular way of forming beliefs will, sooner or later, exhibit epistemic circularity. And the question that poses is as to what alternatives that leaves us. One, such as it is, is global skepticism, which, as we have just seen, means that we join our erstwhile skeptical opponent in that position of frozen immobility just sketched. But that is not a real alternative for us. It is not a position we could possibly occupy. So long as we are alive we cannot help having beliefs, nor can we avoid using them to guide our thought and action. The conditions of human life irresistibly impel us to do so. And even if it were possible, as some of the ancient Greek skeptics supposed it to be, it would be about as unpalatable an alternative as can be imagined. So what live alternatives are there?

They can all be ranged under the following formula. Proceed to form beliefs and rely on them (take them to be credible, take them to be at least probably true), using various modes of belief formation that we find ourselves in possession of and the reliability of which we find ourselves strongly inclined to trust. All this without *already* having shown them to be reliable. This is the only alternative to the frozen immobility of global skepticism. It is the only alternative because, as we have seen, we cannot even begin to try to show that a given way of forming beliefs is reliable without relying on various ways of forming beliefs to give us the premises we would use in the attempt.

But, the critical philosopher might say, isn't that arbitrary, dogmatic, or deserving of some other term of epistemic censure? How can it be rationally acceptable to employ a way of forming beliefs without having established its claim to a sufficient degree of reliability? Well, it must be conceded that this goes against a strong aspiration of epistemology—to refuse to use any way of forming beliefs unless it has successfully run the gauntlet of philosophical criticism. But what we have just seen is that achieving this is strictly impossible, as impossible as squaring the circle or being in two widely separated places at the same time. Hence the better part of wisdom is to recognize that fact and get over the yearning for the impossible.

Moreover, the curse of arbitrariness or dogmatism can be at least diminished by the reflection that once we have a substantial body of beliefs in our repertoire and have committed ourselves to a number of ways of forming beliefs, we can submit any of those beliefs or doxastic practices to critical evaluation. But not all at once. For we can critically evaluate any one of them only by taking for granted, pro tem, a goodly number of the others. That is the fundamental feature of the human cognitive condition that we have been running up against. We can't do a job without some tools. We can't mount an argument without some premises and without taking some way(s) of forming beliefs to be generally reliable.

But recognizing this fundamental feature does not tell us what ways of forming beliefs to credit without having shown them to be reliable. In terms of the myth of a starting point of human inquiry that Descartes and other early modern philosophers have deeply impressed on the modern philosophical mind, which of the possible ways of forming beliefs should we take for granted without prior validation when we begin the task of building up a body of knowledge? This is a myth rather than a real-life situation just because by the time any of us reaches the stage at which the deepest and most basic epistemological questions are raised, we have already acquired a rich repertoire of beliefs and have already been confidently using a wide variety of ways of forming beliefs. As Hegel put it, "The owl of Minerva flies only at the gathering of the dusk". More soberly put, what ways of forming beliefs should we use at the outset, before any critical evaluation of such ways has been possible? Should we follow the Cartesian exhortation to accept only what we see "clearly and distinctly" to be true? Should we accept, also or instead, a reliance on what we know by introspection about our states of consciousness? Should we accept the deliverances of sense perception, memory, and/or various forms of reasoning, and so on? The abstract possibilities are legion.

But, of course, the points already made imply that it is futile to search for *reasons* for preferring some doxastic practices rather than others at the beginning. For at "the beginning" we have absolutely nothing to go on to make a reasoned decision as to which practices to use and which to abstain from. There is no "view from nowhere", to use Thomas Nagle's memorable phrase. So the imaginative exercise of placing ourselves at the beginning of our cognitive life is of no use in organizing our real cognitive life. To be sure, it would seem that some simple ways of forming beliefs are biologically determined, "hard-wired" in such a way that at a certain developmental stage we employ them willy-nilly without having to make a decision, reasoned or otherwise, to do so. The simplest forms of perceptual belief formation presumably fall under this description, and certain basic forms of reasoning and acceptance of testimony, and others may do so as well. But the fact remains that where making a reasoned choice as to what modes of belief formation to employ, there is no question of doing so without already having DPs at our disposal without having chosen them on the basis of reasons. And in real life by the time we reach the stage at which we become concerned with this ultimate epistemological question, if we ever do, we find ourselves with the deposit of not only hard-wired DPs but all the DPs and their doxastic outputs that we have been accumulating for many years. And since it is impossible in principle to make a reasoned choice as to what DPs we should employ without using some DPs to do so and assuming pro tem that they are reliable, it would be arbitrary to pick some smaller selection from the ones we find ourselves attached to at a given moment and give only them a (temporarily) privileged position—keeping in mind that we can critically evaluate any practice or belief at any point, using, of course, other practices and beliefs to do so.

Here I pause in the exposition to relate this "there is no place to start except where we are" point to the response to the epistemic circularity problem in Alston 1991a, chapter 4, and in Alston 1993a, chapter 5. There I deployed what I called a "practical rationality" argument. Faced with the conclusion that any otherwise effective argument for the reliability of a doxastic practice is infected with epistemic circularity, I abandoned the project of trying to establish such reliability and switched to an attempt to show that it was "practically rational", rational as a matter of practice, to employ certain doxastic practices, namely, those that are firmly socially established. And I further argued that if it is practically rational to employ a doxastic practice, it is also practically rational to take it to be reliable. There would be a sort of pragmatic contradiction in employing a way of forming beliefs and denying that it is a generally reliable way of forming beliefs. And so, I maintained, even though epistemic circularity bars us from showing "theoretically" that a given doxastic practice is reliable without relying on others that haven't been shown to be reliable, we can at least show that it is practically rational to take various such practices to be reliable. At least we can show for each socially established practice that it is *prima facie* practically rational to take it to be reliable, though any such prima facie status might be overridden by sufficient contradictions in the output of the practice or sufficient contradictions between that output and the output of more firmly established doxastic practices. And the argument for this conclusion made use of the same kinds of considerations as the present "we have to start from where we are" position. For that conclusion was based on the argument that there is no alternative to employing, and taking as reliable, the practices we find ourselves with at a given time, remembering that any one of these can be subsequently questioned by using some selection from the others to do so.[1] Hence we are forced to settle for a second-best version of the traditional philosophical aim of validating our customary ways of forming beliefs. Though we can't show that any of them are reliable, we can at least show that it is practically rational to take them as such.

I have come to see that this line of argument is defective in more than one way and in addition that it is cumbersome in ways that are not needed to make the basic intuitive point behind it. It is defective because the argument that it is practically rational to employ, and take as reliable, a particular doxastic practice itself has to make use of a practical commitment to the reliability of certain practices (this very one and/or others) and hence itself falls into epistemic circularity. Hence it is no improvement over an otherwise effective straight argument for the reliability of a particular practice. It is unnecessary for making the basic intuitive point because that point is just the one that is set forth in this present exposition, namely, that there is no alternative (practically rational or otherwise) to using in an investigation what we accept at that point as reliable belief-forming practices and probably true beliefs, remembering again that any one of them can be critically evaluated so long as we continue to employ some doxastic practices and take some beliefs as at least probably true. This is a point that is undeniable and that can be set forth very simply, as I did above, without all the cumbersome machinery of the earlier "practical rationality" argument. There are also difficulties in getting straight as to just what 'practical rationality' is supposed to mean in this argument.[2]

iii. Humean Skepticism

Now that we have dispelled the illusion of the possibility of deliberately building up our cognitive equipment from scratch and doing so on the basis of adequate reasons for our choices, let's take a look at the not completely impossible task of taking the reliability of some doxastic practices for granted and on that basis examining the claims to reliability of others. If the DPs we take for granted are scanty enough, we are in danger of falling into what in section i I called "Humean Skepticism". But let's forget Humean and other skeptical positions and confine ourselves to examining the procedure of making a severe restriction in the DPs we take for

---

[1] This is only the barest sketch of the argument for the position set forth in those earlier publications. For the full-dress presentation, the reader is referred to them, especially the version in Alston 1991a.
[2] For some well-aimed shots in this direction, see Plantinga 2000, chap. 4, sec. II.

granted, as contrasted with the more liberal procedure we recommended in section ii. That procedure, remember, involved freely using whatever DPs and whatever beliefs we find ourselves confident of at a given point, using them in whatever investigations we engage in without first having to show the DPs to be reliable and the beliefs to be adequately grounded. This is in contrast to a restriction to a severely limited set of DPs and beliefs that are taken for granted without antecedent support. Hume, for example, worked with DPs of forming introspective beliefs about one's current conscious experiences and forming beliefs about necessary truths on the basis of rational intuition. Other philosophers who take an abstemious route make different choices. There has been no more persistent and effective critic of this "undue partiality" in what is taken for granted than Thomas Reid. Here are two examples.

> The author of the "Treatise of Human Nature" appears to me to be but a half-skeptic. He hath not followed his principles so far as they lead him, but, after having, with unparalleled intrepidity and success, combated vulgar prejudices, when he had but one blow to strike, his courage fails him, he fairly lays down his arms, and yields himself a captive to the most common of all vulgar prejudices—I mean the belief of the existence of his own impressions and ideas.
> I beg, therefore, to have the honour of making an addition to the skeptical system, without which I conceive it cannot hang together. I affirm, that the belief of the existence of impressions and ideas, is as little supported by reason, as that of the existence of minds and bodies. No man ever did or could offer any reason for this belief. . . . A thorough and consistent skeptic will never, therefore, yield this point. To such a skeptic I have nothing to say, but of the semi-skeptic, I should beg to know, why they believe the existence of their impressions and ideas. The true reason I take to be, because they cannot help it; and the same reason will lead them to believe many other things. (Reid 1970, V, 7, 81–82)
> The skeptic asks me, Why do you believe the existence of the external object which you perceive? This belief, sir, is none of my manufacture; it came from the mint of Nature; it bears her image and superscription; and, if it is not right, the fault is not mine: I even took it upon trust, and without suspicion. Reason, says the skeptic is the only judge of truth, and you ought to throw off every opinion and every belief that is not grounded on reason. Why, sir, should I believe the faculty of reason more than that of perception?—they came both out of the same shop, and were made by the same artist; and if he puts one piece of false ware into my hands, what should hinder him from putting another? (1970, VI, 20, 207)

This is in terms of only "reason" being taken for granted and used to judge the reliability of other ways of forming belief, a term that suggests rational intuition of necessary truths. But I suspect that Reid, who had Hume in mind, was thinking of it as also containing the awareness of one's current impressions and ideas, that is, one's current experiences.

Let me take the liberty of putting in my own words, with considerable loss of rhetorical effectiveness, the point that Reid is making in these passages. If we take the reliability of some way(s) of forming belief for granted without recognizing the need of reasons for this, and then hold that any other doxastic practices are to be rejected unless their reliability can be shown by employing the former practices, we are guilty of undue partiality. If it is epistemically allowable to take "reason" to be reliable without offering any reason for this supposition, how can we justify not extending the same courtesy to others that we find ourselves confidently employing— perception, memory, inductive reasoning, and so on? In Reid's terms, we accept the former because "we cannot help it", and in that case we should be equally entitled to accept others we "cannot help" using. More prosaically put, since human existence would be impossible without our forming beliefs in some ways or other, and since we cannot have reasons for forming them in certain ways without using other ways to generate those reasons, we cannot exist without, at the moment, taking some modes of belief formation for granted. This being the case, it would be arbitrary to accord that status to some of those of which we feel confident and withhold it from others. Thus the only nonarbitrary course open to us is to continue to use, and take as generally reliable, all the ways of forming belief we find ourselves inclined to accept as such, remembering that any one of them can be subject to critical evaluation, provided we continue to employ others in order to have some resources for that evaluation.

Please note that I am not arguing for a ban on the project of using some doxastic practices to determine whether certain others are reliable. As I pointed out in Chapter 9, section vi, many attempts have been made to establish the general reliability of sense perception without relying on perception for any of the premises of the argument. I argue in Alston 1993a that those that are not otherwise defective suffer from epistemic circularity. And although I do not believe that tomorrow someone will come up with an argument that escapes this criticism, I cannot prove that it is impossible. Moreover, as pointed out above, even if this were possible for one of the major basic modes of belief formation, we would wind up in a larger circle if we continued to ask the same critical questions about the reliability of the practices employed at each stage of the regress thereby generated.

How significant is this disclaimer of a ban? It may be of some interest to determine whether one can carry out an a priori proof of the general reliability of sense perception, or an empirical proof (not relying at all on memory) of the general reliability of memory. But that interest is likely to dissipate when it is pointed out that even if this can be done in particular cases, it has no decisive bearing on the resolution of global skeptical doubts about the reliability of our belief-forming faculties, because of the ultimate circularity in which we will become enmeshed, as pointed out in Chapter 9, section vi. Hence, as far as the most ultimate questions are concerned, we are thrown back on the position that there is no real alternative to taking for granted, pro tem, what we find ourselves confidently accepting, and working with that to further enlarge and purify our beliefs and our repertoire of doxastic practices.

iv. Skepticism Concerning Various Epistemic Desiderata

This discussion of the most ultimate epistemological questions, and of the various forms of skepticism that provoke them, has been restricted to what I have claimed to be the most fundamental epistemic desiderata for beliefs—having an adequate basis and being formed in a reliable way. I have argued that any attempt to avoid taking for granted and working with what we find ourselves with at a particular time is inevitably infected with epistemic circularity and therefore does not give us what we have traditionally been looking for. But what about the other epistemic desiderata for belief? Do they lead in the same direction? Are we driven there to moderate our philosophical aspirations by taking for granted, prima facie, what we find ourselves with at the moment? Let's consider the matter, beginning with other desiderata in the truth-conducive (TC) cluster.

First, consider S's having adequate reasons (evidence . . .) for a belief that p. This can be construed as leaving it open whether S believes that p and/or if so whether that belief is based on the adequate grounds in question. Since we are restricting the discussion to epistemic desiderata for beliefs, we will ignore cases in which S does not believe that p. (It can easily be brought into the picture as a potentiality for having that ground for an actual belief that p.) We may allow the cases to range over both those in which the belief is based on the ground in question and cases in which it is not, though the ground is there to serve as a basis if called on to do so. (Note that we are violating ordinary usage to the extent of speaking of having a "ground" of a belief even where the belief is not so grounded. That is, the term is being used to range over both actual and possible grounds.) The desideratum so construed can be called *having an actual or possible ground for a belief*, 'APG' for short. Now we can raise the question whether we run into epistemic circularity if we try to show that (possible) beliefs of a certain class are generally such that when people have such beliefs they have APGs for them. We may as well think of this issue in terms of normal perceptual beliefs.

This question can be quickly answered. What possible reason could there be for beliefs of a certain class to be such that it is generally true that those who have them also have adequate grounds for them, except that people who have such beliefs generally *base* them on adequate grounds? If the latter were not the case, then it would be a sheer accident that people who have such beliefs also generally *have* adequate grounds for them. There would be no discernible connection between having a belief of that sort and having adequate grounds unless it were the case that beliefs of that sort are generally based on adequate grounds. What other connection could there be? I can think of no halfway plausible possibility.

But then showing that normal perceptual beliefs are generally accompanied by APGs reduces to showing that they are generally based on adequate grounds. And this means that our previous arguments for the inevitability of epistemic circularity in arguing that beliefs of a certain basic kind are generally based on adequate grounds applies also to the APG case, since we can mount a successful argument for the latter only by deriving it from the former.

The other desiderata in the TC complex, *formed by the exercise of an intellectual virtue* and *forming a belief by the proper functioning of one's cognitive faculties*, can be even more summarily dispatched. As for the former, you will remember that this was admitted to be a TC desideratum only if intellectual virtues were understood as dispositions to form beliefs that were thereby at least probably true. Hence a belief is formed by the exercise of an intellectual virtue of the sort under consideration only if it is so formed in a generally reliable fashion. And so the enterprise of showing that beliefs of a certain class generally exemplify this desideratum presupposes the possibility of showing that they are reliably formed. Hence given that the latter demonstration inevitably involves epistemic circularity, so does the former. QED. A similar point holds for the "proper function" desideratum. That was accorded the status of an epistemic desideratum only if it was so construed as to entail that the belief was formed in a reliable way. And so the inevitability of epistemic circularity in any attempt to show that applies here as well. This completes the case for all TC desiderata being such that attempts to show that the members of a given class of beliefs generally exhibit a particular TC desideratum will be infected with epistemic circularity and hence will give rise to the skeptical problems with which we have been wrestling. And hence there is no escape from the "work with what you have at the moment" position by moving from one TC desideratum to another.

When we move to non-TC desiderata, it is quite a different story. Let's first consider Group III desiderata, which consist of higher-level epistemic knowledge or well-grounded belief or the ready access thereto. Take as our representative of this group *knowing the epistemic status of a belief.* The points to be made about this will readily generalize to other desiderata in the group. Remember that the problems about epistemic circularity arose for TC desiderata because of the fact that to develop an otherwise effective argument for, for example, the adequate grounding of normal perceptual beliefs, it was necessary to include normal perceptual beliefs among the premises; and this meant that to show that such beliefs are generally adequately grounded, we had to make a practical assumption that such beliefs are generally adequately grounded. But to show that beliefs of a certain class are such that subjects of such beliefs will generally know what their epistemic status is, would we have to include among the premises beliefs the subjects of which know what their epistemic status is? To do an ideally thorough job of answering this question, we would have to examine a number of otherwise effective arguments for that conclusion and determine for each of them whether its effectiveness depends on including among its premises items that exhibit this higher-level desideratum. But I am prevented from carrying out this project by my being unacquainted with any arguments for this conclusion that are otherwise effective. In fact, so far as I can see, it is false that there is any major class of beliefs, grouped together on the basis of subject matter or on the basis of mode of origin, which is such that their subjects will generally know what their epistemic status is. It would suffice to demonstrate this falsity if, as I believe to the case, one can have a belief of any of the classes of beliefs specified in one of the ways mentioned above without even having the concept of an epistemic status of belief and/or other wherewithal to have higher-level knowledge of the epistemic status of a belief. This is obvious with respect to the more modest types of belief—perceptual, memorial, introspective, and simple inductive beliefs and beliefs based on rational intuition. But I believe that it also holds for more sophisticated beliefs such as those involved in theology and high-level scientific theories. One can, and sometimes does, believe that a certain cosmological theory best explains the origin of the physical universe without knowing just what the epistemic status of that theory is, how probable the available evidence makes it vis-à-vis its competitors, and so on.

But even if I cannot examine a number of otherwise effective arguments for the conclusion in question, or even one such argument, I can adduce some considerations that render it implausible to suppose that such an argument, in order to be effective, would have to include premises such that one who holds and makes use of the premise would thereby be assuming that he knows what its epistemic status is. The crucial point here is that such higher-level knowledge is by no means necessary for an argument using the premise in question to be cogent. That situation contrasts sharply with the situation vis-à-vis the lower-level TC desiderata of being adequately grounded or reliably formed. Unless the premises of an argument for a conclusion, any conclusion, are adequately grounded, the argument will necessarily lack cogency. But there is absolutely no reason to think that unless the premises of an argument are such that the propounder of the argument knows what the epistemic statuses of those premises are, the argument will thereby lack cogency. That, so far as I can see, has no bearing on the cogency of the argument.

If this doesn't seem obvious to you, consider the following. You have presented an argument for something, for example that the dark ages in western Europe resulted from Muslim domination of the western Mediterranean. I have no doubt that you have based the premises of your argument on adequate grounds. But I ask you, "Do you know or have extremely well-grounded belief that you have based your premises on adequate grounds? Unless you do, there is no reason why I should take your argument seriously". Wouldn't my interlocutor be well within his rights to reject my reservations as not themselves worth serious consideration? "What difference does it make to the cogency of my argument", he might say, "what I do or do not know about the epistemic status of my premises? If my premises are based on adequate grounds, that is enough to take care of the *status of the premises* part of what it takes to make my argument cogent. Why should it also be required for cogency that I have a certain higher-level knowledge of the epistemic status of the premises?" This is just a special application of the obvious point that if a belief does have a particular epistemic status, then it will have that status, and all the implications that carries, whether or not the believer realizes (knows, believes well-groundedly) that it has that status. Unfortunately, the pervasive tendency to level confusions in epistemology leads all too often to a confusion of having an adequate basis for a belief and knowing that one has an adequate basis for a belief, and the consequent tendency to require the latter for something for which only the former is necessary.[3]

Passing now to the "systemic" group of desiderata, we can also summarily dispatch the question whether they run into similar epistemic circularity problems. In the case of coherence, for it to give rise to such a problem, any otherwise effective argument for the coherence of a body of beliefs would have to require some premises that are acceptable as such only if

[3] See Alston 1980.

they are sufficiently coherently integrated into a sufficiently coherent system. Is there any reason for supposing this to be the case? Only, it seems clear, if coherentism is the correct epistemology of what it takes for a belief to be well grounded. I think that there are conclusive reasons for rejecting that, a brief sketch of which I gave earlier, but there is no need to go further into this issue. The crucial point is that whereas our TC desiderata run into epistemic circularity difficulties regardless of what the correct conditions for their application are, the supposition that coherence runs into such difficulties depends on accepting a particular, and highly controversial, account of the necessary and sufficient conditions of the adequate groundedness of belief. In taking this to be a crucially important point, I am, of course, presupposing the thesis argued for in Chapter 3 that the TC desiderata are the most fundamental ones for our cognitive endeavors. But, given that thesis, which is at the center of the position of this book, no further epistemological assumptions have to be made to yield the conclusion of the inevitability of epistemic circularity in attempts to establish the TC desiderata of beliefs of a certain type. Whereas we must make further, quite specific and highly controversial, epistemological assumptions to derive a parallel result for coherence. It is even more obvious, if possible, that the same holds for explanatory power and other systemic epistemic desiderata. The argument for this would take the same form as the above argument for coherence. I leave the extension as an exercise for the reader.

The only other group of alleged epistemic desiderata I have discussed is the deontological one. Since I have already shown that we lack effective voluntary control over belief, I can leave to one side the versions that presuppose such control. That leaves the property of a belief that consists in *its not having been formed under the (even partial) influence of a violation of intellectual duty*. Here the story is parallel to the one with respect to coherence. The only basis for supposing that any otherwise effective argument that beliefs of a certain class will generally exhibit this desideratum will have to have among its premises at least some that exhibit this desideratum, is the thesis that a belief cannot be adequately grounded (or exhibit some equivalent TC desideratum) unless it exemplifies this desideratum. And in this case too that claim depends on a particular, and at best highly controversial, epistemological thesis that truth conducivity depends on the ancestry of the belief's not including any causally indispensable dereliction of intellectual duty. Hence the judgment here will have to be the same as the one on the coherence case. We run into epistemic circularity problems only if this highly dubious epistemology is accepted. And so the situation here differs from the way arguments for TC desiderata generally attaching to members of some large basic class of beliefs lead to epistemic circularity, both because of its dependence on an extra epistemological assumption and because of the questionableness of the assumption, a questionableness much more pronounced than in the coherence case.

The canny reader will have long since noted that the dismissal of any epistemic circularity worries for desiderata of the higher-level epistemic knowledge group, for the systemic group, and for the surviving member of the deontological group is a direct consequence of the assumption that a necessary and sufficient condition for the admissibility of a premise in a cogent argument is its being based on an adequate ground, or some equivalent TC desideratum. Since it is, at best, extremely dubious that any desideratum of these three groups is itself a necessary condition of a belief's being adequately grounded, we can conclude straightaway that there is no significant danger of the conclusion of the argument's being even practically assumed in putting forward the argument. And this might well lead the same canny reader to complain that that general argument could have been presented in one fell swoop, saving us the necessity of slogging through separate arguments for each nondirectly TC group of desiderata. I cannot deny the justice of the charge. My only excuse for the lengthier presentation is that I felt, and still feel, that there is value in exercising our intuitions separately for each the groups discussed, thereby, I hope, rendering the line of argument more convincing. In any event, this canny reader's observations have been useful in bringing out the following basic point. What I believe to be the intuitively compelling thesis that *being adequately TC'ly based is all that it takes for a premise to be admissible* and the thesis for which I have been contending, that *it is only TC desiderata an attempt to give a proof of the general possession of which by some large, basic group of beliefs gives rise to epistemic circularity problems*, mutually reinforce each other. And I am convinced that that tells us something very important about the epistemology of belief. Or at least this pair of theses constitutes an important implication of the most basic thesis in this territory, that *TC desiderata are the most important ones for our cognitive activity, which has as its basic aim a high preponderance of true over false beliefs about matters of interest and importance to us.*

CHAPTER 11

THE EPISTEMIC DESIDERATA APPROACH AND THE OVERALL EPISTEMIC ORGANIZATION OF BELIEF

i. Types of Foundationalism

It remains to consider how the familiar options with respect to the overall epistemic organization of a total system of belief look from the pluralistic epistemic desiderata perspective. The options that have dominated the literature are foundationalism and coherentism, each of which is susceptible of variations. But contextualism, in one sense of that term, also deserves to be considered. I said earlier that in this book I would not get into debates between foundationalism and coherentism. And it is no part of my intention in this chapter to go into all the details that are required to give a convincing resolution of that controversy.

I begin with foundationalism, which deserves to be called *the* traditional position par excellence. The term 'foundationalism' has fallen on hard times, not only because the position is well nigh universally excoriated but also because the term itself is one of the most variously used, and abused, in epistemology. In the hands of one or another writer it is used to designate a commitment to absolute truths (truths not relative to some context, social group, orientation . . .), an uncritical acceptance of dogmas, a realist metaphysics of some sort, etc., etc. I will be focusing on the most sober and most neutral epistemological sense of the term. Foundationalism in this sense consists of viewing the overall epistemic structure of a particular subject's beliefs in the following way. Some of the beliefs enjoy a PES without being based on other beliefs, and hence without owing that status to their relations to other beliefs. That is not to say that they do not owe their PES to being based on anything. A baseless condition is, indeed, one abstract possibility, but it is not at all clear that it is realized by any actual human beliefs. A more common way of being grounded in such a way as to enjoy a PES without being grounded on other beliefs is to be based on experience, where that experience does not itself consist, even in part, in one or more beliefs. Plausible examples of such experience would be feelings of various sorts (feeling depressed, exhilarated, relieved, tense, upset, calm) and perceptual appearances (something's looking round, red, rough, like a maple tree or a computer or a barn). (Note that for the items last mentioned to be pure nondoxastic experiences, looking like a barn must be construed not as seeing something *as a barn*, where that involves taking it to be a barn, that is, believing it to be a barn, but rather as looking the (or a) way a barn typically looks to a normal percipient from such-and-such a distance, angle, in a certain kind of lighting, and so on.) In this rather abbreviated presentation I will ignore other conceivable ways in which a belief could have a PES that is not due, even in part, to being based on other beliefs and focus on the cases in which that status is due to being based on experience. It remains open just how widely the notion of experience extends. Besides feelings and preconceptual perceptual appearances, other possible candidates include bodily sensations, intuitions of self-evidence, senses of obligation or moral rightness, religious experiences, and so on. But just to get a grip on this stretch of the territory we can focus on feelings and nondoxastic perceptual experiences.

We may say that a belief that owes a sufficiently high degree of PES to being based on an experience is *immediately* (*directly*) adequately grounded, or for short is directly grounded ('adequately' being tacitly understood). Such beliefs constitute the foundations, and all other beliefs with PES owe that status to being based, directly or indirectly, on those foundations. These "superstructure" beliefs will be said to be *mediately* (*indirectly*) grounded.[1]

What I have just been describing is the purest, simplest form of foundationalism. There is a sharp distinction between foundations and beliefs in the superstructure. The former owe their PES wholly to the nondoxastic experience on which they are based while the latter owe their PES proximately to other beliefs on which they are based and, in case those other

[1] See Chapter 8, section vi, for an explanation of this terminology.

beliefs are not foundations, ultimately to foundational beliefs, which in turn owe their PES to the experience on which they are based. To turn the foundation metaphor on its head, each indirectly grounded belief stands at the origin of a (more or less) multiply branching tree structure at the tip of each branch of which is a directly grounded belief.

In a moment I will point out some ways in which the clean lines of the above version get blurred by a variety of complications. But first I will note some alternatives that confront us even with this pure format. For one thing, there are choices to be made as to what beliefs can figure as directly grounded. The most traditional version, from the seventeenth century on, restricted these, on the empirical side, to intra-mental items of which one is directly conscious—one's present feelings, sensations, and sensory experiences, and thoughts. This battery of empirical foundations was then sometimes but not always supplemented by self-evident truths. Plantinga introduced the term "classical foundationalism" for the version that limits foundations in this way.[2] These restrictions severely limit what we have to work with to provide indirect grounding for the superstructure. Indeed, it has been the general, though not unanimous, consensus of philosophers that it does not give us enough to provide a sufficient PES for any beliefs at all concerning extra-mental reality, indeed, any beliefs concerning what is beyond the present experience of a particular subject. Thus, unless self-evident truths could provide the bridge to the spatially and temporally external world, a foundationalism with this restricted a set of foundations would, as far as contingent truths are concerned, be in danger of being enclosed in a solipsism of the present moment.

Hence less puritanical foundationalists have been motivated to enlarge the repertoire of foundations to include perceptual beliefs, beliefs about the external environment that are based solely on sensory experience, and, to be able to reach beyond the present moment, memory beliefs as well.

This inflation of the foundational base brings into focus another choice that is called for. Are foundations to be limited to beliefs that are infallible, indubitable, and/or incorrigible, or can they range over beliefs that lack one or more of these "epistemic immunities"? The traditional versions that restrict empirical foundations to those first listed tended to regard such immunities as required for foundations. The names of Descartes and Locke come to mind in this connection, and they have had many followers on this point up into the twentieth century, including Bertrand Russell (at times) and C. I. Lewis. But the twentieth century has

---

[2] In this abbreviated presentation I omit the distinctions Plantinga makes within this genus. See Plantinga 1983, pt. II, sec. C.

also seen sharp attacks on the claim to infallibility, even for beliefs about current experience, from such thinkers as Nelson Goodman and David Armstrong. But however those controversies are settled, once we admit (some) perceptual beliefs about the external environment and (some) memory beliefs into the club, a claim to infallibility, indubitability, and/or incorrigibility loses whatever credibility it had for beliefs of the more restricted class. Therefore, a more relaxed foundationalism will take the foundations to be only *prima facie* adequately grounded by experience, adequately grounded provided that prima facie status is not overridden by things the subject knows or has adequately grounded beliefs about. We may use the term 'modest foundationalism' for the version that recognizes all the foundations from this larger class.

A third set of alternatives open to the foundationalist concerns the admissible ways of deriving superstructure beliefs from the foundations and from each other. A very ascetic position has been embraced according to which only logically valid deduction is countenanced. We find this in Descartes, Hume (of the *Treatise*), and many others. This austere preference runs into the same problems that plague the severe restrictions on foundations—not giving the foundationalist enough to work with in seeking to derive nonfoundational beliefs that seem to be adequately grounded. Hence more generous foundationalists allow various forms of nondeductive modes of derivation. All these are highly controversial, and there would seem to be no principled way to draw the line between sheep and goats except by frankly accepting whatever modes of derivation are needed to get what one has antecedently decided we need, as Chisholm does. Though this is a severe problem for foundationalism, it is by no means restricted to that position. Any reasonable epistemology will have to allow some forms of inference that go from adequately grounded beliefs to other adequately grounded beliefs, and therefore will have to find some acceptable way of deciding which to allow. Epistemic circularity is pervasively present in attempts to solve this problem as well as in attempts to validate noninferential bases of beliefs. The case of enumerative induction is notorious. Again, it seems that we have no reasonable alternative to accepting what we feel confident of at the moment, subject to revision should it be called for.

Now for ways in which the simple unqualified kind of foundationalism we have been considering can be blurred by various complications. In the simple version foundations are based solely on experience, superstructure beliefs solely on other beliefs. But when we recognize mixed cases in which a belief gets part of its support from experience and part from other beliefs, we get a more complex picture. Consider, for example, how a perceptual belief can be partly based on sensory experience (perceptual appearances) and partly on other beliefs. I recognize you across the room at a lecture. But (a) I don't know you well enough to be able to recognize you just from the way you look, and, moreover, I am too far away to tell it is you just by your appearance. However, I have good reason to believe that you are present in the audience, and this when added to the look makes a sufficient basis for my belief.

Can we still apply a foundationalist model to a body of beliefs that contains mixed cases like the above? We can, but not in the simple form we have been working with. For one thing, we could further enlarge the class of foundations to include those that receive an adequate basis only by a combination of experience and other beliefs. But that would have the disadvantage that these "foundations" could not carry out what can reasonably be regarded as a definitive function of foundations, namely, serving as the terminus of a chain of mediate grounding by other beliefs. For such a "foundation", resting as it does partly on other beliefs, would by virtue of that have the status of a link in the chain that depends for its status (partly) on other links. Moreover, even if all mediately well-grounded beliefs could trace their status back to one or more foundations, where those range over these hybrid types as well, this would not serve by itself to avoid an infinite regress. Historically, the main argument for foundationalism is that the only way to avoid both circularity and an infinite regress when we begin tracing back mediate well-groundedness of beliefs is for all such chains to have an origin in well-grounded beliefs that owe *none* of that status to being based on other beliefs. And even if all such chains have an origin in foundational well-grounded beliefs, where that includes hybrids, this will not guarantee that such chains cannot regress infinitely. Hence a better move for the foundationalist would be to treat these hybrids as a third class between the pure foundations and the pure superstructure. The foundationalist position, then, would be that all beliefs that owe any of their PES to having other beliefs as a basis would, in that aspect of their groundedness, be a link in a chain that has as an origin one or more beliefs that owe their PES only to something(s) other than other beliefs. And then the regress argument, in a slightly more complicated form, could still be used as a support for foundationalism.

I will mention only one other complication of the pure foundationalist model. This will introduce coherence, which will be discussed for its own sake very shortly. But I can draw on my citation of BonJour's (1985) explication of the notion of coherence in Chapter 7, section ii, to say something here about how coherence might figure in a mixed basis that is responsible for the well-groundedness of some beliefs. The general idea is this. As long as we are working within a predominantly foundationalist scheme there is no suggestion that fitting coherently into a coherent system is sufficient for a belief's having a high PES. But there could be beliefs that get some support from being based, directly or indirectly, on foundations but where this is not sufficient for being adequately grounded. Then if the belief figures in a coherent system of beliefs all the members of which have at least as much direct and/or indirect foundational grounding as the one in question, this enables the members of the system to reciprocally support each other so as to bring the level of PES of each member up to the required level. The system in question need not be the entire body of the subject's beliefs; it is easier to see this situation exemplified with much smaller local systems of beliefs. Take a case of enumerative induction. The belief contents will be of the form, Most As are Bs, x is an A and a B, y is an A and a B, and so on for many more positive cases. Let's say that each belief receives some support, directly or indirectly, from foundations but not enough in each case to meet some required minimum. They all fit together coherently by mutually supporting each other. More specifically, each is supported by the conjunction of all the others. In that case it would be plausible to take them all as adequately grounded. Each belief would owe part of its PES to foundations and part to its membership in a coherent system of mutually supporting beliefs. This would be, if you like, a mixed structure, in part foundationalist and in part coherentist. But, as I have presented the matter, it is most basically foundationalist because the coherentist factor can make its contribution only if we already have the beliefs in question partly well grounded in a foundationalist way. The coherence factor plays a supplementary role of adding to what the beliefs already have in the way of PES on foundationalist grounds.

ii. Coherentism and Contextualism

Before considering the main issue of this chapter, whether the ED approach to the epistemology of belief has any bearing on the choice between competing accounts of the overall epistemic structure of a body of beliefs, I need to say something about the other competitors—coherentism and contextualism, in that order.

In Chapter 7 I had quite a bit to say about coherentism—how to understand it as an account of what it is for a belief to be adequately grounded or possess some other kind of directly TC desideratum, and why it has grave defects as such an account. That gave a view of the position that covers much of the same kind of ground I have just covered for foundationalism.

But there are some distinctions between versions of coherentism that need to be mentioned.

1. There is a set of distinctions that flow from the fact that coherence is a degree notion. This means that the coherentist has the job of specifying how coherent a system has to be, and how coherently a particular belief has to fit into it, to generate a desired or standard level of PES. And it goes without saying that since coherence is multifaceted and since the facets are specified qualitatively rather than quantitatively, no exact specification of degree is possible. There is also a choice to be made between an absolute and comparative standard of coherence. As an example of the latter, one might require as high a degree of coherence as is obtainable by human beings working at their best.

2. Then there is the difference between taking the required degree of coherence in the abstract and taking it by reference to an actual set of beliefs. By "taking it in the abstract" I mean holding that any possible body of beliefs with the required degree of coherence would, if actualized, be sufficient to render any of its members that fitted into the system with sufficient coherence adequately grounded. This runs into the "mutually incompatible equally coherent body of beliefs" difficulty. It seems that for any degree of coherence there is an indefinite plurality of possible sets of beliefs that exhibit that degree and are such that each of these sets is logically incompatible with some of the other sets. This saddles us with the unacceptable conclusion that incompatible beliefs and conjunctions thereof are all of them adequately grounded. In an attempt to avoid this reductio we could take the theory to be restricted to bodies of beliefs actually held by human beings. This would at least avoid the *necessity* of equally coherent incompatible sets of beliefs, but the theory would still be at the mercy of contingent facts concerning what beliefs are held by human beings. If, as seems entirely possible, there are actual bodies of human beliefs that are equally coherent but logically incompatible, we are still stuck with an unacceptable consequence. So at least the threat of a reductio would remain.

3. The final alternative I will mention is between an internalist and an externalist version of coherentism. 'Internalism' as understood here holds that only what is directly knowable by introspection or reflection has any bearing on the PES of beliefs whereas externalism denies any such *restriction* (without ruling out such influences on PES). So an internalist coherentism would require that the whole body of beliefs and its degree of

coherence be readily knowable just on reflection and/or introspection. It seems clear that this is far beyond the cognitive capacity of any human being. Nevertheless, coherentism has generally been understood internalistically, at least whenever the issue has been raised, as it often has not. It is interesting that BonJour, who in his 1985 has given the most impressive recent presentation and defense of coherentism, became convinced that this requirement was thoroughly unrealistic and as a result gave up coherentism. Thus, when push came to shove, he was more committed to internalism than to coherentism. Though an externalist brand of coherentism might well be worth exploring, that task remains to be undertaken.

Note that we also have a choice between internalist and externalist brands of foundationalism, which has more often been explicitly set forth in an internalist form than coherentism has, and much more often than an externalist foundationalism. Hence incautious writers have not infrequently taken internalism to be an essential component of foundationalism. But if the reader will look back at the characterization of foundationalism in the previous section, she will see that this includes nothing that commits the foundationalist to the view that what makes foundations and superstructure beliefs adequately grounded is known, or knowable, just by introspection or reflection. In any event, since the foundationalist picture of what adequately grounds a particular belief is something restricted to its local epistemic environment rather than something as far-reaching as the coherence of an entire body of beliefs, internalism has seemed more plausible for foundationalism than for coherentism, even though it faces difficulties of its own, particularly with respect to the conceptual development required for a subject's directly knowing that what gives a belief its PES does so.

The only thing left to do with coherentism here is to relate it to the coherence element we saw various epistemologists add as a supplement to a basically foundationalist epistemology. The main thing to say is that the viability of that project in no way depends on a defense of a pure coherentism of the sort I have been portraying. The latter makes the degree of coherence of a complete system of belief crucial for the epistemic status of beliefs in that system. Thus the foundation of the position is a *global* coherence. Whereas a coherentist factor in a foundationalist epistemology makes no claims about the coherence of the subject's total system of beliefs, much less makes this the sole foundation of the epistemic status of particular beliefs. The coherence of small, *local* sets of beliefs makes some contribution to the epistemic status of beliefs in those sets. This amounts to miniature replicas of the way a full coherentism treats the subject's beliefs as a whole; and these mini-coherent sets make only some addition to other contributors to PES.

Thus the objections to full-blown coherentism, depending as they do on the global claims of the position, have no tendency to discredit a coherentist element in a basically foundationalist epistemology.

Let this suffice for a sketch of a coherentist position on what makes a belief well grounded. The last competitor for an account of the overall epistemic structure of a body of beliefs to be surveyed is *Contextualism*. This might be called the "poor man's coherentism". In the form that I will be considering it here it does not exactly fit under the label 'an account of the overall structure of a body of beliefs', for it disclaims any attempt to give such an account. But, as we shall see, along with this disclaimer it does claim to give a picture of inquiry that is designed to be a replacement for such an account, and that leads me to treat it as a competitor to foundationalism and coherentism. In a nutshell, the view is that any inquiry, any attempt to solve a problem or answer a question, takes place in a context that is itself taken for granted with no questions raised about it, though it can be critically evaluated in another context with other things taken for granted. As I pointed out in Chapter 9, section iii, this sounds very much like the "we have to start from where we are" position that I have been arguing is inescapable in our human condition. But, as we shall see in a moment, whereas a full-blown contextualist epistemology applies this point to any inquiry whatever, the form in which epistemic circularity drives us to it is much more restricted.

Contextualism differs from coherentism not only in not proposing any overall account of the structure of a body of beliefs but also in that the contexts relative to which it takes inquiry to proceed are thought of as local, partial, and severely restricted rather than the whole of the subject's beliefs. The context includes only what the inquirer uses, takes account of (or perhaps has available for use), in forming and testing hypotheses concerning the topic under investigation. A third difference is that no constraints are put on what can be part of the context other than its relevance and availability to the subject for this particular investigation. That is, there are no normative constraints on the composition of a context. It may contain ungrounded or poorly grounded beliefs and unreliable modes of inference and ways of forming beliefs, as well as adequately grounded beliefs and reliable modes of belief formation. Thus contextualism is about as far as one can get, in the way of an epistemological position, from a normative epistemological concern to restrict oneself to reliable modes of belief formation and to beliefs that are well supported by adequate grounds. Despite this, it is saved from the depths of relativism, arbitrariness, and irresponsibility by the fact that the contents of any particular context can be subsequently criticized and evaluated relative to some other context if any questions arise about them. But any such subsequent critical scrutiny must be carried out by the use of a context that is itself taken for granted pro tem without any validation of its reliability or well-foundedness.

If the contextualist is upbraided for this pervasive, even if constantly shifting, reliance on unexamined presuppositions and procedures, his response will be, "What's the alternative? What else can we rely on at the moment but what we feel confident of at that moment? If doubts or questions arise about them, we can seek to deal with them, within the framework of some other context, of course". What is behind this attitude is the denial of the possibility of any absolute, privileged, indubitable starting point that carries its own guarantee of truth or reliability. To quote Dewey again, "In the last analysis there is no last analysis". The self-warranted, self-authenticating starting point for all inquiry is a will-of-the-wisp, an illusion. We human beings are thrust into a matrix of uncertainty and fallibility, and the better part of wisdom is to recognize that and make the best we can of it, without wasting time yearning for absolute guarantees outside the activity of human inquiry.

iii. Does the Epistemic Desiderata Approach Make a Difference?

We are now ready for the issue to which all the foregoing was a propaedeutic: Does the switch from justificationism to the ED approach have any implications for what is the correct account of the overall epistemic structure of a subject's beliefs? The short answer is NO. As I have argued, coherentism is subject to fatal defects that in no way depend on that switch. The defects are there whether we are working with a master fundamental positive epistemic status termed 'justified' or whether we are working with the pluralistic approach I have been advocating. In either case the position is impaled on the "multiple equally coherent and incompatible systems" objection and on the "PES in isolation from the general coherence of the larger system" objection, as well as others, including the point that it remains to be shown that coherence in itself implies truth conducivity. And so coherentism falls by the wayside before the contrast between justificationism and the epistemic desiderata approach comes onto the scene. As for contextualism, it opts out of the attempt to give an account of the overall structure of a system of beliefs, and does so on principle. Hence it is not really a competitor for the title of best account of the overall structure of a system of beliefs. It is rather a last resort if all attempts at delineating such a structure fail. It is also worthy of mention that the main rationale of contextualists for the necessity of adopting their position is the impossibility of any direct adequate grounding of beliefs, grounding not by other beliefs, something I take myself to have shown not to have been established. Indeed, careful reflection shows that direct adequate grounding is not only possible but exemplified in multiple ways.

So that leaves foundationalism, perhaps with some subsidiary coherentist element, all alone in the field. Either we quit trying to discern the overall epistemic structure of a subject's beliefs, or we opt for some form of foundationalism, or we develop some alternative hitherto undreamed of. So for all practical purposes our problem boils down to whether adopting the epistemic desiderata approach gives us sufficient reason to accept foundationalism. I cannot see that it gives us sufficient reason either to accept it or to reject it. The viability of foundationalism depends on whether there are enough directly adequately grounded beliefs to yield as derivatives, by acceptable principles of derivation, all the beliefs that are indirectly adequately grounded. To settle that requires a lot of detailed investigation of particular areas of belief and particular modes of derivation of some beliefs from others. That investigation could be carried on, so far as I can see, in terms of any otherwise acceptable account of what TC desiderata for beliefs there are. As I have argued, there are insuperable objections to an account of this in terms of a single master positive epistemic status termed 'justified'. But the arguments for that conclusion were independent of any considerations for or against foundationalism. And the switch from justificationism to the epistemic desiderata approach does not in itself provide either an establishment or a refutation of foundationalism. At most it gives us a better conceptual framework in which to carry on the investigation. And so foundationalists will have to look elsewhere for either salvation or its converse.

iv. Are We Committed to Contextualism?

But one question remains. What are we to say about the apparent coincidence of our "we have to work pro tem with what we are confident of" position on the proper attitude to take with respect to modes of belief formation, and the contextualism described above?

First, let me clear the air by pointing out that the "we have to work with what we have" position does not depend on the pluralistic epistemic desiderata approach rather than a unitary justificationist approach or any other alternative. So long as we are focusing on TC epistemic desiderata of belief we will run into epistemic circularity when we seek to show that such a desideratum is exemplified generally by the beliefs in some large basic group of beliefs. And that is what renders the "we have to work with what we have" position the only viable alternative. Epistemic circularity is inevitable for arguments for the general possession of a TC desideratum, whether that is one of a large plurality of epistemic desiderata, as on my approach, or whether it is construed as the unique epistemic desideratum for belief, as on some forms of justificationism. We can avoid epistemic circularity if we restrict ourselves to nondirectly TC epistemic desiderata for belief, but then we lose contact with the values that are primary in our cognitive endeavors. So even if the "we have to work with what we have" position is a form of contextualism, it is nothing that is necessitated by or distinctive of the ED approach.

But how is this position related to contextualism? It is at least a cousin, for the views are at one in denying the need to validate modes of belief formation before using them. But it is distinguished from the contextualism discussed earlier in a fundamental respect. Contextualism is a global theory in at least this way; it applies to *any* attempt to resolve a problem or answer a question, whatever the type or subject matter involved. But my "start from where you are" position is severely restricted to the question of the epistemic status of allegedly TC ways of forming beliefs. It does not apply to attempts to answer questions as to which first-level (non-epistemic) belief to adopt on some issue or other. It does not touch anything within the vast field of non-epistemic belief, and questions and problems concerning them. There is no reason to suppose that any otherwise effective argument for the claim that my birch tree has lost all its leaves will have to include premises accepting which will practically commit me to the assumption that my birch tree has lost all its leaves. And the same holds for more sophisticated first-level beliefs, such as the big bang theory of the origin of our physical universe. The "you have to start from where you are" position is a response to a very specific problem that arises from a consideration of how to establish certain kinds of epistemic conclusions. It does not even apply to all questions about the epistemic status of epistemic claims, for example, not to attributions of nondirectly TC epistemic desiderata. Nor does it apply to questions about the epistemic status of particular beliefs. It is not the case that any otherwise effective argument that Jim has an adequate basis for his belief that he will be fired from his job next week must use premises that commit him to practically assuming that he will be fired from his job next week. Once we see the narrow corner of our cognitive endeavors to which my "we have to start from where you are" position is restricted, we see the difference between that position and a sweeping contextualist account of all inquiry. But though the territory to which my position applies is relatively small in extent, it is absolutely fundamental to our cognitive endeavors generally. For so long as the reliability of our ways of forming beliefs generally is left in doubt, there is something fundamentally unsatisfactory about our cognitive life.

But though my restricted contextualism about inquiry into the reliability of very general modes of belief formation is distinguished in this way from an unrestricted contextualism about any inquiry, it is like it in another way, namely, in implying a bar to an unrestrictedly general account of the epistemic structure of a person's total body of beliefs. At least that is true if the person in question has beliefs about the reliability of basic general modes of belief formation, such as being based on sense perception, memory, and various kinds of inference. For though I declared earlier that the ED approach is open to the possibility of a foundationalist account of a total body of beliefs, that is true only because of the point made above that the ED approach in itself does not necessitate my position on the epistemic status of claims to the reliability of very wide basic ways of forming beliefs. Once we bring in that position, a rift is created in any alleged overall epistemic structure of a body of beliefs that includes beliefs about the reliability of basic modes of belief formation. For assuming, as we must, that such beliefs cannot have an adequate direct ground in experience or otherwise and hence cannot figure among the foundations of a foundationalist structure, if it could have an adequate indirect grounding, then, assuming that epistemic circular arguments are not countenanced as ways of deriving superstructure beliefs, it would be possible to give an argument for such a belief that does not lead to epistemic circularity, contrary to what was argued above. Therefore, the *reliability of very wide basic modes of belief formation* component would fall outside what can be accommodated in a foundationalist model. And so, assuming that coherentism has been disposed of, we are left with a (modest) pluralism of the structure of an overall body of belief, as well as a (much more sweeping) pluralism of epistemic desiderata. Beliefs other than those concerning the reliability of wide basic ways of forming beliefs can, if the relevant detailed facts dictate it, fit into a foundationalist structure. But those beliefs that will not fit require a local contextualist account. And so we find ourselves forced to a bi-level structure—foundationalism on the bottom, so to speak, a very wide bottom, and contextualism for certain restricted kinds of epistemic beliefs.

ENVOI

I very much hope that this book gives some idea of what the epistemology of belief would look like if approached from the epistemic desiderata point of view—both how it would be different from a justificationist approach and how similarities would remain. I will end the book by recalling the main points under each heading.

By far the most prominent difference is that we would be free from the burdensome and conflict-generating necessity of determining what it is for a belief to be justified and what are the necessary and sufficient conditions of the enjoyment of that status. And it is not just a matter of saving us a lot time and a lot of frustrating and sometimes puzzling controversy. It leaves us free to appreciate and explore a variety of epistemic desiderata of beliefs and to explore them in their own terms, without either ignoring or downgrading any that do not make the grade as giving us the right answer as to what it takes for a belief to be "justified". I hope this book gives enough examples of this activity to make clear the advantages it brings. Here are a few reminders. It enables us to grasp the epistemic value of having sufficient evidence for a belief even if the belief is not based on that evidence, at the same time bringing out genuine epistemic values that we miss in case the belief is based on some less adequate ground. It also frees us up to explore the epistemic value of the coherence of a system of beliefs, even though, from a justificationist standpoint, there are fatal objections to supposing that this is either necessary or sufficient for the justification of a belief in the system. And it enables us to bring out the epistemic value of higher-level knowledge of the epistemic status of beliefs and what is responsible for that, and the epistemic value of the availability of such, without worrying about whether this is necessary for the justification of the belief. And from a justificationist standpoint there are strong reasons for denying that it is necessary for justification.

This pluralist "Let a thousand flowers bloom" orientation has many other payoffs as well. What I take to be one of the most important results of the discussion in this book is the virtual equivalence of a belief's being formed by a reliable belief-forming process and the belief's being based on an adequate ground. I won't go so far as to claim that it would be impossible to reach this insight if one was clinging to the supposition that 'justified' picks out a unique centrally important epistemic desideratum of beliefs. But I will testify that it was only after I had adopted the ED approach that this became clear to me. The key to the discovery was the construal of a belief-forming process as a psychologically realized input–belief output function, and the identification of such inputs with "grounds" on which beliefs are based. Once those steps have been taken, then it takes only the assumption that every belief is based on a ground to yield the conclusion that *being formed by a reliable belief-forming process* and *being based on an adequate ground* are two sides of the same coin. I can see how a preoccupation with what it takes for a belief to be justified naturally leads to a supposition that these two features of beliefs are in competition for the honor of constituting justification. And this has an inhibiting effect on coming to the realization of their substantial identity.

I won't claim that all the important points made in the book about the epistemology of belief stem from the ED approach. I arrived at the treatment of alleged "deontological" desiderata for beliefs and their vicissitudes, which makes up Chapter 4 of the present volume, while I was still heavily embroiled in the quest for the right theory of epistemic justification, though fortunately these results translate nicely into the ED approach. Likewise I don't see how the search for the best construal of *epistemic probability* in Chapter 5 couldn't have been undertaken in the context of chasing epistemic justification, though in fact that is something that was worked out in the course of writing this book. And I am inclined to think that the freedom from worrying about the conditions of epistemic justification may have made a substantial contribution to whatever merit there is in what I had to say on that topic.

I turn now to the similarities or, perhaps better, overlap. Let me recall what I said in Chapter 3 about the main headings under which an exploration of epistemic desiderata would be conducted: Explication, Viability, Interrelations, and Importance. The question is whether what has gone on in the last forty or so years under the aegis of theories of epistemic justification has any bearing on those explorations. You bet it has. Just because the desiderata I have identified and discussed have each been affirmed, and denied, as conditions of justification, those discussions have much to contribute to the ED approach. In terms of the above list of rubrics under which I said that an investigation of epistemic desiderata should be conducted, it is with respect to Explication and Viability that the ED approach can make most fruitful contact with theories of justification. We naturally don't find much there on Interrelations because justificationists are typically not interested in organizing a plurality of epistemic desiderata. And the attention on the epistemic importance of various features of belief tends to be narrowly focused on what they tell us about justification.

We can most profitably tackle Explication and Viability together. There was an extended example of borrowing material on these topics from justification theory in the chapter on deontological alleged epistemic desiderata. The results there were mostly negative. But more positive material emerges for other desiderata. A large proportion of the discussion in this book has focused on *being formed by a reliable belief-forming process* and *being based on an adequate ground*. Have these desiderata figured in the quest for a theory of epistemic justification? Most certainly. Both have been strongly defended and strongly attacked as accounts of what it is for a belief to be justified. As a result much work has been done by justificationists on their explication and their viability. Remember that my work on the reliability of belief-forming processes in Chapter 6 was conducted in conversation with justificationists, both friends and foes of a reliabilist account of justification. A great deal of attention has been lavished on what it is for a belief to be formed reliably and on whether it is possible to arrive at a satisfactory account of this. I was not completely happy with any of the existing views on these matters, but the fact remains that, as is often the case in philosophy and elsewhere, I was building on the results of their labors, both positively and negatively. You will remember that I took the germ of my account of belief-forming processes from Goldman, developing it in ways he did not, and constructed a defense of the viability of the notion of a belief's being formed in a reliable way from that. This is perhaps the major example of achieving positive results in this book with the assistance of previous work by justification theorists. Other significant examples include the discussion of how to understand 'probable' in thinking of an adequate ground of belief as one that renders the belief probably true, and the idea that a belief's being formed by the exercise of an intellectual virtue is a genuine epistemic desideratum.

This book is only a beginning of an epistemology of belief carried out in terms of a plurality of epistemic desiderata and without any supposition of a uniquely central epistemically valuable property of beliefs picked out by 'justified'. Some parts of a thoroughgoing treatment have been gone into in some detail, particularly the kinds and vicissitudes of deontological features of beliefs, beliefs being based on adequate grounds, and beliefs being formed in a reliable way. But the other desiderata mentioned here deserve much fuller treatment—particularly intellectual virtues and their role in belief formation, higher-level knowledge and well-grounded belief about the epistemic status of lower-level beliefs and the cognitive access thereto, the place of coherence in epistemic evaluation, and foundationalism and other views of the overall structure of a subject's system of beliefs. And all that needs to be integrated with an acceptable account of propositional knowledge. So do not lose heart, pioneers of the ED approach, if any of you are out there. There is still much work to be done. The harvest is large, and laborers are needed.

BIBLIOGRAPHY

Alston, William P. 1976. "Self-Warrant: A Neglected Form of Privileged Access." *American Philosophical Quarterly* 13:257–273. Reprinted in Alston 1989.
———. 1980. "Level Confusions in Epistemology." *Midwest Studies in Philosophy* 5:135–150. Reprinted in Alston 1989.
———. 1985. "Concepts of Epistemic Justification." *The Monist* 68:57–89. Reprinted in Alston 1989.
———. 1986a. "Epistemic Circularity." *Philosophy and Phenomenological Research* 47:1–30. Reprinted in Alston 1989.
———. 1986b. "Internalism and Externalism in Epistemology." *Philosophical Topics* 14:179–221. Reprinted in Alston 1989.
———. 1988a. "The Deontological Conception of Epistemic Justification." *Philosophical Perspectives* 2:257–299. Reprinted in Alston 1989.
———. 1988b. "An Internalist Externalism." *Synthèse* 74:265–283. Reprinted in Alston 1989.
———. 1989. *Epistemic Justification: Essays in the Theory of Knowledge*. Ithaca: Cornell University Press.
———. 1990. "Externalist Theories of Perception." *Philosophy and Phenomenological Research*, Supplement, 50:73–97.
———. 1991a. *Perceiving God: The Epistemology of Religious Experience*. Ithaca: Cornell University Press.
———. 1991b. "Higher Level Requirements for Epistemic Justification." In *The Opened Curtain*, ed. K. Lehrer and E. Sosa. Boulder: Westview Press.
———. 1993a. *The Reliability of Sense Perception*. Ithaca: Cornell University Press.
———. 1993b. "Epistemic Desiderata." *Philosophy and Phenomenological Research* 53:527–551.
———. 1995. "How to Think About Reliability." *Philosophical Topics* 23:1–29.

———. 1996a. *A Realist Conception of Truth*. Ithaca: Cornell University Press.
———. 1996b. "Belief, Acceptance, and Religious Faith." In *Faith, Freedom, and Rationality*, ed. Jeff Jordan and Daniel Howeard-Snyder. Lanham, Md.: Rowman & Littlefield.
———. 1998. "Perception and Conception." In *Pragmatism, Reason, and Norms*, ed. Kenneth R. Westphal. New York: Fordham University Press.
———. 1999. "Back to the Theory of Appearing." *Philosophical Perspectives* 13:81–103.
Armstrong, D. M. 1961. *Perception and the Physical World*. London: Routledge & Kegan Paul.
———. 1973. *Belief, Truth, and Knowledge*. Cambridge: Cambridge University Press.
Battaly, Heather D., and Michael P. Lynch, eds. Forthcoming. *Perspectives on the Philosophy of William Alston*. Lanham, Md.: Rowman & Littlefield.
Bogdan, Radu J., ed. 1982. *Henry E. Kyberg Jr. and Isaac Levi*. Dordrecht: D. Reidel.
BonJour, Laurence. 1985. *The Structure of Empirical Knowledge*. Cambridge: Harvard University Press.
BonJour, Laurence, and Ernest Sosa. 2003. *Epistemic Justification: Internalism vs. Externalism, Foundations vs. Virtues*. Oxford: Blackwell.
Carnap, Rudolf. 1950. *The Logical Foundations of Probability*. Chicago: University of Chicago Press.
Chisholm, Roderick. 1968. "Lewis' Ethics of Belief." In *The Philosophy of C. I. Lewis*, ed. P. Schilpp. La Salle, Ill.: Open Court.
———. 1977. *Theory of Knowledge*, 2d ed. Englewood Cliffs, N.J.: Prentice-Hall.
———. 1989. *Theory of Knowledge*, 3d ed. Englewood Cliffs, N.J.: Prentice-Hall.
Dretske, Fred. 1971. "Conclusive Reasons." *Australasian Journal of Philosophy* 49:1–22.
Feldman, Richard. 1985. "Reliability and Justification." *The Monist* 68:159–174.
———. 1988. "Having Evidence." In *Essays Presented to Edmund Gettier*, ed. David Austin. Dordrecht: Kluwer.
Feldman, Richard, and Earl Conee. 1985. "Evidentialism." *Philosophical Studies* 48:15–34.
———. 1998. "The Generality Problem for Reliabilism." *Philosophical Studies* 89:1–29.
———. 2001. "Internalism Defended." *American Philosophical Quarterly* 38:231–260.
Foley, Richard. 1985. "What's Wrong with Reliabilism?." *The Monist* 68:188–202.
———. 1987. *The Theory of Epistemic Rationality*. Cambridge: Harvard University Press.
Fuller, S. 1988. *Social Epistemology*. Bloomington: Indiana University Press.
Fumerton, Richard. 1995. *Metaepistemology and Skepticism*. Lanham, Md.: Rowman & Littlefield.
Ginet, Carl. 1975. *Knowledge, Perception, and Memory*. Dordrecht: D. Reidel.
———. 1985. "Contra Reliabilism." *The Monist* 68:175–187.
Goldman, Alan. 1988. *Empirical Knowledge*. Berkeley: University of California Press.
Goldman, Alvin. 1977. "Perceptual Objects." *Synthèse* 35:257–284.
———. 1979. "What Is Justified Belief?." In *Justification and Knowledge*, ed. G. Pappas. Dordrecht: D. Reidel. Reprinted in Goldman 1992a.

———. 1980. "The Internalist Conception of Justification." *Midwest Studies in Philosophy* 5:27–53.
———. 1986. *Epistemology and Cognition*. Cambridge: Harvard University Press.
———. 1988. "Strong and Weak Justification." *Philosophical Perspectives* 2:51–69. Reprinted in Goldman 1992a.
———. 1992a. *Liaisons: Philosophy Meets the Cognitive and Social Sciences*. Cambridge: MIT Press.
———. 1992b. "Epistemic Folkways and Scientific Epistemology." In *Liaisons: Philosophy Meets the Cognitive and Social Sciences*. Cambridge: MIT Press.
———. 1999a. *Knowledge in a Social World*. Oxford: Clarendon Press.
———. 1999b. "Internalism Exposed." *Journal of Philosophy* 96:271–293. Reprinted in Goldman 2002.
———. 2002. *Pathways to Knowledge*. New York: Oxford University Press.
Govier, Trudy. 1976. "Belief, Values, and the Will." *Dialogue* 15:642–663.
Harman, Gilbert. 1973. *Thought*. Princeton: Princeton University Press.
Heil, John. 1983. *Perception and Conception*. Berkeley: University of California Press.
Jeffreys, Harold. 1939. *Theory of Probability*. Oxford: Clarendon Press.
Keynes, John Maynard. 1921. *A Treatise on Probability*. London: Macmillan.
Kvanig, Jonathan. 1992. *The Intellectual Virtues and the Life of the Mind*. Lanham, Md.: Rowman & Littlefield.
Kyberg, Henry E., Jr. 1974. *The Logical Foundations of Statistical Inference*. Dordrecht: D. Reidel.
Lehrer, Keith. 1990. *Theory of Knowledge*. Boulder: Westview Press.
Maitzen, Stephen. 1995. "Our Errant Epistemic Aim." *Philosophy and Phenomenological Research* 55:869–875.
Meiland, Jack. 1980. "What Ought We to Believe? The Ethics of Belief Revisited." *American Philosophical Quarterly* 17:15–24.
Monmarquet, James A. 1993. *Epistemic Virtue and Doxastic Responsibility*. Lanham, Md.: Rowman & Littlefield.
Moser, Paul. 1985. *Empirical Justification*. Dordrecht: D. Reidel.
———. 1989. *Knowledge and Evidence*. Cambridge: Cambridge University Press.
Pendlebury, Michael. 1987. "Perceptual Representation." *Proceedings of the Aristotelian Society* 87:91–106.
Pitcher, George. 1971. *A Theory of Perception*. Princeton: Princeton University Press.
Plantinga, Alvin. 1983. "Reason and Belief in God." In *Faith and Rationality*, ed. Alvin Plantinga and Nicholas Wolterstorff. Notre Dame: University of Notre Dame Press.
———. 1988. "Positive Epistemic Status and Proper Function." *Philosophical Perspectives* 2:1–50.
———. 1993a. *Warrant: The Current Debate*. New York: Oxford University Press.
———. 1993b. *Warrant and Proper Function*. New York: Oxford University Press.
———. 2000. *Warranted Christian Belief*. New York: Oxford University Press.
Plantinga, Alvin, and Nicholas Wolterstorff, eds. 1983. *Faith and Rationality*. Notre Dame: University of Notre Dame Press.
Pojman, Louis. 1986. *Religious Belief and the Will*. London: Routledge & Kegan Paul.

Pollock, John. 1986. *Contemporary Theories of Knowledge*. Totowa, N.J.: Rowman & Littlefield.
Putnam, Hilary. 1981. *Reason, Truth, and History*. Cambridge: Cambridge University Press.
Quine, Willard Van Orman. 1969. *Ontological Relativity and Other Essays*. New York: Columbia University Press.
Radcliffe, Dana. 1996. "Beliefs, Grounds, and the Basing Relation." Ph.D. dissertation, Syracuse University.
Reid, Thomas. 1970. *An Inquiry into the Human Mind*. Chicago: University of Chicago Press. Originally published 1764.
Runzo, Joseph. 1977. "The Propositional Structure of Perception." *American Philosophical Quarterly* 14:211–220.
———. 1982. "The Radical Conceptualization of Perceptual Experience." *American Philosophical Quarterly* 19:205–217.
Schmitt, Frederick F., ed. 1994. *Socializing Epistemology: The Social Dimensions of Knowledge*. Lanham, Md.: Rowman & Littlefield.
Searle, John. 1983. *Intentionality*. Cambridge: Cambridge University Press.
Sosa, Ernest. 1991. *Knowledge in Perspectives: Selected Essays in Epistemology*. Cambridge: Cambridge University Press.
Steup, Matthias. 1988. "The Deontic Conception of Epistemic Justification." *Philosophical Studies* 53:65–84.
Stich, Stephen. 1990. *The Fragmentation of Reason*. Cambridge: MIT Press.
Stove, D. C. 1986. *The Rationality of Induction*. Oxford: Clarendon Press.
Swain, Marshall. 1981. *Reasons and Knowledge*. Ithaca: Cornell University Press.
Swinburne, Richard. 2001. *Epistemic Justification*. Oxford: Oxford University Press.
Unger, Peter. 1975. *Ignorance: A Case for Scepticism*. Oxford: Clarendon Press.
Williams, Bernard. 1972. "Deciding to Believe." In *Problems of the Self*. Cambridge: Cambridge University Press.
Williams, Michael. 1991. *Unnatural Doubts: Epistemological Realism and the Basis of Skepticism*. Oxford: Blackwell.
Williamson, Timothy. 2000. *Knowledge and Its Limits*. Oxford: Oxford University Press.
Winters, Barbara. 1979. "Believing at Will." *Journal of Philosophy* 76:243–256.
Wittgenstein, Ludwig. 1953. *Philosophical Investigations*. Trans. G. E. M. Anscombe. Oxford: Blackwell.
———. 1969. *On Certainty*. Trans. Dennis Paul and G. E. M. Anscombe. Oxford: Blackwell.
Wolterstorff, Nicholas. 1983. "Can Belief in God Be Rational if It Has No Foundations?." In *Faith and Rationality*, ed. Alvin Plantinga and Nicholas Wolterstorff. Notre Dame: University of Notre Dame Press.
Zagzebski, Linda Trinkhaus. 1996. *Virtues of the Mind: An Inquiry into the Nature of Virtue and the Ethical Foundations of Knowledge*. Cambridge: Cambridge University Press.

INDEX

Readers are advised to familiarize themselves with the Table of Contents. It lists 11 chapters divided into 61 sections, each with a title that indicates what is presented there.

Adequacy of grounds, 36
   a degree notion, 94–95
   internalist construals of, 92–94
   maximal degree of, 100–104
   truth-conducive form of, 92
   See also Beliefs: based on adequate grounds
Armstrong D. M., 54, 120–21

Basing relation, 81–82
   causal account of, 84–85
   conscious and unconscious forms of, 86–87
   internalist accounts of, 85–86
   involves sustenance and preservation, 84
   as mode of defending the belief, 86
   as taking something to support the belief, 85–86
   See also Grounds of beliefs
Belief-forming processes as psychologically realized functions, 125–29
   boundaries thereof, 119–22

   cases of extended deliberation, 142–43
   earlier stages of belief formation that are epistemically relevant to the final product, 143–45
   influence of cognitive capacities of the subject on the epistemic status of the final product, 146–47
   influence of evidence one does not possess on the epistemic status of the final product, 145–46
   overdetermination cases, 142
   resultant solution of problem of generality, 129–32,
   resultant solution of the reference class problem for frequency probability, 133–34
   objections to these solutions and answers thereto, 138–42
   See also Reliability of belief formation
Beliefs
   based on adequate grounds, 36, 43, 92–98, 132–38
   confers probability on belief, 94
   merely having an adequate ground, though a desideratum is less desirable than basing the

Beliefs (continued)
    belief on an adequate ground, 91–92
    where it is of special importance, 172
    epistemic evaluation of, 5–6
    currently in terms of "justification", 3, 11
    about the epistemic status of beliefs not susceptible of immediate grounding, 179
    epistemology of is focus of book, 5–6
    See also Epistemic conditional probability of beliefs; Reliability of belief formation
BonJour, Laurence, 12–13, 30, 42–43, 53–55, 166–68, 237

Chisholm, Roderick M., 13, 69–71, 92–94, 164, 233
Coherence
    alternative to linear model of support, 195–96
    contributors to, 166
    explanation of, 166–67
    forms of, 236–37
    as necessary and sufficient for epistemic justification, 167
    objections to, 167–68
    as supplement to foundationalism, 234–35, 237–38
Contextualism, 196, 238
    and coherentism, 238
    and overall organization of belief, 238–39
    and the "we have to start with where we are" position, 240–42

Deontological conceptions of epistemic justification, 12–14, 15–17
    derived from application to action, 16, 59
    forms of, 45, 58
    locutions that suggest this, 59–60
    See also Deontological desiderata; Deontological statuses
Deontological desiderata, 45, 58–60, 72–78, 228–29
    where of special importance, 174–75
Deontological statuses
    presuppose voluntary control, 60
    required-forbidden-permitted, 59
    See also Deontological desiderata

Deontology
    sense in which it is used here, 58–59
Descartes, René, 214, 219, 233
Dewey, John, 196, 239
Doubts
    ways of stilling, 196–97
Doxastic practices, 197–201
    of various degrees of generality, 198
    ways of individuating, 198–99

Epistemic circularity, 201–10
    attempts to avoid, 204–7
    defined, 202
    pervasiveness of, 207–10
    and Pyrrhonian skepticism, 215–20
    robs arguments of desired force, 202–4
    and various epistemic desiderata, 224–29
    See also Epistemic skepticism
Epistemic conditional probability of beliefs, 95–100
    conditional on being based on a certain ground, 95
    differences from usual probability theory account, 96–100
    objective and subjective construals of, 104
    See also Adequacy of grounds; Beliefs: based on adequate grounds
Epistemic desiderata
    approach to epistemology of belief, 39
    advantages, 243–44
    borrowings from justificationism, 244–45
    and overall organization of belief, 239–40
    supported by diversity of contexts in which one or another desideratum is most important, 175–76
    aspects of to be examined, 47–49
    being able to effectively defend a belief, 43–45
    where of special importance, 174
    (directly) truth-conducive, 36, 43, 81, 224–25
    most fundamental, 47, 50
    features of systems of belief, 45–47, 163–69, 227–28
    interrelations of, 49–51
    knowledge of epistemic status of beliefs, 43–45, 162–64, 226–27
    where of special importance, 172–73

INDEX

list of, 39–47
relations to truth goal, 43–45, 46–47, 163–64, 165, 168–69
truth as an epistemic desideratum, 40–42
See also Epistemic justification
Epistemic evaluation
objects of, 37–38
power and speed, 37
Epistemic folkways, 156–57
Epistemic justification
abandonment of makes philosophical epistemic evaluation of beliefs more complicated, 176–78
attempts to identify, 23–26
being justified and activity of justifying, 18, 86
concepts of, 11–19
deontological and truth-conducive groups of, 15–17
conditions for, 19–21
a definition of, 159
highly accessible internal conditions as necessary for, 56–57
propositional/doxastic forms of, 18
reasons for denying existence of, 23–28
reliable belief formation as necessary for, 55–56
reliable belief formation as sufficient for, 53–54
responsible belief holding as necessary for, 54–55
Epistemic point of view, 29–31
See also True belief as basic goal of cognition
Epistemic skepticism
degrees of severity in criteria for the status it is about, 213–14
particular (local) or general (global), 212–13
substantive or challenge, 213
ways of supporting it
  inability to rule out all alternative possibilities (Cartesian), 211–15
  no adequate grounds for beliefs of a certain kind (Humean), 215
  no adequate grounds for presupposed epistemic assumptions (Pyrrhonian), 215–16
what status it is about, 212

See also Responses to skepticism; Skepticism; Ways of supporting substantive epistemic skepticism
Epistemology, 1–5
and cognitive psychology, 4
definition, 2–3
forms of, 3–5
no precise boundaries, 1–2
practical, 40–42
See also Naturalistic approach to epistemology
Evidence, 82
as beliefs, 83
and facts, 82–83
See also Grounds of beliefs; Reasons
Explanation, 165–66

Feldman, Richard, 116–20
Feldman, Richard and Earl Conee, 15, 138–40
Final settlement of epistemic issues, impossibility of, 194–95
See also Epistemic circularity
Foley, Richard, 14, 55–56, 93–94
Foundationalism, 230–35, 240–42
classical, 232
with coherence, 234–35, 237–38
defined, 230–31
and internalism/externalism, 237
mixed, 233–35
and overall organization of belief, 242
pure, 231–33
types of, 231–35
Frequency construal of conditional probability, 109–12
decision on range of cases, 110–11
decision on reference classes, 110–11
generalization from particulars basic for, 109–12
parallels with determining reliability of a process of belief formation, 111–12
See also Epistemic conditional probability of beliefs
Fumerton, Richard, 107–8

Ginet, Carl, 12, 145, 163–64
Goldman, Alan, 13
Goldman, Alvin, 4–5, 13, 26–28, 35–37, 56–57, 120–23, 126, 132, 145, 156–57, 161, 245
Grounds of beliefs, 81, 83

Grounds of beliefs (continued)
  defined in terms of basing, 82
  direct/indirect, 178–79, 231–32
  do all beliefs have them?, 97–99
  See also Evidence; Reasons

Harman, Gilbert, 91
Hegel, Georg Wilhelm Friedrich, 219
Hume, David, 215, 233

Indirect voluntary influence on beliefs, 73–80
  activities that can exert it, 75–76
  analogues to, 74
  can be sufficient for blame, 74
  doesn't apply "required, forbidden or permitted" to beliefs, 74–75
  an intellectual but not an epistemic desideratum, 78–80
  not sufficiently truth-conducive, 78–80
Inquiry, conduct of, 4
Intellectual virtues, 152–61
  acting from (exercise of), 152, 154–55
  a truth-conducive desideratum, 155–57
  defining motivation of, 159–61
  definitions of, 154–55, 157–58
  and reliability of belief formation, 153
  See also Virtue epistemology
Internalism
  counterexamples for sufficiency for justification, 56–57
  different construals of, 52
Internalism/Externalism
  how the contrast is conceived here, 52–53
  how controversies over this are treated in a justificationist and in an epistemic desiderata approach, 53–57
  different construals of, 52

Knowledge, 34–35, 158–59
Kyberg, Henry, 135

Logical account of epistemic probability, 104–9
  arguments for, 105, 107–8
  on model of logical implication, 104–5
  problems with, 105–7
  See also Epistemic conditional probability of beliefs

Maitzen, Stephen, 35–37

Moser, Paul, 13, 14, 29–30

Nagle, Thomas, 219
Naturalistic approach to epistemology, 7–8, 201
  dissatisfaction with, 191–93
  and non-epistemic investigations, 192–93

Perception
  adverbialism, 182–83
  direct realism, 182–83
  perceptual experience, 181–87
  place of conceptualization and belief in, 180
  presentational, doxastic, and conceptualist views of, 180–84
  See also Perceptual beliefs
Perceptual beliefs
  can have both doxastic and experiential grounds, 178–79
  definition of, 180–82
  self-warrant of, 178
  truth-conducive grounds for, 184–87
  best shown by presentationalism, 185–87
Plantinga, Alvin, 12, 15, 87–89, 105–7, 117, 135–36, 140–42, 148–52, 178, 232
Pollock, John, 14
Prima facie status, 200
  presupposes "overrider system", 200–201
Probability of truth of belief, 95
Propensity construal of conditional probability, 109–10
Proper functioning of cognitive faculties, 148–51
  See also Warrant of beliefs
Propositions, 82
Psychological realism, 139–42
Pyrrho of Elis, 215

Quine, Willard van Orman, 8, 30

Reasons, 81–83
Reid, Thomas, 222–23
Reliability of belief formation, 36, 43
  belief-independent and belief-dependent processes, 122
  counterexample to necessity for justification, 55–56
  counterexample to sufficiency for justification, 53–55

generalization from particular case is crucial, "The Problem of Generality", 114–19
includes strengthening and preserving, 115
indicator and process reliability, 112–13, 136–37
parallels with adequacy of grounds, 122–25, 135
perfect reliability not possible, 200
problem of range of cases, 123–25
"Single Case Problem" and track record approach, 119–20
where input (ground) is doxastic, its epistemic status is relevant as well as the input-output relationship, 137–38
where of special importance, 172
See also Belief-forming processes as psychologically realized functions
Reliability of cognitive subjects, 152
where of special importance, 171
Responses to skepticism
Humean, 221–24
Pyrrhonian, 217–21
See also Epistemic skepticism; Skepticism

Skepticism, 7–8, 193, 211–24
See also Epistemic skepticism; Responses to skepticism
Social epistemology, 4–5
Sosa, Ernest, 154–56, 161
Starting point for inquiry, 218–21
and contextualism, 240–42
and practical rationality, 220–21
Swain, Marshall, 14
Swinburne, Richard, 138–40

True belief as basic goal of cognition, 29–31, 158–59
and other goals, 34–37
refinements of, and qualifications to, 31–34
See also Epistemic point of view
Truth
epistemic conception of, 31
realist conception of, 31
See also True belief as basic goal of cognition

Undue partiality in what is prima facie taken for granted, 222–24

See also Starting point for inquiry
Unger, Peter, 213–14

van Inwagen, Peter, 207–9
Verificationism, 186–87
Virtual identity of reliable belief formation and belief based on adequate ground, 124–36
qualification to this, 136
See also Adequacy of grounds; Beliefs: based on adequate grounds; Reliability of belief formation
Virtue epistemology 3–4, 153–61
types of, 153
See also Intellectual virtues
Voluntary control, 60–75
of actions and states of affairs, 61
and free will, 61
indirect, 67–68, 69
long-range, 69
nonbasic immediate, 67–68
requires control of alternatives, 61
at will (basic), 62
See also Deontological desiderata; Voluntary control of belief
Voluntary control of belief, 59–73
and of acceptance, 62n 3
less implausible where belief is not obviously true or false, 64
locutions suggesting this, 62
long range, 69–73
confused with other things, 69–71
not often successful, 71–73
more plausible construals of, 65–72
non basic immediate, 68
better construals of, 68–69
not restricted to beliefs formed by a voluntary act, 61
and of other propositional attitudes, 60–61
presupposed by required, forbidden, and permitted, 60
at will (basic), 62–67
attacked as logically and as psychologically impossible, 62–63
extends to the obviously true, 63
See also Deontological desiderata; Voluntary control

Warrant of beliefs, 148–52
conditions for, 148–51

Warrant of beliefs (continued)
  defined, 148
  differences from functional account of belief forming processes, 151–52
  directly truth-conducive, 149–50
  and knowledge, 148–51
  and proper functioning of cognitive faculties, 148–51
Ways of supporting substantive epistemic skepticism
Ways of supporting substantive epistemic skepticism (continued)
  inability to adequately support epistemic assumptions (Pyrrhonian), 215–21
  and epistemic circularity, 215–17
  inability to find adequate grounds for beliefs of a certain type (Humean), 221–224
  inability to rule out alternative possibilities (Cartesian), 214–15
  See also Epistemic skepticism; Skepticism
Wittgenstein, Ludwig, 207–9
Wolterstorff, Nicholas, 12

Zagzebski, Linda, 15, 157–61

www.ingramcontent.com/pod-product-compliance
Lightning Source LLC
Chambersburg PA
CBHW020113010526

44115CB00008B/812